CONTEMPORARY ART

FROM CRESCENT MOON PUBLISHING

The Art of Andy Goldsworthy: Complete Works: Special Edition
by William Malpas

The Art of Andy Goldsworthy
by William Malpas

Andy Goldsworthy: Touching Nature
by William Malpas

Andy Goldsworthy In Close-Up
by William Malpas

The Art of Richard Long
by William Malpas

Constantin Brancusi: Sculpting the Essence of Things
by James Pearson

Alison Wilding: The Embrace of Sculpture
by Susan Quinnell

Eric Gill: Nuptials of God
by Anthony Hoyland

The Erotic Object: Sexuality in Sculpture
From Prehistory to the Present Day
by Susan Quinnell

Minimal Art and Artists in the 1960s and After
by Laura Garrard

Land Art, Earthworks, Installations, Environments, Sculpture
by William Malpas

Land Art: A Complete Guide to Landscape, Environmental,
Earthworks, Nature, Sculpture and Installation Art
by William Malpas

Richard Long In Close-Up
by William Malpas

Land Art In Close-Up
by William Malpas

Colorfield Painting: Minimal, Cool, Hard Edge, Serial
and Post-Painterly Abstract Art From the Sixties to the Present
by Laura Garrard

Mark Rothko: The Art of Transcendence
by Julia Davis

ERIC GILL

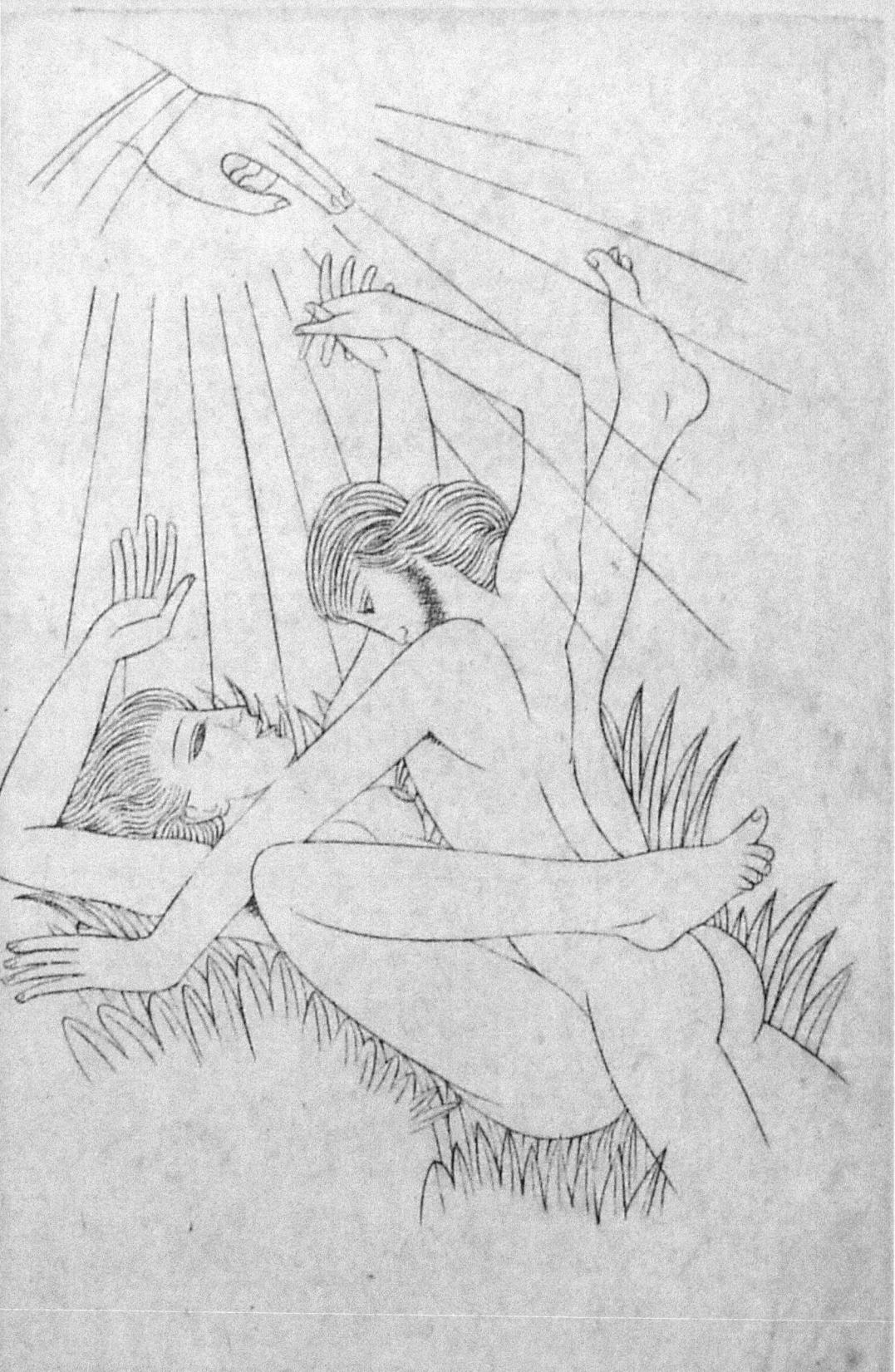

First published 1994. Second edition 2008. Fourth edition 2011. Fifth edition 2012.
© Anthony Hoyland 2012.
Photographs of Eric Gill's art by Jeremy Robinson.

Printed and bound in the U.S.A.
Set in Joanna 10 on 14pt and Gill Sans display.
Designed by Radiance Graphics.

British Library Cataloguing in Publication data

Hoyland, Anthony
Eric Gill, 1882-1940 – Criticism and Interpretation
I. Title
709.2

ISBN-13 9781861713216 (Pbk)

ISBN-13 9781861713551 (Hbk)

Crescent Moon Publishing
P.O. Box 1312
Maidstone, Kent
ME14 5XU, U.K.
www.crmoon.com

Contents

Abbreviations

A   *Autobiography*, Eric Gill

M   Fiona MacCarthy, *Eric Gill*

Y   Malcolm Yorke, *Eric Gill: Man of Flesh and Spirit*

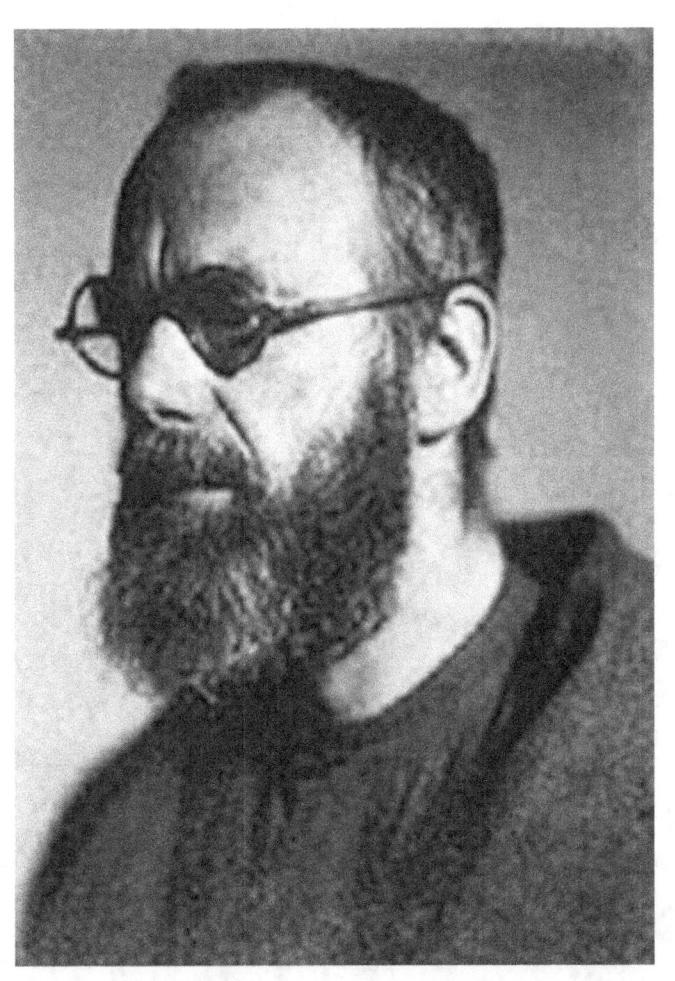

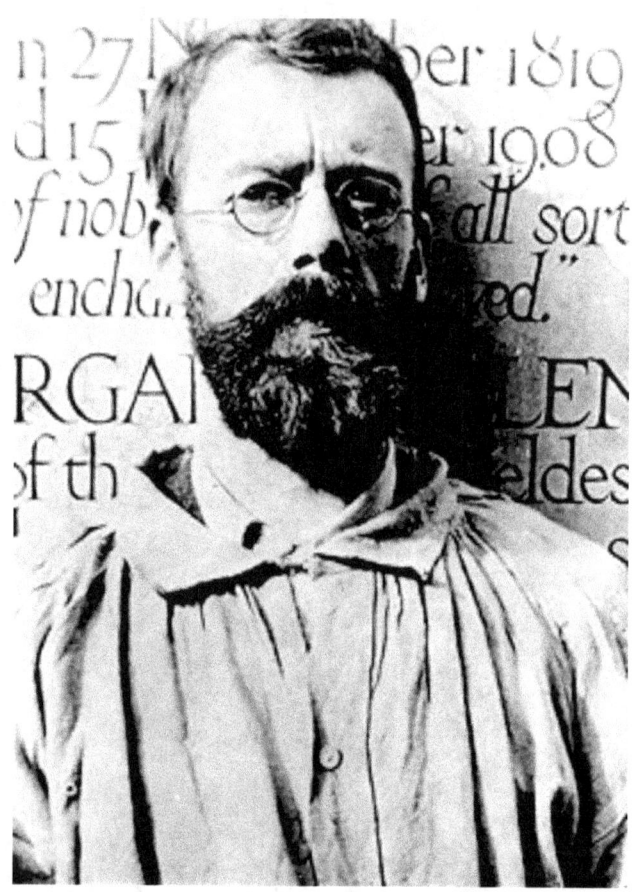

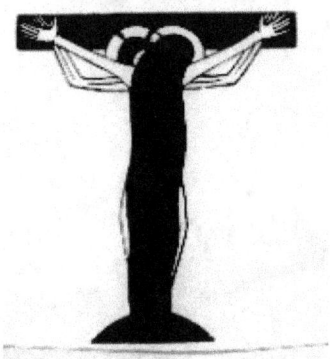

Eric Gill's Nuptials of God, 1922.

An extraordinary image, by any standards,
it depicts Mary Magdalene making love
to Christ on the Cross.

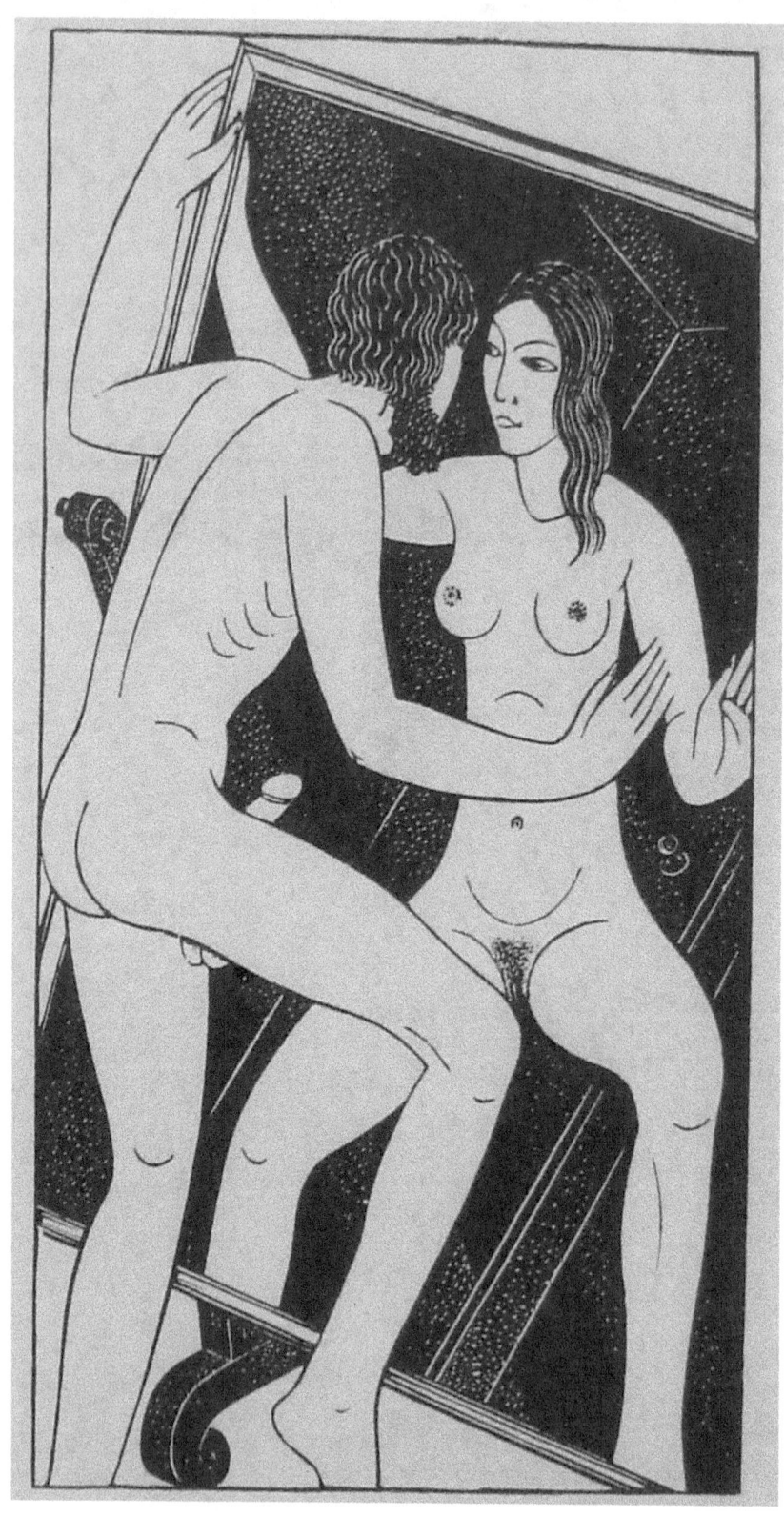

Eric Gill, Artist and Mirror, 1932

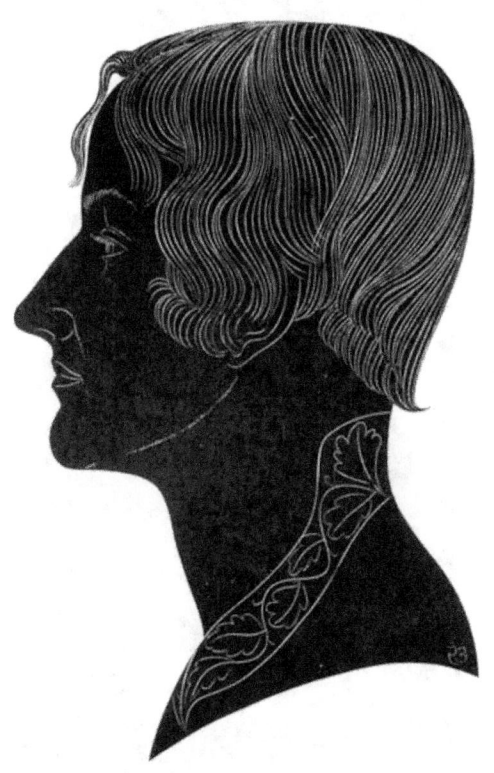

Two of the women in Eric Gill's life: his wife Ethel (below), and Beatrice Warde in 1929 (left).

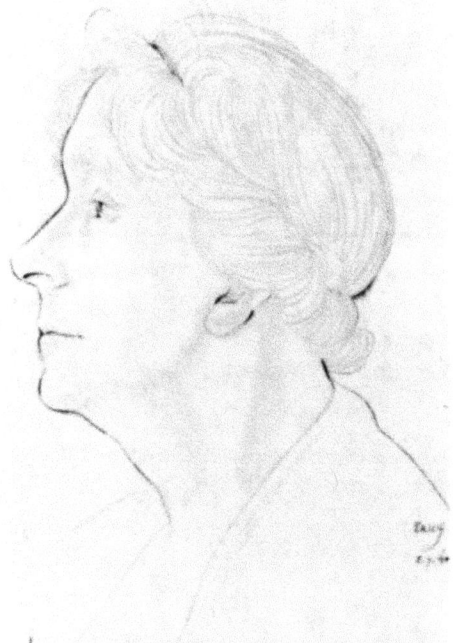

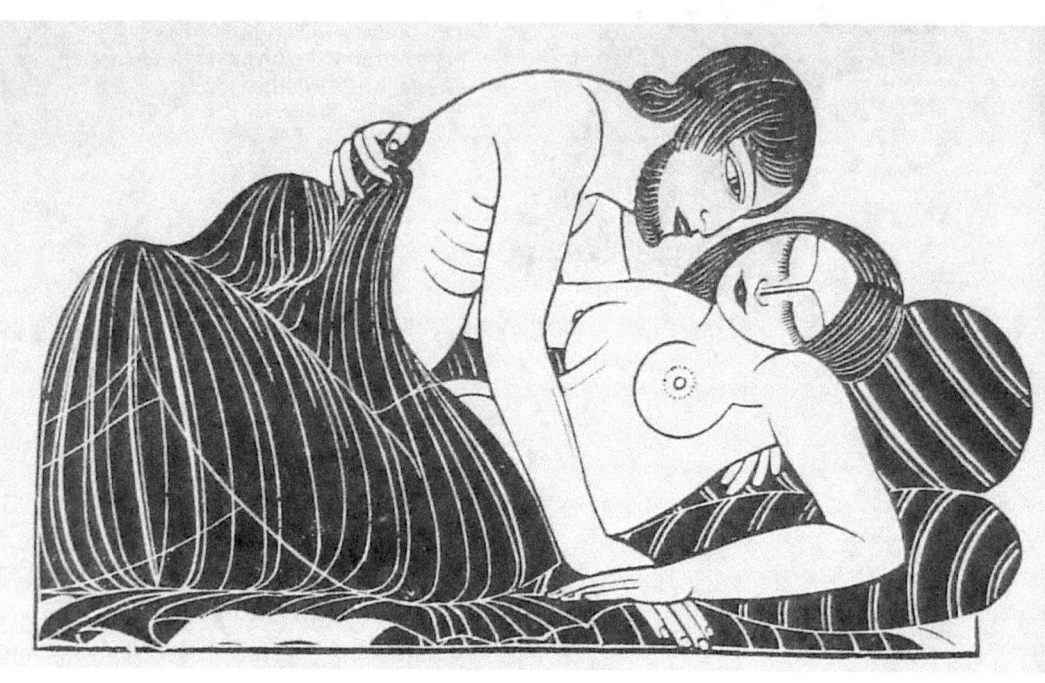

Eric Gill, The Juice of My Pomegranates, 1925

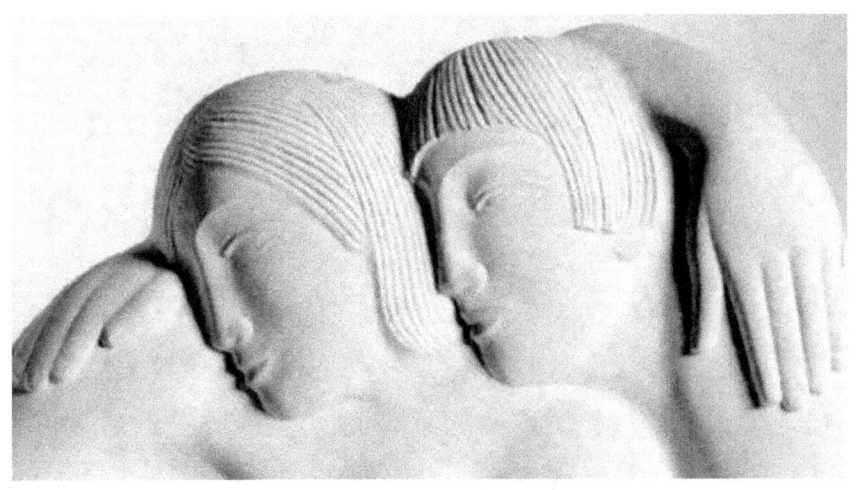

Eric Gill, Tobias and Sarah, 1926, private collection (above).
Eric Gill, Ariel Learns Celestial Music, 1932, Broadcasting House, London (below).

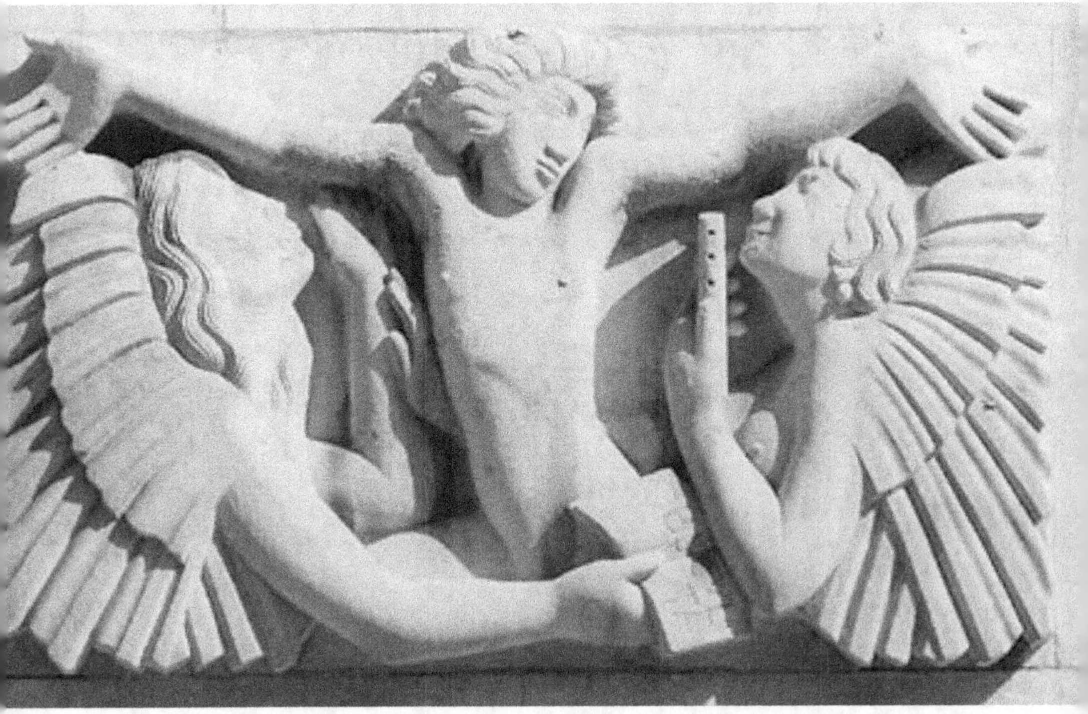

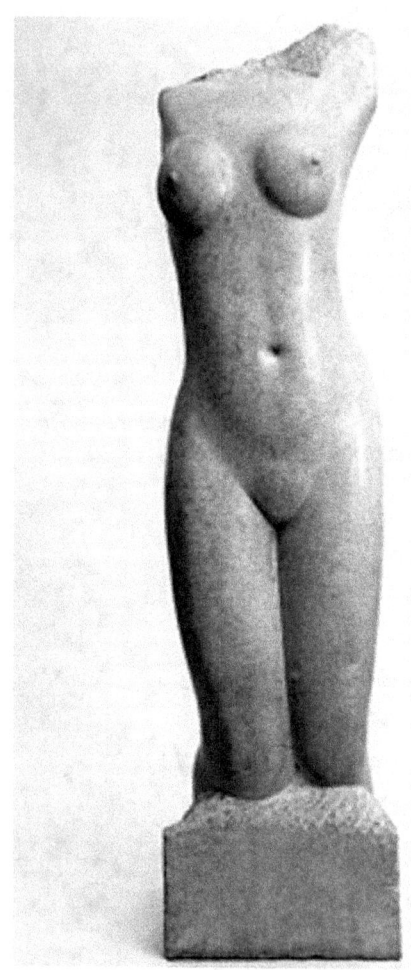

Eric Gill, Mankind,
Victoria & Albert Museum

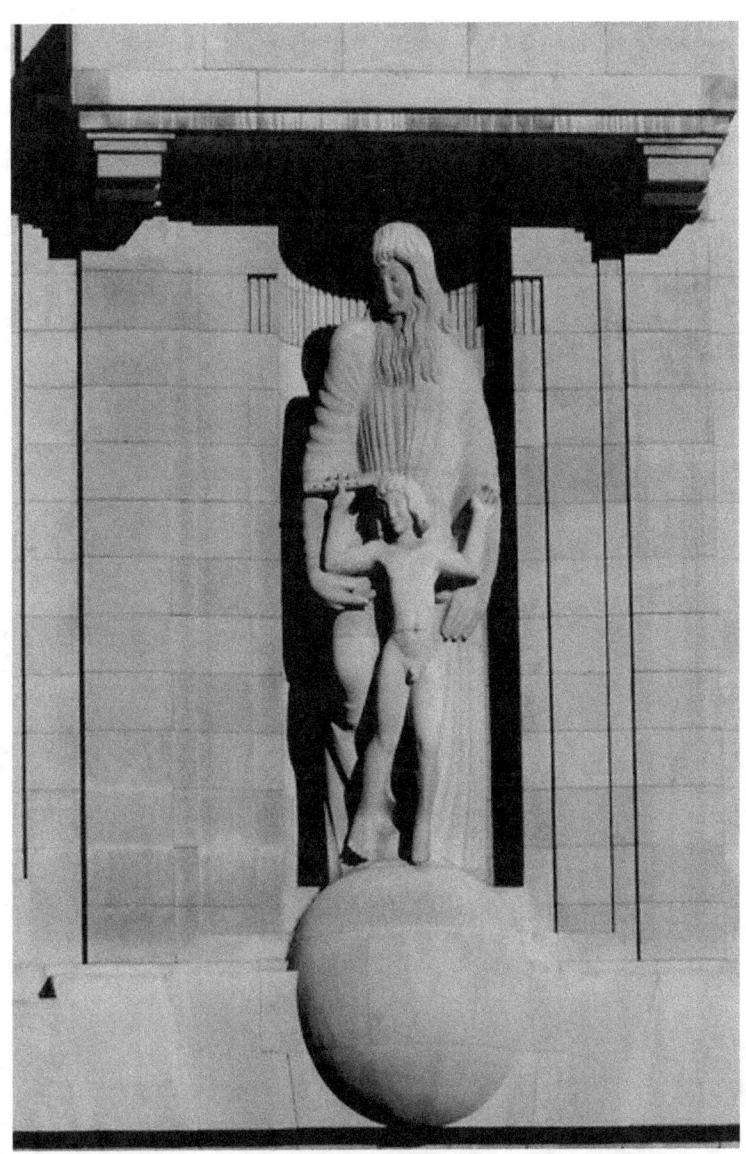

Eric Gill at the BBC

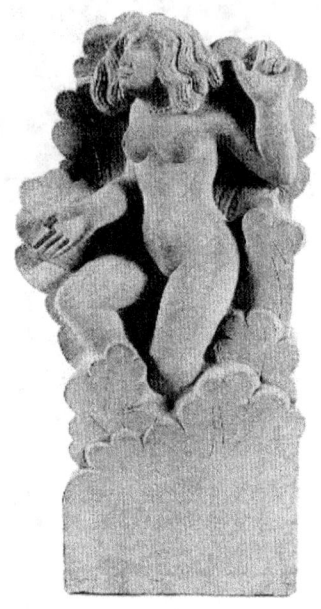

Eric Gill, Caryatid, stone

AaBbCcDdEeF
fGgHhIiJjKkLl
MmNnOoPp
QqRrSsTtUuV
vWwXxYyZz

Examples of Eric Gill's fonts
(this page and over)

Golden Cockerel Roman

Golden

Golden Cockerel Titling

GOLDEN

Golden Cockerel Italic

Golden

Golden Type Black

Golden

Gill Sans

Aa Qq Rr
Aa Qq Rr

a

COLLEGIUM

abcdefghijklm
nopqrstuvwxyz
0123456789

ABCDEF

PQRSTU

fghijklmn

ing should be left to the imagination of the sign-
writer or the enamel-plate maker. In this quality of
'fool-proofness' the Monotype sans-serif face
(figure 15) is perhaps an improvement. The letters

ABCDEFGHIJKLM
NOPQRSTUVWX
Y&Z 1234567890
abcdefghijklmno
pqrstuvwxyz

Figure 15: Monotype sans-serif

are more strictly normal — freer from forms depen-
ding upon appreciation and critical ability in the
workman who has to reproduce them.

I

INTRODUCTION

ERIC GILL (1882-1940) is one of the major erotic artists of the 20th century, and one of the major British 20th century artists. Wyndham Lewis called his work 'excellent and ribald', while influential critic Roger Fry, one of Gill's supporters, said Gill's sculpture was 'the outcome of a desire to express something felt in the adventure of human life.'[1] In a gushing review in the Nation, Fry emphasized the innocence in Gill's art. Augustus John was more cutting, writing:

> He is much impressed by the importance of copulation possibly because he has had so little to do with that subject in practice, and apparently considers himself obliged to announce the gospel of the flesh, to a world that doesn't need it.[2]

Eric Gill's life has been well-documented elsewhere, in biographies and memoirs by, among others, Malcolm Yorke, Robert Speaight, Cecil Gill, David Kindersley, Donald Potter, John Rothenstein, J. Thorp, Beatrice Warde, Donald Attawater and Fiona MacCarthy.

A brief biography is offered here: he was born Arthur Eric Rowton Gill on February 22, 1882, at 32, Hamilton Road, Brighton. He was named after Eric, or Little by Little, by Dean Farrar (1858). He was born into a large family – with six brothers and six sisters.

Religious matters were deeply engrained in his family: his father, Arthur Tidman Gill, had been a Congregational minister (in Burnley) and in Brighton became a clergyman in the 'Countess of Huntingdon's Connection', part of Calvinist Methodism. In 1896, Arthur Gill again changed his religious allegiance, and joined the Church of England. Gill described his father thus: 'a rather good-looking, bald-headed clergyman with a trim beard. A very kind man and a conscientious visitor of the poor' (A, 43). Eric Gill's grandfather, George Gill, was a Congregational minister; both his grandfather and great uncle had been missionaries. Gill's sister Madeline, 'the bookworm of the family', became a Church of England nun; his brothers Cecil and Romney became Anglican missionaries in Papua New Guinea.

In his *Autobiography*, Eric Gill described how important Chichester was for him, in particular its mediæval street plan and cathedral. By comparison, Gill found his hometown of Brighton ugly and sprawling, with a street plan and architecture largely influenced by the railway (however, Gill loved locomotives, and some of his earliest lettering jobs were designs for locomotive names). Chichester, though, satisfied Gill's desire for a religious, unified, human-scale environment. In his *Autobiography*, Gill described Chichester as nothing less than 'the human city, the city of God, the place where life and work and things were all in one and all in harmony' (A, 76-77). It was the beauty of the town, not the sense of history, Gill explained, it was that Chichester was

> *a thing planned and ordered — no mere congeries of more or less sordid streets, growing, like a fungus, wherever the network of railways and sidings and railway sheds would allow... Chichester was what Brighton was not, an end, a thing, a place, the product of reason and love. For love too was visible.* (A, 77)

Eric Gill even drew a street plan of (parts of) Chichester and Brighton to illustrate his argument. Chichester cathedral became one of Gill's favourite haunts in his youth; after the head verger had been persuaded to give him the keys, Gill explored every nook and cranny. Significantly, it was in Chichester cathedral, the centre of Gill's 'city of God', that he met his future wife, Ethel Moore, the daughter of the sacristan; she had already been courted by a Sussex teacher before she met Gill. (Eric Gill's first love was at art school, Winifred Johnson, a platonic affair). Later, the area around Lincoln's Inn Fields acquired the same sort of ordered, cloistered environment that Gill loved.

The broad outlines of Eric Gill's life include:

✽ had an architectural apprenticeship in London

✽ set up as a stone-mason and letter-cutter in 1903

✽ at this time he was living in Hammersmith, with his wife Ethel and their daughter Elizabeth

✽ Gill was involved with the Fabian Society, the Arts and Crafts Exhibition League, the Housemakers' Society, the Calligraphers' Society, and the Art Workers Guild

✽ the Black Lion Lane and Hammersmith milieu, where Gill lived, was influenced by William Morris and the Arts and Crafts movement

✽ Morris's Kelmscott House was on the riverside at Hammersmith (the Socialist League used to meet there)

✽ among Gill's artistic neighbours in Black Lion Lane were Morris's daughter May, Emery Walker, Edward Spencer (from the Artificer's Guild), and Edward Johnston, the Arts and Crafts calligrapher

✽ Gill's socialist views were generally the standard ones: '[j]ustice and equity and fair dealing' between all people, the 'greatest good for the greatest number', food, shelter, clothing for everyone, no privilege, better pay and less hours, sanitation, books for all, and so on (A, 152)

✽ Gill's socialism also extended to go outwardly against the Church and Christianity, because Christianity was aligned with corporate capitalism, which employed 'mechanized war to preserve mechanized living'

✽ Gill said he believed that 'capitalism is robbery, industrialism is blasphemy and war is murder' (A, 257)

✽ Gill admired John Ruskin's philosophy, particularly for its spiritual and moral aspects

✽ another of Gill's friends around this time was H.G. Wells, one of the stars of the Fabian Society ('a great influence on my mind', Gill remarked [A, 271]), and also George Bernard Shaw

✽ Gill was one of the founders (with Holbrook Jackson and Jean Orage) of the Fabian Arts and Philosophy Group (in 1907)

✻ Gill developed his æsthetics of the everyday function and clarity of art early on in his career, backed up by Arts and Crafts æsthetics

✻ Gill espoused an art of craftsmanship, work, honesty, functionality and clarity (which can be easily seen in his Gill Sans typeface, his lettering, his woodcuts and his stone carving)

✻ in his *Autobiography* Gill spoke at length of the pleasure of working with a pen and ink

✻ he worked on many wood engravings and illustrations from the 1900s onwards

✻ he emphasized the simple but deep pleasures of work, whether it was sculpting, stone carving, letter-cutting or drawing

✻ Gill converted to Catholicism in 1913 (he was converted, he said, because of love: 'I became a catholic because I fell in love with the truth. And love is an experience. I saw. I heard. I felt. I tasted. I touched. And that is what lovers do' [A, 247])

✻ in 1907 Gill and his family moved to Ditchling in Sussex

✻ he created three main artistic communities – at Ditchling in Sussex, at Capel-y-ffin in the Black Mountains of Wales, and at Piggots near High Wycombe

✻ he collaborated with publishers and institutions such as the Hampshire House Workshops, Cranach Press, Golden Cockerel Press, St Dominic's Press and Count Harry Kessler, of Insel-Verlag

✻ some of his more well-known commissions included: the *Stations of the Cross* for Westminster Cathedral, a giant relief for the League of Nations building in Geneva, statues of Prospero and Ariel for the BBC at Broadcasting House in Langham Place and at tube stations for London Underground (St James). The Westminster *Stations of the Cross* were 14 stone relief panels for the cathedral, an important commission for Gill, and one of his major works.

On the internet, useful websites include the Eric Gill Society (ericgill.org.uk), ericgill.com, and the Tate Gallery (at tate.org.uk).

✻

Eric Gill has become a familiar figure in British modern art and life. He certainly looked the part of the Bohemian artist with his little skull caps, imitation monk's habits, artist's smocks and his penchant for bare feet and sandals (an early hippy? Yep). In his Fabian Society, Arts and Crafts and socialist period, Gill was described (in Blackfriars, 1941) by John Middleton Murry, a key member of D.H. Lawrence's circle, as a 'silent figure in a shabby mackintosh' who rolled his own cigarettes.

Gill the Monk. Saint Gill.

Eric Gill stands out in most of his photographs: in the photo of Gill standing next to the Flying Scotsman steam engine, flanked by various London and North Eastern Railway dignitaries in their suits and bowler hats (taken to advertize Gill's typeface for LNER, Gill looks distinctive in his beret, scarf and long coat. René Hague, Gill's collaborator and later son-in-law, said Gill looked like a 'Dutch missionary'. A photograph by his friend Howard Coster shows Gill in a black hat, with his thick-rimmed round spectacles, and sporting a cigarette holder. In the photo of Gill at the Pigotts sculpture studio (1937), he stands confidently in a stone-mason's smock, beside the large carving of Creation. Then there are the many pictures of Gill in his monk's habit, thick leather belt, beret and bare feet at work in his various studios, often bent over an engraving.

Eric Gill was a tireless worker, an embodiment of the Protestant work ethic, filling all his available hours with 'making, mending, setting things to right', as someone who worked with him remarked (M, 24). He worked on engravings, drawings, sculpture, typography, lectures, essays, plus the daily Catholic rituals, the family life, and recreations such as tennis, swimming, walking, drinking, poetry, singing, music and of course talking.

Count Kessler described Gill as a 'Tolstoy-like figure in a smock and cloak, half-monk, half peasant' (Kessler, 1971). As well as a monk's habit (!), Eric Gill also wore the 'girdle of chastity', sported by the Dominican Confraternity of the Angelic Warfare members; the girdle of chastity derived from the Angelic Warfare cord of St Thomas Aquinas, the white cord which two angels had put around the saint after he had seen off a young woman's advances. It was typical of Gill, a self-confessed sexual obsessive, to wear a symbol of chastity (!).

In photos of Eric Gill with his family, still dressed in his monk's garb, he sports a wide-brimmed straw hat. The hat, round glasses and beard picked him out from the various family members and grand-children. Gill comes across as the family patriarch, presiding over an extended household of children, grand-children, relatives, collaborators and friends. Large family gatherings were a staple part of Gill's life. In many pictures, Gill is smoking. In some he wears the square cap he constructed. In one photo (1924), Gill is wearing a wool jerkin and felt hat that his daughter Petra made for him.

Eric Gill was fastidious about clothes, as his life, art and writing demonstrate. He produced books such as *Trousers and the Most Precious Ornament*, *Clothes*, and *Clothing Without Cloth*. He saw clothes as unnecessarily covering up the body and its sexual organs, particularly in adolescence, 'with all its budding sexual enthusiasm'; he called clothes the 'first privy – private parts, in fact privy parts' (A, 50). In *Trousers and the Most Precious Ornament*, Gill wrote passionately about how women should hide their desirousness, which included

> scents, paint, closely clothed hips and croups, a swaying walk, immense care of the face and hair, short skirts in the street, diaphanous clinging drapes in the evening, bare backs and chests. (2)

It was OK for men to be vain, narcissistic, and self-preening, with peacock displays of clothes, but for women it was 'a sign of degradation, a proof of departure from the divine plan'' (from *Art-Nonsense*, 22). Eric Gill's fastidiousness extended throughout his art as well as his life: he was meticulous, for example, in recording and cataloguing his art, labelling his engravings in their many states, and writing in his diary.

Some of Eric Gill's key books (among 55 publications) included: *Autobiography*, *Art-Nonsense and Other Essays*, *Beauty Looks After Herself*, *An Essay on Typography*, *Last Essays*, *Sculpture*, *Sculpture and the Living Model*, *Money and Morals*, *Work and Property*, *Unemployment*, *Work and Leisure*, and his diaries. Some of his important illustrated volumes include: *The Canterbury Tales*, *Troilus and Criseyde*, the *Bible*, *Canticum Canticorum*, *Twenty-Five Nudes* and the editions of William Shakespeare's plays.

Some of Eric Gill's pet subjects, aside from the main ones of sex, religion, Catholicism, work, art, and so on – included plainchant, shorthand, postage stamps, naturism, social credit, spelling reform, custard powder and insurance. Gill contributed to many publications, including the *Times, The L.N.E.R. Magazine,* the *Slough Observer, The Schoolmaster & Woman Teacher's Chronicle, Ireland Today, The Engineer, Music and Liturgy,* various Catholic magazines and the *Socialist Review.*

Eric Gill's *Autobiography* is more a series of essays on Gill's favourite topics (architecture, urban planning, sex, religion, work, the family, nature, socialism) than a personal account of a life. At times in the book Gill reminds himself of the task he's consistently veering away from. 'I did inscriptions and tomb-stones. I begot three lovely daughters. I carved all sorts of comic statues – good, bad and indifferent' (A, 171).

Eric Gill was an artistic and spiritual leader for some; his admirers gathered around the patriarch and called him saintly. Gill believed in the idea of the artist

> *as prophet and seer, the artist as priest – art as man's act of collaboration with God in creating, art as ritual – these things I believed very earnestly.* (A, 173)

Like many other artists, Eric Gill had a vision of an arts and crafts community, and succeeded in some way in creating it at Ditchling, Capel-y-ffin, and Piggots, High Wycombe. A Gill admirer, Desmond Chute, wrote that Gill was a 'dear and holy man', and life at Ditchling Common was 'almost monastic', with Catholic rituals occurring daily, such as the ringing of the Angelus, the singing of the Compline and the Rosary (M, 137).

Eric Gill organized Ditchling like a spiritual retreat, complete with Tertiary meetings; vacations for the workshop on devotion and obligation days; and a chapel choir (Gill designed the chapel). Conrad Pepler described life at the Dichtling commune as baking cakes in brick ovens, making butter, pig-killing, harvesting, amateur dramatics, music-making, wine-making, and Catholic rituals, in amongst ponies, pigs, goats, cows and poultry (Y, 33). Cars, telephones and gramophones were not allowed (only later, at Piggots, were they approved). Inevitably, some visitors were not so taken with the Gillian version of commune life, and complained about the cold rooms, draughts, no electricity, frozen water, smoky fires, and the dilapidated buildings (Y, 34).

In his *Autobiography* Eric Gill was not kind about the group of artists he helped to found.

> I believed in religion and was desperately trying to find it, and they seemed to regard religion as being essentially nonsense but valuable as a spur to æsthetic experience and activity. (A, 173)

Capel-y-ffin was the most remote of Eric Gill's monastic, arts-and-crafts retreats, a Welsh village 14 miles outside Abergavenny, in the Brecon mountains, with the nearest railway station 10 miles away, and the nearest doctor in Hay-on-Wye. In his *Autobiography* Gill said:

> what I hope above all things is that I have done something towards the re-integrating bed and board, the small farm and the workshop, the home and the school, earth and heaven. (A, 282)

As Eric Gill explained in his *Autobiography*, Capel-y-ffin was four miles N.W. of Llanthony in the Ewyas valley. It had been built by 'Father Ignatius', an Anglican preacher, in the 1860s (A, 216). Gill said that 3 families, 7 children (from 5 to 19 years old), a pony, chickens, cats, dogs, goats, ducks, geese, and 2 magpies travelled from Ditchling to Capel-y-ffin. 'I say it was a good life, and it was, and it was a natural life' (A, 228).

Life at Capel-y-ffin was basic; too rough for a motor car, much of the travelling and carrying was done by pony and cart. Gill said his daughters enjoyed living in the Black Mountains:

> They used to ride the fifteen miles into Abergavenny to do the shopping and when I had to go to London, as happened every month or so, we had to drive the eleven miles to Llanvihangel Crucorney (the nearest station) with great nicety of calculation so as just not to miss the train. Many a time we would see the smoke of the train approaching us with another half-mile to gallop. (A, 218)

Among Eric Gill's many collaborators was Robert Gibbings, a founder of the Society of Wood Engravers, who took over the Golden Cockerel

Press, for whom Gill did some of his best graphic work, including *Sonnets and Verses* (by his sister Enid), the *Song of Songs* (1925), *Troilus and Criseyde* (1927), *Canterbury Tales*, and *The Four Gospels*. Other collaborators included Desmond Chute, John Skelton, Jacob Epstein, Beatrice Warde, Stanley Morison, David Jones and Douglas Cleverdon. Cleverdon ran an antiquarian bookshop off Park Street in Bristol; Gill painted the sign for Cleverdon's bookshop; Cleverdon was involved in various ventures with Gill, including publishing Gill's *Art and Love*.

Jacob Epstein's art (and personality) chimed with Eric Gill's at various points: both had 'enlightened' views on the eroticism of art; both adored the female body; both produced erotic art, with nude forms, that created controversies; together, around 1910, they planned a 20th century Stonehenge, in the Sussex countryside, which would feature giant figures, some of them nude. Ananda Coomaraswamy was another important friend (and influence), discussed below. Gill was also associated with the Neo-Pagans, the intellectual, free-thinking Cambridge circle, who included Rupert Brooke, Edward Marsh and the Cornfords.

When Petra Gill died (in January, 1999), her obituaries were inevitably illustrated with an illustration by Eric Gill. The obituary in *The Independent* (January 9, 1999), by Lottie Hoare, described Petra Tegetmeier as the 'perfect adolescent muse' for her father; Hoare discussed Petra's unusual childhood, growing up at Ditchling Common, the self-sufficiency, the Catholicism, the erratic education she received from Gill and various artists; her escape from her 'patriarch's territory' to become a weaver; her engagement to David Jones in 1923; her marriage to Denis Tegetmeier, the Trappist monk, cartoonist, engraver and letterer, which lasted until his death in 1987.

Eric Gill enjoyed scandals and shocking people with his art; one of the most famous is his BBC commission to carve Prospero and Ariel at Broadcasting House in London: after a preview, Gill was asked by the BBC's governors to make Ariel's genitals smaller. An MP, G.G. Mitcheson, complained about Gill's Ariel, calling for the Home Secretary to have it removed. At Jesus College, Cambridge, Gill was asked to reduce the angels' buttocks in his carving over the gateway. Gill's art was the subject of banning and censorship during (and after) his life. The archbishop of Westminster Cathedral, for example. ordered the monkey in Gill's statue of St Thomas More to be taken away. His *Ck. and Balls* was banned from Shanks Bathroom fittings' showroom in Bond Street.

And then there's sex. Eric Gill and sex. Sex, sex, sex.

There's always a flavour in Eric Gill's art and writing of quaint Englishness. You can spot it right away, in so many details. And it's very appealing. I think of a sexed-up Ealing comedy, or a *Carry On* movie which includes hard-ons as well as boobs.

Eric Gill's social background in regard to sex was of the Victorian fire and brimstone kind, where sex and masturbation was never spoken about, something kept secret, linked with shame, guilt, sin and perversion. Gill said in his *Autobiography* that he had tried talking to his parents about sex, but had been told that bringing up such subjects would result in a thrashing 'and, if we persisted, 'consumption', madness and death' (A, 53). So when Gill finally discovered sexual pleasure, he was ecstatic (note the emphasis on genitals):

> ...how shall I ever forget the strange, inexplicable rapture of my first experience? What marvellous thing was this that suddenly transformed a mere water tap into a pillar of fire — water into an elixir of life? I lived henceforth in a strange world of contradiction: something was called filthy which was obviously clean; something was called ridiculous which was obviously solemn and momentous; something was called ugly which was obviously lovely. Strange days and nights of mystery and fear mixed with excitement and wonder — strange days and nights, strange months and years. It was a blessing that this intellectual puzzlement and emotional exaltation was balanced by a good healthy rabelaisianism. (A, 53-54)

A footnote to the above passage in *Autobiography* justifies how 'natural' masturbation must be; nearly all young people do it, Eric Gill contends, and if it gives 'a pleasure so ecstatic', all the better. It is not harmful, and should be indulged in. Gill also gives the topic of masturbation a classist aspect:

> the 'working' and 'country' classes don't suffer much from excessive masturbation — they know enough about sex not to be excessively curious and imaginative and in such circles there is less unnatural pudicity and puritanism. The 'middle-class' is naturally much more ignorant and therefore much more secretly vicious. (A, 54-55).

For Eric Gill, the sin and guilt and self-condemnation of Christianity was deadening; instead of placing one's trials and troubles at the feet of Christ, for him to purify and redeem, perhaps one could make them 'occasions of thanksgiving', because '[t]here can be no movement of the flesh or of the imagination which cannot thus be sanctified and turned to sweetness' (A, 224).

2

SEX AND TEXTS

Eric Gill created some superb and much-used typefaces, what he called 'absolutely legible-to-the-last-degree letters', including Solus (1929), Perpetua (1925) with its elegant sloping italic, Joanna (1930), named after his daughter, and Gill Sans (1927 and after), based on Edward Johnston's 1913 font. Joanna (1930) and Bunyan (1934) were designed for Hague & Gill; Monotype made their version of Joanna in 1937. Golden Cockerel (1929) was made for the Golden Cockerel Press; Aries (1932) was made for the Stourton Press; Jubilee (1934) was designed for Stephenson & Blake; and Hebrew (1937) was made for Monotype.

For Gill Sans, Eric Gill developed Johnston's London Underground that Frank Pick had commissioned. The commission to produce Gill Sans for Monotype came from the London and North Eastern Rail company (LNER), as part of their total corporate design. LNER were trying to found a national transport network, which required a standardization in typefaces. Like Johnston's typeface, Gill Sans was intended to be simple and clear, easy for signwriters to paint, and easy for printers to use. Beatrice Warde emphasized its functionality and clarity; it would give rail travel a continuity, she said, so that passengers could see the same font used in timetables, promotional leaflets, station signs, destination boards and posters; her partner at Monotype, Stanley Morison, pointed out that the roots of Gill Sans were in classical architecture: the original letters were carved on ancient Greek and Roman buildings. Gill Sans is still in use by private rail companies today. The Gill Sans commission enhanced Gill's reputation. Gill was critical of the publicity campaigns of Monotype, the way his typefaces were used for advertizing and commercial enterprises, even though he profited from them (C. Badaracco, 104).

Gill Sans was Eric Gill's most popular font by a long way, and is still being used in thousands of places. Gill Sans has become a design 'classic', much admired by typographers and designers, with its modernist, Art Deco echoes. Although it is used as widely as fonts such as the Swiss Helvetica and Morison's Times New Roman, it retains its æsthetic credibility. Detractors of Gill Sans said because it was sans serif it was associated with advertizing and commercial printing, as sans serif faces had been used for commercial applications in the 19th century. By 1940, around 60% of goods used sans serif typefaces. By 1960, it was 87% of the market.

Some of Eric Gill's fonts were designed for Stanley Morison of the Monotype Corporation; some were for his own use; some were for Hague & Gill. Critics were not so keen on Gill's Perpetua, which took 13 years to complete; they said it was too spindly and delicate to be a useful bookface (C. Badaracco, 94). However, Morison was full of praise:

> There was never anything of that kind before Gill did this, and never has been anything since. The capitals that he did, I think, will be immortal. They'll be used as long as the Roman alphabet is ever used anywhere. (BBC radio, 1969)

Certainly Perpetua is a beautiful typeface, like Joanna and Gill Sans, and all of Eric Gill's other typography. With his work for Monotype and his elegant titling and engraving, Gill's typography has become an important part of modern design. Gill's place has become assured in any history book on 20th century typography, alongside famous typographers such as Frederic Goudy, Jan Tschichold, Stanley Morison, El

Lissitzky and Hermann Zapf.

Designing fonts and letters was very important for Eric Gill, as any look at his art shows: there are letters and words everywhere in his work, carved into stone, cut into engravings, sketched in pencil, drawn in ink, printed as posters. His engravings show his love for designing decorative capital letters and monograms, as well as alphabets. He designed the title pages and look of many books, including editions of the Bible, Virgil, Rainer Maria Rilke (Duino Elegies and Gesammelte Gedichte, for Cranach Press, 1930), Johann Wolfgang von Goethe (poems and Faust), Paul Valéry, John Keats, Homer, Hugo von Hofmannsthal, Geoffrey Chaucer, Percy Bysshe Shelley, William Shakespeare and the Song of Songs.

Eric Gill made Christmas cards, often depicting the Madonna and Child, with inscriptions around the figures (for example last of all in these days he has spoken to us by his Son, Christmas card, 1935, and et tuam ipsius animam pertransibit gladius on a Christmas card for the Peace Pledge Union, 1938). He designed maps and lettering, such as the one showing Piggots near High Wycombe (1928) in its local surroundings and for Beatrice Warde of Pimlico wharf (1935). He made stamps (such as the commemorative stamp for the League of Nations Union, 1939). He designed monograms and colophons using his hand-lettering, including for the British Medical Association, St Bartholemew's Hospital Journal, Petersfield Music Festival, Cambridge University Press, and book-plates, for people such as Morley Kennerley, Nigel Warren, Wilma Mairi Cawdor, Gerald Stephen Hughes, Everard Meynell, Anne Robinson, Thereze Mary Hope, Jacob Weiss, Bridget Grant, John Maurice Rothenstein, Miriam Rothschild, A.H. Tandy and Gladys Huntington.

Many of Eric Gill's designs involve figures entwined with capital letters, sitting on them (such as the decorations for The Canterbury Tales, The Four Gospels and the Song of Songs). The figures in The Four Gospels, made for the Golden Cockerell Press in 1931, are very intricately interwoven with the giant capital letters: engravings such as Mary Magdalene, Christ and the Leper, Herod's Feast and The Visitation portray the human figures entangled with the capitals, their limbs are sometimes either side of the letters. In The Deposition, one of the main illustrations in The Four Gospels (along with

The Nativity, The Burial of Christ, The Creation and Christ Crowned), one of the male figures taking down the dead Jesus from the Cross (perhaps Joseph of Arimethea) is impossibly entwined with the giant capital 'A', in the manner of M.C. Escher's puzzle drawings.

In The Canterbury Tales (1929), the main decorative device is a spray of leaves:

❋ the figures climb the stem (Girl With Lace-edged Drawers, Woman Climbing, Cupid Above, Man Climbing to Girl On Spray);

❋ die in the spray (Naked Man Dead and Man Dead);

❋ write beside it (Chaucer Writing At Foot of Spray);

❋ sit under it (Man Drunk, Man Dead Drunk and Man Drinking);

  sleep in its branches (Cuckold Asleep, Lovers Above);

❋ are murdered in it (The Martyrdom of St Thomas of Canterbury);

❋ make love in it (The Miller's Tale, The Reeve's Tale, The Merchant's Tale, The Shipman's Tale);

❋ Christ dances in it (Christchild);

❋ angels appear in it, as do the Devil (The Devil On Dead Branch), Pegasus, and horsemen (The Squire's Tale);

❋ and lovers pursue in it (Youth Blowing Kiss, Naked Boy Looking Up to Hermaphrodite, Man in Love).

There are many voluptuous nudes in The Canterbury Tales illustrations — such as the image of a beautiful sleeping Venus in Initial Letter H, and Venus and Cupid With the Golden Cockerel, the coy Venus in Initials H and O With Venus Modestly Holding Spray, the long-legged Naked Woman Holding Spray, the shy, coyly smiling nude women, with protuberant nipples and buttocks (Naked Girl in Spray, Head Thrown to Left, Naked Girl in Spray, Head Thrown Back to Right, Naked Girl in Spray, Head Thrown Back to Left and Naked Girl, Hands over Head), and nudes such as The Cook's Tale, Naked Young Woman Sitting On Branch, the two Women Growing Out of a Tree, and the humiliated Delilah, hiding her face (though not so deep in shame she can't show off her hips and bottom). In one of the Geoffrey Chaucer pictures, the spray of leaves becomes a Gill phallus: Woman Climbing Floreated Phallus; in another, a snake entwined in the spray is given a 'phallic head'.

In Eric Gill's art, humanity and typography, sex and letters, intertwine, recalling French feminism and postmodern criticism which speaks of the 'sexuality of texts' and the 'textuality of sex', what French philosopher and feminist Hélène Cixous calls the *jouissance* of writing (the orgasmic quality of poetry). She also uses the term the 'libidinal economy' of literature. From Roland Barthes' work, Julia Kristeva developed her notion of the 'jouissance of the text', the text as *jouissance*, especially as found in modern *avant garde* literature.

For Eric Gill, letters themselves were beautiful things — 'things, not pictures of things' (A, 120); for him, letter-cutting and designing was a solid, honest, useful trade which served society. In his *Autobiography* Gill spoke in ecstatic terms of the first time he saw Edward Johnston, his teacher at Central School, produce calligraphy:

> ...the first time I saw him writing, and saw the writing that came as he wrote, I had what otherwise I can only remember having had when first I touched her body or saw her hair down for the first time (Lord! what the young men have lost since women bobbed their hair!), or when I first hear the plain-chant of the Church (as they sang it at Louvain in the Abbey of Mont César) or when I first entered the church of San Clemente in Rome, or first saw the North Transept of Chartres from the little alley between the houses... I did not know such beauties could exist. I was struck as by lightning, as by a sort of enlightenment. There are indeed many other things as good; there are many occasions when, in a manner of speaking, you seem to pierce the cloud of unknowing and for a brief second seem to know even as God knows — sometimes, when you are drawing the human body, even the turn of a shoulder or the firmness of waist, it seems to shine with the radiance of righteousness. But these more sudden enlightenments are rare events, never forgotten... (A, 119)

For Eric Gill, trades such as letter-cutting and stone carving were not only socially valuable, they were also holy trades. And for Gill, the sacred also meant the sexual: hence he spoke of the phallic energy needed to pursue this kind of work. The 'perpetual seethe of tumescence', he called it, where the 'exuberance of nature is a factor of paramount importance'. Gill used a vivid metaphor to explain his view: the 'urine of the stallion fertilizes the fields more than all the chemicals of science. So, under Divine Providence, the excess of amorous nature fertilizes the spiritual field' (A, 122-3).

The interweaving of eroticism and typography, sex and letters, occurs also in Eric Gill's life: he did much of his work for the Monotype Corporation, and had an affair with Beatrice Warde, the independent-minded American publicity officer of Monotype (she was called the 'First Lady of Typography'); in turn, Warde had a life-long affair with Stanley Morison, Gill's boss at Monotype.

Beatrice Warde (1900-69) was a strong individual who operated in the largely masculinist world of design and typography. She had a male pseudonym for her professional persona, 'Paul Beaujon', which she used for her lengthy, learned trade articles. For years Warde edited Monotype's trade journal, *Monotype Recorder*. Warde also had an affair with another of Gill's collaborators and friends, Douglas Cleverdon. Warde was the model for some of Gill's *Twenty-Five Nudes*, and appears in many of Gill's portraits.

3

WOMEN

For Eric Gill, eroticism was a vital part of life, and should be openly displayed in art. He moved from nudes to Madonnas easily and simply: sex and religion were part of the same mystery for him. Seen in Lacanian theory, the female model becomes the 'obscure object of desire', feared and desired, ever unreachable, the manifestation of eternal loss.[1] The problematic and erotic relation between life and art, between the human beloved and the art object, is vividly expressed in the way Eric Gill started working in sculpture. The very reason that Gill turned to sculpture, so he says, was sexual: his wife was pregnant with their third daughter, Joanna, and because of the 'enforced abstinence', i.e., no sex during pregnancy, Gill turned to stone carving:

> ...as I couldn't have all I wanted in one way I determined to see what I could do about it in another – I fashioned a woman of stone. Up to that time, I had never made what is called an "erotic" drawing of any sort and least of all in so laborious a medium as stone. And so, just as on the first occasion when with immense planning and scheming, I touched my lover's lovely body, I insisted on seeing her completely (no peeping between the uncut pages, so to say), so my first erotic drawing was not on the back of an envelope but a week or so's work on a decent piece of hard stone. I say this seems praiseworthy, and so it is... no one would guess the fervours which conditioned its making. But there it was; it was a carving of a naked young woman and if I hadn't very

much wanted a naked young woman, I don't think I should ever have done it. Lord, how exciting! — and not merely touching and seeing but actually making her. I was responsible for her very existence and her every form straight from my heart. A new world opened before me. My Lord!... A new alphabet — the word was made flesh. (Autobiography, 158-9)

Deprived of sex in real life, Eric Gill turned to creating sex in art. Instead of 'possessing' the real woman, he could 'possess' the created woman, the woman in stone, ink, text. Instead of putting his hands on flesh-and-blood breasts, he could put his hands on breasts made of stone. '[N]ot merely touching and seeing but actually making her' as he put it (A, 159). A stone woman, as Pygmalions throughout history have known, does not answer back, nag or moan. She does whatever one likes.

There are many female nude sculptures in Eric Gill's œuvre:

❊ *Dancer* (1913) .

❊ *Contortionist* (1912), a woman bending over, arching her back, clasping her knees, displaying her breasts and pubis .

❊ *A Roland For Oliver* (1910, University of Hull) .

❊ *Anadyomene* (1920, Texas) .

❊ *Gingerbread Woman — Eve* (1920), a beautiful headless torso in Bath stone, emphasizing the breasts, hips and pubis .

❊ *Small Female Torso* (1924, Texas) .

❊ *Adam and Eve* (1920), a double relief, headless, showing the first couple embracing .

❊ *Headless Female Torso Relief*, a voluptuous version of the *Gingerbread Woman* .

❊ *Nude Girl With Hair* (1925), a dreamy nude image with an amazing abundance of long hair, made at Capel-y-ffin out of a piece of stone found in the Welsh hills .

❊ *Standing Nude With Hair* (1922).

❊ *Torso — Woman* (1913), in which a woman clasps her breasts, a favourite Gill gesture .

❊ *Tobias and Sara* another version of Gill's 'divine lovers' theme .

❊ *The Bath* (1920), a double relief, showing a naked woman crouching in a tub from the front and back .

❀ *Caryatid* (1927, UCLA), a large wooden sculpture of an idealized female nude.

❀ *Belle Sauvage* (1930, Cecil Higgins Art Gallery), another long-haired female nude, this one surrounded by foliage (Gill carved another one in the same year).

❀ In *The Rower*, a woman displays her buttocks, when the sculpture is positioned upright.

❀ *Chloe* (1930, Fogg Art Museum), made for Leonard Woolf (Virginia's husband).

❀ *Memento Mori Stone for a Garden* (1939), a gravestone incorporating a female nude.

Mankind (1928, Tate Gallery) was a large Hoptonwood stone piece, superbly finished, carved in Chelsea for Eric Gill's 1928 Groupil Gallery show. Fiona MacCarthy found *Mankind* a little bland and anonymous (220), but I think this classical style torso is one of Gill's finest sculptures, at once imposing and tender, monumental and maternal (and it's not anonymous — it's instantly recognizable as an Eric Gill sculpture). The critics liked it (including the *Observer* and the *Daily Mail* newspapers, though Whipsnade Zoo rejected it). *Mankind* has an assurance and a simplified economy, stripping down the human form to a near-abstract beauty. (Recently, it's been well presented in the Victoria & Albert Museum — see the illustrations).

By far the most common subject in Eric Gill's sculpture, though, was religious (and Christian): the nudes, acrobats, contortionists and divine lovers may receive more attention in art criticism, but the religious and Catholic sculptures are more numerous: there are *Depositions*, *St Sebastians*, *Annunciations*, *Crucifixions*, *Holy Faces*, *Mary Magdalenes*, angels, crucifixes, memorials, headstones, altarpieces, many *Madonna and Childs*, and of course the *Stations of the Cross* series.

Just as typical as the female torsos and lovers fucking are sculptures such as *Christ and the Money Changers*, *Holy Water Stoup With Crucifixion*, *Christ Giving Sight to Bartimaeus*, *Christ the King Seated*, *Paschal Lamb Relief*, *St Joseph and Jesus*, *St Joan of Arc*, *Agnus Dei Relief*, and *St Anthony of Padua*. Of course, most of Eric Gill's religious sculptures are infused with his heightened sense of eroticism, his blending of the sacred and the sexual, his sensualization of

Christianity. Perhaps the most common of all Gill's religious sculptures are his *Madonna and Childs* and *Christs*, as one would expect, for these are the two most common images in Western art, certainly in Western art from mediæval and Renaissance times onwards.

Also, as one would expect, Eric Gill eroticized the mother-child relation in his many *Madonna and Child* sculptures: there are many images of Mary suckling the baby Jesus, in some she squeezes her breast, holding it to his mouth (as in *Madonna and Child Relief*, 1912, *Madonna and Child 1*, 1912, and *Mother and Child Relief*, 1917). Some of the *Madonna and Child* works feature a naked Virgin – an image that certainly hardly (if ever) occurs in mediæval or Renaissance art. It is not wholly peculiar to Gill, the naked Virgin Mary, but it is a subject he makes his own: in *Madonna and Child 1* (1910), *Madonna and Child 2* (1910), *Naked Mother and Child* (1913), and the two *Mother and Childs* (both 1913). In one of the nude *Madonna* sculptures Gill has sit with her thighs apart, so the viewer can see her genitals.

One can see elements of the Lacanian lack, desire, repression, mirror stage, Symbolic Order and œdipal anxiety in the modern artists who create specifically erotic images. In artists such as Eric Gill, Pierre Renoir, Henri Matisse, Aristide Maillol, Auguste Rodin, Gustav Klimt, Amedeo Modigliani and Pablo Picasso, one finds loss, desire, repression and anxiety quite clearly. The art they produced was fiercely heterosexual, glorifying women, even as, in some cases (Picasso) the paintings seem to denigrate women. Renoir, in paintings such as *Bather Arranging Her Hair*, and Lawrence Alma-Tadema in *In the Tepidarium*, produced works that exalt women as sexual objects. The soft flesh is available but also distinctly not available.[2] These nude paintings remain chimeras, never to be possessed, always to be yearned for. As Nicholas Poussin wrote of painting: '[p]ainting is nothing but an imitation of human actions, which alone are, properly speaking, inimitable' (in R. Goldwater, 154). Poussin recognizes that painting is always an imitation, a mirror; the real thing can never be possessed in art. It is the same in erotic art – indeed, it is most dramatically expressed in erotic art – this paradoxical fear and desire, this simultaneous desire and loss, this ambiguous conflict between possession and dispossession.

4

NUDES

Many of Eric Gill's female nude engravings are simple, tender studies of women. The Thorn in the Flesh (1921) shows just the female torso, the large breasts and belly very prominent; On the Tiles depicts a nude woman crouching, knees drawn up, recalling the melancholy woman in Vincent van Gogh's nude drawing; some of Gill's nude studies are simple and anonymous (such as Yahoo, 1926, Nude Study and Woman, 1926).

Some of Eric Gill's depictions of nude women are studies of the women in his life (such as his daughters): ✻ Hair Combing (1922) shows his nude daughter Petra tending her very lengthy tresses; ✻ Girl in the Bath (1922 and 1923), again of Petra, is all limbs; ✻ taken from a Daily Mirror photograph, The Tennis Player (1923), depicts a standard Gillian scene: a nude woman bending over from behind.

Eric Gill portrayed women's asses in many drawings and sculptures: like Mellors in Lady Chatterley's Lover, Gill was very fond of women's behinds. He liked to portray women bending over (in The Chinese Maidservant, Woman Bending [1926] and The Tennis Player); Eve sticking her tush out with the snake between her thighs (1935); two 'experiments with a multiple tool', Woman (1926 [P412]) and Sculpture No. 2 (1930 [P629]), in the latter engraving the buttocks are impossibly spherical, like two footballs; and the rounded bottom of *Naked Girl With Back Turned* from *Troilus and Criseyde* (1927).

Women's bottoms are prominently displayed in many of the *Twenty-Five Nudes* (such as *Female Nude, Standing, From Behind, Female Nude, Kneeling* and *Female Nude, Lying*). The latter engraving in *Twenty-Five Nudes* concentrates solely on the butt: this reclining nude recalls some of Gustav Klimt's and Auguste Rodin's studies, where the hips and bottom become the subject, or Gustave Courbet's infamous painting *The Creation of the World* (1866), showing just the torso of a woman, with her legs wide open.

The female nudes in the book *Twenty-Five Nudes* are delicate, tender, somewhat idealized, the forms delineated with Eric Gill's usual economy of means: there are just outlines for the limbs, sometimes a faint line to indicate details of the body, such as the folds of skin around the stomach; little squiggles indicate the belly button. Only a few of the nudes have shading to indicate volume. Gill makes sure that the erogenous zones are clearly defined: the nipples and breasts, the hips and buttocks, the conch and pubes. Vulvas, pubic bushes and nipples receive special care. Many of the *Twenty-Five Nudes* depict women without heads, or with their faces turned away; Gill is not interested in particular personalities here, but in the body in different poses.

The female nudes assume classic and more unusual poses: standing, seated, stretching, reclining. *Twenty-Five Nudes* are erotic but also innocent, sexualized but also idealized, bodies with bulges but largely without blemishes. The headless, idealized female form also occurs in Eric Gill's sculpture *Mankind* (1928), a modernist female study recalling those of Auguste Rodin, Jacob Epstein, Aristide Maillol and Henri Gaudier-Brzeska. The nude women Gill engraved for the borders of the Golden Cockerel edition of Geoffrey Chaucer were heavily idealized, and eroticized: the *Naked Girl With Back Turned* coyly shows off her protuberant globes; the *Naked Girl Facing Left* has *Playboy*-style pert breasts; the *Naked Girl Facing Right* (all 1927) also has prominent nipples and buttocks.

The *Twenty-Five Nudes* commission is full of sexualized, nude women: from the harpies squatting atop trees to various women cavorting amongst the branches. A pencil drawing of the Twenties (*K.L. on Sofa*, National Portrait Gallery, London) shows a nearly-nude woman reclining in a more obviously pornographic pose, her legs spread for the viewer, her cooch visible under the semi-translucent clothes. The engravings for *Clothing Without Cloth* depict more idealized women, the standing nudes in *Venus* and *The Bee Sting*, the sitting nude in *Girl on Bank* (all 1924). In *Clothing Without Cloth* illustrations, the women have their arms raised, to reveal their bodies.

5

ERIC GILL
AND CONSTANTIN BRANCUSI

Although he was a hugely significant sculptor, working at the same time as Eric Gill, according to some critics (J. Collins, 1998, 34), there is no record that Gill discussed Constantin Brancusi in his letters or essays. Brancusi's most erotic sculpture was one of his early pieces, which turned up in various forms: *The Kiss* (for example, *The Kiss*, 1907-8, stone, Museum of Art, Craiova, Romania and *The Kiss II*, c.1908, private collection). Unlike Auguste Rodin's *tour-de-force* depiction of erotic passion (*The Kiss*, 1886, Musée Rodin, Paris), Brancusi's *The Kiss* is a 'primitive', non-naturalistic square block of stone, very far indeed from Michelangelo Buonaroti, Gian Lorenzo Bernini or Auguste Rodin, but much closer to Gill's *Divine Lovers* and *Ecstasy*. For Brancusi *The Kiss* was his 'road to Damascus', a key work (quoted in H. Roche, 26f).

The different versions of Constantin Brancusi's *The Kiss* aim to depict that intimate erotic experience of love-making, symbolized by a kiss. The two people – male and female, of course – are shown kissing face-on, their bodies fused together. It is a modern version of spiritual union, that dream of Plato, the love which is 'two-in-one', and celebrated through post-classical Western history. The Platonic *syzygy* or 'two yolks (or souls) in one egg (life)' aspect is underlined by the fact that these two lovers are made out of one block of stone.

Like Eric Gill's different depictions of lovers embracing, Constantin Brancusi's *The Kiss* is distinctly gendered, with many details that describe the man and the woman not apparent from just a brief glance. The hair, for instance, is parted on the woman but pulled back on the man; the man's hands are on her shoulders, while hers are pressed against the back of his head; the woman is clearly sexualized by her breasts, as ever in masculinist art; the eyes and lips (there are no ears) seem to be the same, though the man is shorter than the woman. In subtle ways, Brancusi delineated the psychology of his male and female figures. They are at once flawed individuals and generalized (idealized) forms. Gill's standing copulating figures are similarly idealized like Brancusi's, but Gill makes more of the erotic aspects of their bodies. For example, while Brancusi carved a slight bump to indicate the woman's breast, Gill portrayed the whole breast and nipple.

The later Constantin Brancusi *Kisses*, the column and the gate, are monumental versions of the Platonic soul union, but erotic and cosmological versions. The 'eyes' are biological 'cells', as Brancusi explained. They are the basic form of life, the organic cell, from which all life grows. These 'eyes' are also circles, and in *The Column of the Kiss* and *The Gate of the Kiss*, Brancusi uses the circle as the prime symbol of life. He cuts it in two, and so those two semi-circles become the perfect symbol of the Platonic souls finding their 'other half'. Circles split in two also have sexual associations, hinting at the genitals of men and women. The bisected circle can be, if one likes, labia, or testes, or glans, and so on. Brancusi explained the meaning of the 'eyes':

> *What is left behind when you are no more? It is the memory of the eyes, of your looks that imparted love for man and people. These figures are a representation of the amalgamation of man and woman through love.* (in B. Brezianou, 1976, 143)

The 1912/16 *The Kiss*, in limestone, is a further 'rationalization', as critics say, of the first *The Kiss*. There is a clear line marking the narrow space between the figures, who are shown down to the waist. The 1923-

5 limestone The Kiss returns to the shortened version of 1908. It is rounded, making the two figures into an oval shape. In Constantin Brancusi's vision of the supreme erotic moment, the unio mystica as Catholic mystics and theologians call it, the two figures are clasped together so tightly nothing gets between them. It is a pure fusion of body and soul: their eyes touch, their faces touch, their mouths touch, their bodies touch.

In later versions of The Kiss, such as the one in Montparnasse Cemetery (1909, stone, 35.2 inches high, Paris), Constantin Brancusi showed the whole body of the two eternal, archetypal lovers. Sidney Geist wrote of the Montparnasse The Kiss:

> The initial innocence of The Kiss has given way to the image of pagan frankness. In the total embrace of the Montparnasse Kiss we witness a scene so sweet and stately that it is often not recognized for what it is. In all except primitive art, there is probably no representation of the sexual act that is at once so undisguised and so discreet. Although the lovers in this Kiss are revealed in a passional act, its intensity is mitigated by a new rigour of design and execution. The broad facades are, for all purposes, identical. (1978)

In some of Eric Gill's images it is not always recognized that the lovers are copulating. In the Divine Lovers image (1922), for example, only the heads and upper torsos are seen; however, knowing Gill's art from images such as the sculpture Fucking and the illustrations to the Song of Songs, it's obvious that the couple in Divine Lovers are making love.

A later, intaglio version of Divine Lovers (1926) shows a little more of the bodies (down to their waists). In all versions, the woman's breast is visible, her nipple touching his. In the later version, the woman's head is behind the man's; with his short beard and long hair, the man looks like Gill's Jesuses. Divine Lovers, then, shows Christ making love, an image which recalls Gill's Nuptials of God. In his illustrations for the Song of the Soul (1927), Gill provided more restrained images of lovers embracing – with clothes on (in The Soul and the Bridegroom), and in A Symbol of Divine Love (from Art & Love, 1927).

Sex and Christianity fuses again in Eric Gill's illustrations for Troilus and Criseyde (1927): in Man and Girl On Way From Church, a young couple are shown leaving church, with the priest behind them waving goodbye; in the next image, further down the plant stem of Gill's vertical borders, the couple are shown embracing; in the third stage, they are nude, making love.

Approaching Dawn from *Twenty-Five Nudes* is one of Eric Gill's most successful and lavish engravings, the eroticism of the entangled lovers is enfolded by layers of sheets and bed covers which Gill drew in waves of stripes echoing the forms of the couple. The skilful patterning seems to radiate outwards from the lovers, like a magnetic field of black-and-white stripes. For David Jones, one of Gill's followers, Constantin Brancusi and Henry Moore were æsthetically linked, but Gill's sculpture created a 'different kind of otherness'.

★

Constantin Brancusi's *The Kiss* is a sculpture that is meant to represent by its solid mass a timeless erotic union. *The Kiss* is nothing less than a representation of that central 'act' of humans – making love. It's the act that forms the foundation of Eric Gill's art – love between mothers and children, love between couples, even love between the faithful and the Saviour. Brancusi's and Gill's is a cosmic vision of togetherness, a vision that goes down to the fundamental, organic levels of life. Brancusi used the image of two halves melding into one in his monuments at Tirgu Jiu.

Asking the American sculptor Malvina Hoffman what she thought of the columns, she said: 'I see the forms of two cells that meet and create life. The beginning of life… through love. Am I right?' Brancusi replied:

> *Yes, you are… and these columns are the result of years of searching. First came this group of two interlaced, seated figures in stone… then the symbol of the egg, then the thought grew into this gateway to a beyond.* (1939, 53)

There are similarities between Eric Gill and Constantin Brancusi, though both Auguste Rodin and Aristide Maillol are more obviously associated with Gill. Both Gill and Brancusi made erotic art; they both created a series of sculptures and drawings showing a heterosexual couple in the act of love; they both used direct carving; they both had idealized and Platonic as well as earthy and realistic views of art; they were both somewhat ascetic and uncompromising in their artistic practice (if not in their lives); they both admired religious carving; and they both leant towards Oriental art and philosophy. Brancusi spoke of trying to reach the form buried in the stone, and of trying to achieve the 'essence of things' in sculpture. Gill spoke in very similar terms in his *Autobiography*:

> stone carving is conceiving things in stone and conceiving them as made by carving. They are not only born but conceived in stone; they are of stone in their inmost being as well as their outermost existence. (A, 161)

In Constantin Brancusi's art, there is always a striving for some realm greater than his immediate milieu of the first half of the 20th century. The sculptural space for Brancusi is not that of sculptors such as Michelangelo Buonaroti, Donatello, Gian Lorenzo Bernini, Antonio Canova or Auguste Rodin, it is both fashionably 'primitive' in the *avant garde* Parisian sense, as found in the paintings of Pablo Picasso or Henri Gaudier-Brzeska's sculptures, and also archaic, shamanic, magical, Platonic, mystical; a space where there is only *essence*, the 'essence of things'. This is, finally, Brancusi's desired world, a Paradise of 'essences'. An otherness that is utterly *real*, an abstraction that is pure reality. Nature not artifice, reality not fantasy, touch and objecthood, not ethereality and insubstantiality. In Brancusi's art, the emphasis is on the poetics of nature, not the nature of poetics, the mysticism of actualities, not the actualities of mysticism.

A paradox, in the end, for the more he stresses 'essence' and Platonic philosophy, the further Constantin Brancusi moves away from nature and reality. It is a paradox he celebrates, criticizes, reviews, has doubts about and continued to explore throughout his career. It is the paradox of all sculpture (and all art): the paradox between something being there (the art object) and something not being there, which is 'represented' (the 'content', 'theme' or 'subject'). The paradox is a dichotomy never resolved into a (Platonic) unity. Yet Brancusi seems to have got closer than most to some kind of resolution, although he maintained, rightly, that no work of art is ever 'finished'.

Constantin Brancusi's sculpture was, finally, far more radical than Eric Gill's art; Gill always kept to the human form, and never moved into total abstraction, while Brancusi progressively reduced his sculptures to their simplest form. Yet Gill chimes with Brancusi's æsthetics when he said:

> I just wanted to make in solid stone, round and smooth and lovely images of the round and smooth and lovely things which filled my mind. (A, 163)

6

GILL, RODIN, MAILLOL, KLIMT AND SCHIELE

There are a number of modern artists who are unrestrained in their exaltation of women. Auguste Rodin is a typical example. Of the *Venus de'Medici*, Rodin wrote: '[n]otice all the voluptuous curvings of the hip... And now, here, the adorable dimples along the loins... It is truly flesh... You would think it moulded by caresses!' (in R. Goldwater, 325). Rodin is the classic womanizer artist, who made love to his models physically as well as psychologically and æsthetically. Eric Gill too did this. Rodin's models, like Gill's, became his mistresses (such as Camille Claudel). Like many artists, Rodin produced erotica for private consumption. But enthusiastic eroticism infuses everything Rodin created. A sculpture such as *The Metamorphoses of Ovid* is typical[1] – it depicts two lovers embracing. Gill's *Lovers* sculptures have affinities with this Rodinesque æsthetic.

Auguste Rodin's sculpture *Christ and the Magdalene* (1894) is more controversial, for it depicts Mary Magdalene sexually embracing the crucified Christ. The image is blasphemous, fusing sex and religion in an age-old fashion. This eroticization of Mary Magdalene occurs also in the art of Félicien Rops and Eric Gill.

Much of Auguste Rodin's art pivoted around female sexuality, as in Eric Gill's art. Rodin produced drawings of women masturbating (for example, *Reclining Female Nude*, *c.*1900, Musée Rodin, Paris), which influenced Gustav Klimt's images of autoerotic women. Rodin's *Oceanides* (1905, Musée Rodin, Paris), like his *Gates of Hell*, depicts lovers entwining in a series of fluid lines and sensuous forms. Rodin's depictions of *The Kiss* centre around the voluptuousness of eroticism, on the beauty of bodies clasped together in complex poses. Rodin's *The Kiss* is the height of modern figurative sculpture, Michelangelo made modernist and more explicitly erotic.

Other sculptors produced similarly sensuous, entwined *Kisses*, with the man always on top, always bearing down onto the woman, always enveloping, always controlling the kiss: M.L. Bégine's *The Embrace* (1906), Jules Dalou's *The Kiss*, Edvard Munch's *The Kiss* (1895, private collection), Gustav Klimt's *The Kiss*, F. Voulot's *The Kiss* (1905), Pablo Picasso's *The Embrace* (1900), William Zorach's *The Embrace* (1933) and E. Derré's *La Grotte d'Amour* (1905).

Love infuses every gesture Aristide Maillol makes, an artist Eric Gill admired, as it does with Gill. 'Aristide Maillol is the greatest man in the world,' Gill wrote, after working with him (quoted in Y, 197). Maillol and Gill collaborated on engravings and designs for a book from Cranach Press, published in 1927. Count Kessler brought Gill and Maillol together (A, 179).

There are no blemishes, no irregularities, no awkward poses in Eric Gill's or Aristide Maillol's city of women. Each figure is softly rounded, softly drawn or sculpted. It seems as if male artists have loved creating rounded forms in women since time immemorial – large-hipped women appear not only throughout Western art (in the works of Peter Rubens, Titian, Rembrandt van Rijn, Henri Matisse) but also in prehistoric imagery, in the faceless "Stone Venuses". These ancient women are not potential lovers but mothers. They seem to conform to the Freudian and Lacanian emphasis on the mother as the male's first lover. The large women in the art of Pablo Picasso, Henri Matisse, Auguste Rodin, Paul Gauguin, Pierre Bonnard, Jacob Epstein, Aristide Maillol and Eric Gill are motherly, so clearly the mother figure of psychoanalysis, and the

Goddess of ancient mythology. In her far-reaching essay on Giovanni Bellini and Renaissance art, Julia Kristeva describes the relationship between the marginality of the maternal and the artistic enterprise:

> The language of art, too, follows (but differently and more closely) the other aspect of maternal jouissance, the sublimation taking place at the very moment of primal repression within the mother's body, arising perhaps unwittingly out of her marginal position. At the intersection of sign and rhythm, of representation and light, of the symbolic and the semiotic, the artist speaks from a place where she is not, where she knows not. (1982, 242)

The artist has to make the ungraspable graspable, as Kristeva notes: '[t]he artist, as servant of the maternal phallus, displays this always and everywhere unaccomplished art of reproducing bodies and spaces as graspable, masterable objects, within reach of his eye and hand' (1982, 246).

※

Egon Schiele, like Pablo Picasso or Eric Gill, was one of the great modern erotic artists. Schiele is dæmonic compared to Gill and Gustav Klimt, producing angular, nervy and melancholy art where Klimt is rounded, relaxed and uplifting (O. Benesch, 1950; 1958, 9-10). The influence of Klimt's decorative, Art Nouveau style is very much apparent in Egon Schiele's early painting; similarly, Gill's art shows the influence of William Morris, John Ruskin, Art Nouveau, and the Arts & Crafts movement. Schiele's view of sex, which chimes with Gill's, is the usual male Existential, bourgeois one that sex = pain and pain = being truly alive. Schiele said: 'I am a human being. I love death and I love life' (in F. Whitford, 193). Schiele wrote from prison in 1912: 'I believe that man must suffer from sexual torture as long as he is capable of sexual feelings' (in ib., 119).

Egon Schiele's art is a mass of Expressionist meditations on the painful moments of life – sex, death, birth and violence. Eric Gill's art is much less angst-ridden and melancholy than Schiele's, though for both artists, as for other European modernists Auguste Rodin, Gustav Klimt, Pablo Picasso, Amedeo Modigliani, Hans Bellmer and Henri Matisse, (heterosexual) eroticism is the vehicle for much of their exploration of art and life. Like Gill and Klimt, some would say Schiele was obsessed with sex. Like Rodin, Klimt, Maillol and Gill, Schiele produced many drawings and paintings of nude women.

Like Eric Gill, Egon Schiele explored the theme of motherly love, and painted many mothers and children. Like Gill, Schiele was narcissistic, and was self-conscious about his image (look at Schiele's photographs). Both Gill and Schiele were fastidious about clothes, as their art and lives show. Both Schiele and Gill drew their penises and images of themselves sexually aroused.

Another æsthetic Eric Gill shared with the Expressionists was a love of acrobats, athletes, and circus performers; (German) Expressionists and artists such as Max Beckmann, Georges Rouault, Pablo Picasso, James Ensor, and Marc Chagall depicted many clowns, dancers, masks, circuses, performers, harlequins and carnivals. In the Expressionists, life was depicted as a bitter carnival, a masquerade of nightmares. Gill, on the other hand, wallowed far less in Existential suffering and Middle European angst; instead, he was drawn to acrobats and dancers largely because of their sense of movement. He corresponded with people like Laura Knight and Duncan Grant about acrobats.

Gustav Klimt is one of those 'acceptable' erotic artists, whose art is consumed these days as mild porno. Klimt never strayed from the heterosexist norm of soft-core pornographic consumption. Klimt was vigorously heterosexual in his art. Like Rodin, Epstein, Maillol and Gill, Klimt passionately adored women, and his art is a modernist summary of all male artists who have loved and painted women since Classical times.

In paintings such as *Danae* (c.1905, Galerie Weltz, Salzburg), *The Kiss* (1907-8, Österreichische Galerie, Vienna) and *Woman* (1913, Vicktor Fogarassy Collection), Gustav Klimt produced luxuriant, post-Symbolist, post-Byzantine icons of femininity in the Art Nouveau style of the Viennese 'Secessionstil'. Decadence or over-indulgence is one of Klimt's hallmarks.

At times, only Gustave Moreau seems more luxuriant. Gustav Klimt depicts naked or half-naked bodies flowing over each other, entwined and writhing but also half-asleep, their eyes closed or half-open, as if stuck in some slow motion opium orgy (see, for instance, Klimt's The Virgin, 1912-3, Narodny Galerie, Prague). Stylistically, Gill preferred clear, simplified lines to the compositional complexity of Klimt. Both artists, though, explored the possibilities of frontal, decorative art.

Like Eric Gill, Gustav Klimt flattened every element of his representations onto one picture plane, and turns the image into pure ornamentation and decoration. Klimt was supremely stylish, and rarely allowed any evil serpent to slither in and spoil his basically tame, nostalgic paradises. In his friezes, one sees the epic grandeur asserting itself. Klimt's art is relentlessly ornamental. He dispenses with three dimensionality, and goes for an abstract flatness, as in The Fulfilment (c. 1905-09, Musée des Beaux Arts, Strasbourg), which features an erotic embrace like that depicted in The Kiss – where the background is a mosaic of swirls. Klimt's art is utterly sensual, in its intent, and the signals it gives off: the lush colours, the profuse use of gold, the swirling shapes, the intricate patterns, the flowing lines and the exaltations of the human form. The sexuality depicted in Klimt's art, as with Gill's, is fully in tune with the art of, say, Titian, Correggio, Jean-Dominique Ingres, or the anonymous Greek sculptors of Classic times.

In Gustav Klimt's drawings the eroticism is more specific: he drew women reclining, legs drawn up, masturbating, their hands moving dreamily over their vulvas and clits as they look at the viewer. They have titles such as Reclining Woman, or Seated Woman, with Open Legs (Reclining Woman, 1912-18, Grapische Sammlung Albertina, Vienna). Auguste Rodin was the precursor of Klimt's masturbating nudes (such as in Rodin's Reclining Female Nude, c.1900, Musée Rodin, Paris). Klimt had seen Rodin's erotic drawings, and they inspired him. As with the images of mainstream pornography, these are anonymous women, any women, with faces but no names, and no personalities (Seated Woman, with Open Legs, 1916/17, Recumbent Semi-Nude, 1914/15, Historical Museum, Vienna). These are orgasmic images, celebrating female jouissance.

This form of eroticism is not confined to the 'private' drawings, drawings which can be seen as a private form of pornography: Gustav Klimt's famous Judith (1901, Österreichische Galerie, Vienna) stares voluptuously at the viewer with her eyes half-closed, in a orgasmic state. It is a pose cultivated by Hollywood stars, the seductive, luscious look to camera. Klimt's drawings of women lying back with their legs spread are pure erotic – the *Seated Nude*, for example. *Goldfish* (1901/02, Dübi-Miller Foundation, Kunstmuseum, Solothurn) depicts in oil a woman, nude of course, squatting, buttocks prominent. While Klimt, Schiele and Rodin drew women masturbating, Eric Gill preferred to show women making love with men, if they were involved in a sex act. Gill's studies of nude women are rarely pleasuring themselves; if they're on their own, they will be sleeping, brushing their hair, standing, or posing.

7

FUCKING

Eric Gill built eroticism into most of his depictions of people. 'Quite mad on sex', Gill wrote of Jacob Epstein, the sculptor, in his diary (December 9, 1913). The statement might equally apply to Gill. He thought of sex a lot. In his *Autobiography*, he wrote:

> How many times a day do men think, perhaps only momentarily, of the shape and attributes of female flesh? How many tiny interstices are thus filled? How often and how vehemently do we look forward to going to be bed – but not to sleep?... I can only confess that, judging from my own experience and having no reason to think that others are different from me, the thought or memory of that activity of our bodies which is only acknowledged openly between lovers... and which reaches its fulfilment in physical union and orgasm, does in fact occupy, in greater or lesser degree, very many of the interstices of our waking lives and thus colour and inform and perfect or, it may be, mar our doings. (222-3)

Eric Gill set up mirrors to watch his love-making, collected erotic photographs and books, drew genitals in detail (his own and other people's), wrote up his sexual exploits in his diary, copied out extracts from Havelock Ellis, studied animals mating and recorded their activities in his diary, spent a day photographing himself and the Epstein family nude, played tennis in the nude, made a good deal of erotic art, and spied on people having sex (as in Hyde Park). Robert Speaight said Gill was 'prey to an obsessive curiosity' (179)

Despite his self-confessed obsession with sex and human bodies, some critics remarked that Eric Gill was also curiously reticent about it, perhaps due to his Victorian and Nonconformist childhood; he was also seen as being ignorant of women's bodies (M, 262). Gill's ethical view of sex in art is essentially that of the pornographer: people fuck, so why not show them fucking in images and texts? It's natural, so it's natural people should depict fucking in art. Gill wrote in his *Autobiography*:

> ...even pornographic photographs are generally photographs of things very good in themselves. I mean: what's wrong with a naked girl that you shouldn't look at the photograph of one? What's wrong with sexual intercourse that it should be considered damnable? (97)

Eric Gill loses himself here in the art versus pornography debate, an extremely complex area where the relations between art and life, between politics and the body, between things-in-themselves and representations of them, are complicated by all manner of elements. Gill did not have the clarity of understanding to unravel every strand of this multi-layered, tangled discourse. He could not reconcile to his own satisfaction, as with so many artists and liberals, the conflicts between liking erotica but disliking pornography (but that didn't stop him concentrating on sex throughout his artistic career). The art vs. porn debate much exercised feminists and critics in the 1970s and 1980s, but seems to have been forgotten about now. Pornography appears to be accepted, or simply ignored, these days. Social debates have moved on.

Eric Gill continually drew attention to a figure's genitals. He writes, for instance, of sex often, as in this account of love-making with his wife Ethel:

> The roundness and largeness of her legs and thighs and hips, the sudden smallness of her waist and splendid fatness and softness of her buttocks, the thick hair on her belly are beautiful and very exciting. (diary, in M, 59)

In other diary entries, Eric Gill describes the joy of making love with

Mary (as Ethel became): how he had a 'great time in bed' with Mary (March 3, 1915); how she came down in the evening with no knickers on; how they made love in a hay rick; how they got freaky in a wood while walking back from Hay-on-Wye.

During the happy periods in Eric Gill's life, he and Mary had sex every day (M, 200). 'Have you felt the smooth whiteness of the flesh between her thighs and the dividing roundness? Such thoughts are kindling to our fires', wrote Gill (A, 227).

Eric Gill was obsessed, for instance, by pubic hair, and drew attention to it (or the lack of it) in countless drawings. In his *Autobiography*, Gill described the

> day when, as the result of being shown a photograph, I discovered that the adult human female has a bush of hair on its belly! This knowledge pervaded my mind, filled all the nooks and crannies of thought, both day and night, for several months – and added a lot of fuel to the fire. (A, 85)

I'm reminded of the French filmmaker Jean-Luc Godard, who said that nudity in his films had to include pubic hair – having actors topless wasn't enough. In *He and She* (April, 1913), Gill described taking Mary early on in their relationship to a Fleet Street hotel. As she undressed, Gill wrote:

> for the first time I saw that she was a woman. I saw the dark full growth of hair on her belly. I touched it and kissed her. By now she was naked. Her breasts – her little tender nipples were against me – Her hair down and covering my face – our lips kissing. So we lay together for the first time.

Particularly hairy works, with the bush minutely emphasized, include many of the *Twenty-Five Nudes*; *Artist and Model I*; *The Skaters* (1926), an engraving which in its first state showed the figures' genitals with thick pubic hair at the centre of the composition; *Earth Waiting* (1926), showing the nude woman kneeling on grass; *Ecce Tu Pulchra Es* (1929), an engraving not used in *Canticum Canticorum*; and *The Dancer* (1925, from the *Song of Songs*), where the nude woman raises her arms and legs, revealing her body.[1]

Some of Eric Gill's engravings and drawings show different versions of the same subject, often portraying clothed and unclothed variants: in *The Skaters* (1926), for example, taken from a *Daily Mirror* photograph, Gill depicts them nearly nude, clad in see-through skirts; in another variant, the male and female skaters form a cross with their limbs, but are now naked, their genitals at the optical centre of the picture. *The Artist and Model* comes in clothed and nude variants; in *Nature and Nakedness* (from the book *Clothes*, 1930), two women are contrasted, one clothed, the other revealing her body. In the book *Clothes* Gill produced engravings entitled *Clothes as Houses, Clothes as Churches and Town Halls,* and *Clothes as Workshops.*

8

PHALLUS

Eric Gill was fascinated by the penis, particularly his own. He had what psychoanalysts call a 'phallic fixation'. But that is putting it mildly. He drew his penis countless times, and even carved a life-size marble sculpture of his penis, 'a perfect copy with dimensions meticulously taken and relayed to his acquaintances with satisfaction', as Fiona MacCarthy puts it (115). One is reminded of the Plastercasters, the rock groupies from Chicago, who took a cast of the members of pop stars. In his *Autobiography* Gill cited the painter Pierre Renoir, who said that he made his art with his penis. 'Let his confession suffice for me' (A, 122).

So many male artists have drawn, painted or sculpted their penises: Jasper Johns, Egon Schiele, Pablo Picasso, Hans Bellmer, Robert Rauschenberg, Salvador Dali and Tom of Finland. The penis is supreme amongst many male artists. Male artists are sometimes obsessed by their members. As were some ancient peoples: from the Cerne Giant in Dorset, with its 30-foot long phallus, to ithyphallic cave paintings of the palæolithic era. There are phalluses and wombs, men dressed in animal skins, with the phallic horns or antlers on their head, men as ithyphallic hunters or shaman. Phallic art can be found in many cultures throughout history, not only in the prehistoric era: sometimes the phallic fetishes have a magical or religious aspect, as in ancient Rome. During the ancient Roman honeymoon, for instance, the bride was expected to sit on the erect phallus of a statue of the god Tutinus, before going to the marriage bed.

Eric Gill thought of the genitals as the flower of the human body, the apotheosis of it, 'precious ornaments' which should be cherished:

> What are those lovely creatures which we delight to fill our gardens with and to display on our tables? What are they indeed but the sex organs of the plants they adorn. So that it is neither dramatic nor even an exaggeration to say that while from one point of view the country hedgerow is filled with savage creatures armed to the teeth — with poison and thorns and spikes and every sort of offensive and defensive weapon (in this respect perfect models for all modern nations), so from another, it is nothing but an uproarious exhibition of desire for fruitfulness and multiplication. (introduction to Drawings From Life; and A, 225)

Despite being open about sexuality, Eric Gill did keep some of his art secret. There are private drawings in the collections of the Victoria and Albert Museum and the British Museum in London, which depict, for instance, people fucking, masturbating, sucking, and so on (often in what some call 'Oriental' sex positions). There are some seventy drawings of penises. The drawings are careful anatomical studies, of penises in various states, complete with measurements. The titles of the drawings are funny: Eric Erect, A Bird in the Hand, Actual Size Approx and Man Root. It's all harmless fun.

Some of the drawings in the British Museum in the folders 'Studies of Parts' and 'Love Drawings etc' show penises and vaginas together; some feature penises being masturbated; only a few (four) have the yoni on its own; three drawings contain masturbating women. Eric Gill's Studies of Parts include measurements such as '6.5" to 7" up, 3.5" or 4" to 4.5" down' (M, 205). It's so important, isn't it, the size of the 'male member'? So Gill crawled around on his hands and knees, with a ruler or a tape measure, gathering statistics on penises. A bizarre but oh so crucial scientific activity. For Gill was always strict, always went for mathematical exactness in all things, from size of penis to vastness of ego. Strict delight was one of his favourite mottoes, meaning that pleasure must be ascetic as well as luscious (M, 135). A sheet of four drawings of penises were titled 'Leslie' (French, an actor), 'Douglas' (Cleverdon), 'Joseph' (Cribb), and 'self'.

Some of Eric Gill's erotic drawings have their humorous side, like schoolboys' exercise book doodlings: some of the penises have arms and heads, another shows the Devil's tail as, yes, a penis. One drawing of a female nude reclining shows the woman pointing to her vulva with the caption 'That's your Master' (stating the obvious).

Some of the phallic drawings show Eric Gill masturbating, or on a bed, or in a mirror. Sometimes the drawings of penises enter the critically acceptable arena, as in the prints entitled The 'Most Precious Ornament' (1937).[2] These show just the torso of the male body, the leg lifted so that the erection and testicles are the centrepiece. Few artists have been so obsessed with their penis as Arthur Eric Rowton Gill. And he seems to have given as free rein to his horsey cock in his life as in his art. On June 22, 1927, Gill wrote in his diary:

> A man's penis and balls are very beautiful things and the power to see this beauty is not confined to the opposite sex. The shape of the head of a man's erect penis is very excellent in the mouth. There is no doubt about this. I have often wondered – now I know.[3]

The penis in Eric Gill's work is an object of reflectivity, of vanity, a mirror, a mythicizing mirror, as in the Lacanian psychoanalytical system, where the phallus is essentially that 'obscure object of desire', the displaced body of the mother. Gill's cult of the phallus is the product of (yawn) masculine narcissism, that vanity that relates everything, ultimately, to itself.

In Eric Gill's art, the phallus is 'the most precious ornament'. It is the most revered object, to be treated as an object of 'high art', a symbol and a reality to be worshipped. Kneel down and worship the phallus! cries Eric Gill. Connie Chatterley does just that in the most ridiculous scene in Lady Chatterley's Lover. Look at me, mom, I've got a wiener! yelps the little male – it is the familiar cry not only of boys of all ages but of artists such as Robert Mapplethorpe, Jasper Johns, Egon Schiele, Hans Bellmer and others (see I. Lippman, 1975).

In one of Eric Gill's 'humorous' drawings (The Domestic Hose, 1929), a man dressed as a flower holds out his penis, which also has a flower on it.[2] The rider reads: 'the domestic hose comes out well in time of drought'. Gill means that the penis can 'water' the world in drought. The implication, as ever in Gill's art, is that the penis can rejuvenate life, that the penis is at the centre of life, that the penis helps everything to grow, to achieve itself.

9

MIRRORS AND LOOKING

Men looking at women. Mirrors. The phallus. Luce Irigaray and other feminists have criticized the Freudian-Lacanian emphasis on the phallus as the 'transcendental signifier', as the measure of authentic sexual pleasure.1 The Lacanian Look emphasizes eroticism. Seeing is erotic, the eye becomes a kind of phallus, caressing the obscure object of desire, which it can never 'possess'. As the poet Rainer Maria Rilke wrote '[g]azing is a wonderful thing.'2 The act of looking eroticizes the object. Jack Zipes explains:

> For him [Lacan], seeing is desire, and the eye functions as a kind of phallus. However, the eye cannot clearly see its object of desire, and in the case of male desire, the female object of desire is an illusion created by the male unconscious. Or, in other words, the male desire for woman expressed in the gaze is auto-erotic and involves the male's desire to have his own identity reconfirmed in a mirror image.3

The Look is an assertion of male power and sexuality. For the gaze is male or masculine, and feminists have grappled with the notion of a 'female' gaze.4 'Male desire is presented as a response to female beauty', writes Andrea Dworkin (1988, 114). In the Jungian system, Beatrice, Laura, Cleopatra, Isolde, Eurydice, Ariadne and all those women of myth, poetry and legend, are incarnations of the *anima*, which is, as Carl Jung explains, something all males possess: '[e]very man carries with him the eternal mage of woman, not the image of this or that particular woman, but a definitive feminine image.'[5] The *anima* is 'a personification of the unconscious in a man, which appears as a woman or a goddess in dreams, visions and creative fantasies', write Emma Jung and Marie-Louise von Franz.[6] Male painters throughout history have depicted their version of the *anima*, it seems. For painters, this idealized *anima* figure seems to be another manifestation of that obscure object of desire, the eroticized woman, a mirror for male lust. The equation is: the more sublime and voluptuous the woman is painted, the more sublime and voluptuous is the artist's desire. The artist's model, then, can be seen as a Jungian *anima*, heavily eroticized, a Lacanian phallic mirror.

In Eric Gill's work there are many instances where the female model becomes a phallic mirror, reflecting back the creator's erotic desires. One engraving demonstrates this really powerfully – the *Artist and Model I* (intended for Gill's 1932 book *Sculpture and the Living Model* but not used).[7] Here, a naked man stands in front of a full-length mirror, but the reflection is... a naked woman. It is a perfect example of Lacanian psychology and Jungian *anima* theory, where the male creates the idealized female (sex) object. In a variant of *Artist and Mirror I*, the man has an erection, as if to make the circularity of desire obvious to the viewer (in the other variant, just the man's testicles are shown). The version that was used in *Sculpture and the Living Model* (*Artist and Mirror II*, 1932) shows the artist and female reflection clothed.

10

DESIRE

In Lacanian psychology, desire, which is the foundation of the system, is enmeshed with speaking, with creativity and art. The œdipal crisis and the repression of the desire for the mother occurs with the entry into the Symbolic Order, and the entry into language. As Toril Moi crystallized Lacan's thought so concisely: '[t]o speak as a subject is therefore the same as to represent the existence of repressed desire' (1985, 99-100) The links between seeing and erotic pleasure, between the eye and the phallus, are found in much of Western 'high culture': not only in the history of painting, but also in the great works of poets such as Dante Alighieri, Francesco Petrarch, William Shakespeare and the troubadours. In the 'classic' book of pornography, Georges Bataille's *The Story of the Eye*, there are eyes placed in mouths, vulvas and anuses. Bataille takes the Sadeian ethic of the pornographic Look to its logical, literal extreme.

Men gaze at women and manipulate them into erotic poses. Larysa Mykyta wrote that

> The sexual triumph of the male passes through the eye, through the contemplation of the woman. Seeing the women ensures the satisfaction of wanting to be seen, of having one's desire recognized, and thus comes back to the original aim of the scopic drive. Woman is repressed as subject and desired as object in order to efface the gaze of the

Other, the gaze that would destroy the illusion of reciprocity and oneness that the process of seeing usually supports. The female object does not look, does not have it own point of view; rather it is erected as an image of the phallus sustaining male desire.[1]

The pleasure of the text, whether the text is a painting, film, magazine, photograph, or piece of theatre, comes, according to Roland Barthes, when the Look of the spectator is aligned with that of the author.[2] People can get uncomfortable when they are forced by the text to align themselves with a certain viewpoint. They become discomfited when they look at erotic art, at Gill's drawings, for instance.

What feminist criticism has done is to question the masculine 'pleasure of the text', arguing for a feminist reading of the traditional masculinist or patriarchal view of texts. For some feminists, however, there can be no true 'feminist gaze', because the Look is always masculine, ultimately. This is true in Eric Gill's work, where the spectator is situated firmly within a heterosexist, masculine viewpoint. If the spectator is a 'gendered object', suggests Annette Kuhn, then 'masculine subjectivity [is] the only subjectivity available'.[3] The politics of representation, which are central to the consumption of pornography and art, are weighted firmly in favour of men and patriarchy. As John Berger writes: 'men act and women appear'.[4] As Catherine King notes: 'most images in masculine visual ideology are created to empower men as spectators – that is, to see themselves as endlessly important with things laid out for their desire'.[5]

Clearly, erotica is a series of texts or representations that maximizes the pleasure of the (often) male spectator. The female nude painting does the same. Eric Gill's work is pornographic, then, in this second wave feminist view, for it is a series of texts (sculptures, drawings, engravings, writings, calligraphy) that maximizes the pleasure of the (male) voyeur at the expense of the (female) object. The female nudes in Gill's art are not 'female subjects' but more like 'female objects'. The real 'subject' of Gill's art is, as with the art of Henri Matisse, Pablo Picasso, Egon Schiele, Gustav Klimt, Jacob Epstein, Aristide Maillol and Auguste Rodin, the male artist. The true 'subject' of heterosexual erotic art is not a description of the female body, but a record of the inscription of male desire upon the female body.

✻

Eric Gill was meticulous in his recording of sexual activities. His private writings reveal a secret code for acts such as anal intercourse (diary entries read: 'stayed 1/2 hour – put p. in her a/hole' (diary, January 12, 1920). A cross with four dots appears in his diary to denote sex. 'BAD' was a frequently occurring reference to masturbation, which appeared in Gill's diary from the Chichester days onward.

Typical diary entries include: 'Bath after supper and dancing (nude). R & M fucked one another after, M. holding me the while' (diary, November 30, 1925). Another incident, with Clare Leighton, is recorded in Eric Gill's strange matter-of-fact, unemotional fashion, a little like a schoolboy writing up an experiment in the physics lab:

> We talked a lot about fucking and agreed how we much we loved it. Afterwards we fondled one another a little and I put my penis between her legs. She then arranged herself so that when I pushed a little it went into her. I pushed it in about 6 times and we kissed and went into lunch. (diary, August 24, 1932)

Fiona MacCarthy comments:

> The evidence in Gill's diary is that his sexual behaviour was, by conventional standards, extraordinary. Some of the entries have been obliterated but enough of them remain, almost clinical in the accuracy of their description... when Betty was sixteen, Gill records how one afternoon while Mary and Joan were in Chichester he made her 'come', and she him, to watch the effect on the anus: '(1) Why should it,' he queries, 'contract during the orgasm, and (2) why should a woman's do the same as a man's?' This is characteristic of Gill's quasi-scientific curiosity: his urge to know and prove. (155-6)

Eric Gill was often adulterous, having sex, for example, with Lizzie, a maid. He asked her to sleep with him, as his wife was pregnant: 'I said to her, wd. she let me lie with her as Ethel was with child. She agreed' (diary, June 14, 1906, in M, 75). Gill's attitude is that of the male predator: he has to have sex, his lust is so great it simply cannot go unsatisfied, so he expects women to lie down and accept him. Is this being unfair to Gill? Not really, his writings and his art glorify the 'right' of men to have women, to have sex when and where and how they like. Many women, for instance, were persuaded to 'experiment' sexually with Gill. His lust could not be stopped: he *had* to have his way, as they say, with women. He is, like characters in the fiction of Marquis de Sade or Henry Miller, like Casanova or Don Juan, the libertine, the sexually aggressive liberal who advocates lashings of sex, but who is also a purist, even ascetic. He visited prostitutes. In his diary he relates how, after a Hilaire Belloc lecture, he 'gave a woman 2/- to feel her between the legs and she me. No connection. No orgasm. Am I mad!' (M, 126).

Another love affair was with Elizabeth Bill, an independent-minded woman, who had sophisticated tastes (including for pornography), with an illegitimate son, who came to Capel-y-ffin. Bill became one of Eric Gill's principal models, as well as his mistress. He introduced her to the Gillian way of life, which included modelling, measuring his penis, looking at slides of sperm under a microscope, and stone-carving.

Other model-mistresses included Lillian Meacham, Daisy Hawkins and May Reeves. Other dalliances included Cicely Marchant, of the Groupil Gallery; and Clare Leighton. Eric Gill's relationship with Lillian Meacham began in early 1907; she was a Fabian 'New Woman', tall, intellectual, the daughter of a company director; they both loved Friedrich Nietzsche, and read *Thus Spake Zarathustra* together (oh happy days!); they attended lectures (such as William Rothenstein at the Fabian Arts Group on "Art and Religion" and Jean Orage at the Theosophical Society on "Human Consciousness"); in March, 1907, Gill and Meacham went to Chartres ('a New Woman's holiday, free love and architecture' [F. MacCarthy, 76]). In his *Autobiography* Gill said that the 'young Fabian woman', love, socialism and Nietzsche were bound up together, making 'a pretty complicated entanglement' (A, 271). Gill tried to organize outings with Meacham and his wife Ethel, but they didn't really work: the emotional tensions were too strong.

As one would expect, recalling Eric Gill's rapturous descriptions of Chichester Cathedral, he fell in love with Chartres Cathedral. It became one of his models of architectural perfection. As Fiona MacCarthy suggested, Gill's enraptured view of Chartres Cathedral was bound up with the erotic vacation with Lillian Meacham. The passionate affair eventually burned itself out. In the *Autobiography* Gill said he went away for a week 'and thus, having cleared away the passionate side of the matter, was in a clear frame of mind'. Friedrich Nietzsche and socialism, Gill said, were no substitutes for a family and a loving wife:

> I was too deeply in love with the mother of my children and too deeply in love with the Christian idea of the family and the home and parental love, thus to throw everything away. (A, 271-2)

Daisy Hawkins became part of Eric Gill's Pigotts household; she was something of a daughter and maid figure for Gill; when Gill had a two-year affair with her, in the late 1930s, she was 19, he was in his fifties. Gill drew Hawkins obsessively; she became one of his last model-mistresses; he carefully recorded their love affair in his diary, even writing down where they made love: in Gordian's room (his adopted son), in Dr Flood's room, in the bathroom, in his studio, and on the landing.

Eric Gill pursued Daisy Hawkins to Capel-y-ffin, too, after she had left Pigotts because of tensions between her and Gill's wife; at Capel-y-ffin, Gill made love to her in the school room, in Elizabeth Gill's room (his daughter), and in the hills. Hawkins was one of the models in the *Twenty-Five Nudes* and *Drawings From Life* (1940).

Eric Gill also experimented with bestiality (such as with dogs), homosexuality, voyeurism, incest, and group sex (M, 1989). He had an incestuous relationship throughout his life with his sister Gladys (it began around the time she modelled for his sculpture *Fucking (Ecstasy)*, 1911). He also probably had an incestuous relationship with his sister Angela.

Eric Gill used to visit Gladys and sleep with her when she lived alone with her daughter in West Wittering. 'Bath and slept with Gladys', he noted in his diary (M, 239). In his *Autobiography* Gill wrote of the innocent pleasures of childhood friendship, including his sisters ('it is not exaggerating to say that on the whole we were enraptured with life' [A, 41]), but with an overtone of incest:

> ...those friendships of childhood were even better than any others, clearer, brighter,

lovelier, more unselfish, more unalloyed. *They were a union of minds, of souls. And they were human too. There was nothing of the disembodied spirit about them. In a real sense we enjoyed one another's bodies too. We shared the same games and enjoyments. We did the same things, went on the same walks, enjoyed the same sights and sounds. We were in complete accord... We loved the flowers and the hills. We loved the sunsets and the birds and beasts. We loved one another.* (A, 37)

Arthur Eric Rowton Gill had incestuous relations with his daughters as well as his sisters. In his diary he recorded experimenting with dogs: '[c]ontinued experiment with dog after [bath] and discovered that a dog will join with a man' (ib.).

When Eric Gill portrayed animals, such as dogs or horses (they were usually male), he often made sure their genitals were visible (such as the animal penises in *Pegasus*, 1931; *The Lion of St Mark*, 1931; *Two Deer*, 1932; *Hound of St Dominic* (1923), with its large penis; *Unicorn*, 1931; *Griffin and Motto*, 1937; *A Hart*, 1939; and *Horse Prancing*, 1930).

Eric Gill was a voyeur (but then just about everyone is in one way or another). But Gill recorded his voyeurism in detail, along with the rest of his sexual experiences. Some of Gill's diary entries reveal him to be watching people having sex, or being watched by other people. Group sex in Gill's life was not uncommon (often with a husband and wife).

The act of looking is crucial for most artists, and especially for the artist who depicts sex acts. In Eric Gill's life, the act of seeing and the eye had a particular religious emphasis: in Gill's childhood household his father Arthur Tidman Gill told his offspring that God was watching them. Gill's father put a sign up in the house with an eye on it. 'Thou God seest me' read the legend. Gill drew a symbol for himself showing an eye in a palm (*Hand and Eye*, 1908). On the verso of a sketch showing two people fucking in Hyde Park, Gill wrote:

> ...*seen in Hyde Park (abt. 20 yds from pathway) 14.5.25 10.0pm summertime i.e. not quite dark. Note well: the couple were watched afterwards and were discovered to be quite obviously an ordinary couple of good middle class young people genuinely in love – he about 25-30, she abt. 20-25. He looked like a student or journalist – she like a girl in business.* (in Y, 113)

Despite what he practised in his private life, in his public writings

Eric Gill was hypocritical about sexuality. For example, he condemned homosexuality as the 'ultimate disrespect both to the human body and to human love' (in *Clothes*). He said female adultery was worse than male. He publicly disapproved of over-dressing, make-up and perfume in women, yet in private enjoyed such things. Despite his Victorian prudery, he was aroused by tight clothing, bare arms, and even shop window displays (Y, 54). Divorce was out ('a phantasy of disordered imagination'). He said nudist colonies 'induced frigidity'! Some of Gill's views are wonderfully bonkers.

He was against contraception, which he termed 'simply masturbation *à deux*'. According to Eric Gill in a letter to Doctor Helena Wright, a proselytizer of contraception, the 'sex act with contraception is the same as homosexuality'.6 Gill proposed birth control by other means: (1) karezza; (2) abstinence; (3) withdrawal; (4) condoms. 'I don't think 3 And 4 are good', commented Gill.

I don't think abstinence from orgasm is necessarily a bad thing. It depends on the state of mind and states of mind can be cultivated. (Anyway there's no point in ejaculating seed into a woman who doesn't welcome it can go without, if they don't want our spunk they needn't have it.) (ibid.)

I I

LADY C

Of all love poets, we are the love poets. For our religion is loving. To love passionately, but completely, is our one desire.

D.H. Lawrence, *"Georgian Poetry: 1911-1912"*

In Eric Gill's art one finds all the usual tensions of Western art: such as the relation between women and fertility, agriculture, nature and nurture; the constant eroticization of people, the reduction to sexual identities; and the idea that sex can instigate a social and spiritual renewal or revolution.

Eric Gill's sense of sexuality is distinctly heterosexual, as with other campaigners for sexual liberty, such as D.H. Lawrence (the attitudes towards sexuality of both Gill and Lawrence were ambiguous, not straightforward). When D.H. Lawrence died in 1930 Gill offered mass for him in the Pigotts chapel. Later, in 1933, Gill began corresponding with Frieda Lawrence. Like Lawrence, Gill exalted women and the idea of 'woman'; both were visual and verbal artists (Lawrence painted, and valued painting highly; Gill wrote at length); like Lawrence, Gill secretly admired the male form: in both Gill and Lawrence there is an emphasis on the phallus, the symbolic erect phallus, which meant religious rebirth, as Lawrence showed in *The Escaped Cock*, a novella of the 'phallic' man, the new Adam.

Eric Gill and his Bohemian cronies discussed the possibility of a 'new religion', just as D.H. Lawrence had done with his Cafe Royale disciples. Gill's 'New Religion' 'took the form of a Neo-Nietzschean cult of super-humanity under the sign of the Ithyphallus', wrote Augustus John (1952). Eric Gill formulated his 'New Religion' with people like Jacob Epstein, Ambrose McEvoy and John, during meetings at John's studio in the King's Road. Like many others (such as Nietzsche), Gill was after a philosophy of integration, in which sex would fuse with religion:

> I wanted to achieve an integration of all things but had not yet come to see that man was not only not integrated in himself but was not integrated with the world he lived in. (A, 157)

Like D.H. Lawrence and Friedrich Nietzsche, part of Eric Gill's project was to create a new religion. 'I said I invented a new religion. Well, I had to do so', confessed Gill in his *Autobiography* (164), because the existing religions were so unsatisfactory.

D.H.L.'s way of depicting sex and relationships has become famous. In "Excurse" in *Women in Love*, Ursula and Birkin make love in a highly emotional manner, familiar now because of Lawrence's use of language. Unable or unwilling to be specific, to write about genitals, Lawrence paints bodies clothed in darkness and mystery. It is a form of writing about sex that has been parodied endlessly since *Women and Love* and *Lady Chatterley's Lover*. Here, Lawrence gives sex a religious treatment:

> They threw off their clothes, and he gathered her to him, and found her, found the pure lambent reality of her forever invisible flesh. Quenched, inhuman, his fingers upon her unrevealed nudity were the fingers of silence upon silence, the body of mysterious night upon the body of mysterious night, the night masculine and feminine, never to be seen with the eye, or known with the mind, only known as a palpable revelation of mystic otherness.
> She had her desire of him, she touched, she received the maximum of unspeakable communication in touch, dark, subtle, positively silent, a magnificent gift and give again, a perfect acceptance and yielding, a mystery, the reality of that which can never be known, mystic, sensual reality that can never be transmuted into mind content, but remains outside, living body of darkness and silence and subtlety, the mystic body of reality. (403)

Too much sex and too much dwelling on sex is bad, Bertie Lawrence claimed. Yet he filled most of his novels with sex: *Sons and Lovers*, *The Rainbow*, *Women in Love*, *Aaron's Rod*, *Lady Chatterley's Lover* – these are all books which examine sexual relations in detail. In his essays too Lawrence discusses sexuality at great length: the psychology of it, how it works in nature, in symbolism, in emotion, etc.

D.H. Lawrence's testament of erotic revolution, *Lady Chatterley's Lover*, was admired by Eric Gill, and he lent it out to his apprentices. Gill illustrated it (*Lady C*, 1931),[1] depicting Mellors and Connie making love, kneeling in grass, in an extremely idealized, tender manner, in that soft, distinctive, curving white line against black, with the bodies posed for the benefit of the viewer, to expose their genitals. (As usual in Gill's art, the centre of the *Lady C* composition is the man's penis disappearing inside the woman).

Both the *Lady C* and *Mellors* prints are in the usual white line on solid black, but Eric Gill has added stipples and dots on the bodies, to evoke volume. His more usual technique was to use a single line to define a limb; the *Lady Chatterley's Lover* engravings looked more worked and developed than many of Gill's other prints. When Gill illustrated William Shakespeare's *Sonnets* for the British publisher Cassell, he chose to depict two naked heterosexual lovers (*Man and Woman in a Garden*, 1933), despite the fact that most of the *Sonnets* are passionately homosexual, addressed by the older poet to the young aristocratic man.

For Bertie Lawrence and Eric Gill, the phallus was holy, a religious object. Fiona MacCarthy writes:

> To Gill the erect phallus came to have a particular symbolism as the image of God's own virility, the potency of holiness. It became the basis of a quite elaborate theory of human love being a participation in and glorification of divine love. (162-3)

At the end of *Lady Chatterley's Lover*, which is the British novel of sexual liberty, verily a sexual/ poetic manifesto for Eric Gill and others like him, a vision of the world is offered by Mellors. Mellors is of course the archetypal Gill-man (when Gill drew Mellors, he used himself as the model [*Mellors*, 1931]),[2] the man who is a healthy phallus ranging over the world, deeply in touch with nature and tenderness, the man as lusty phallus, who tups whatever and whenever he likes. Mellors proposes a world in which men go about in tight red trousers, tight to show off their buttocks, cocks and balls. Sadly, one senses that good old Mellors, trusty fucker that he is, is not being ironic here. He really does want men to walk around in tight red trousers!

This hilarious view, though, is also Eric Gill's, really. In Gill's book arguing for the reinstatement of masculinity, *Trousers and the Most Precious Ornament*, Gill advocates the reinstatement of the penis, which, Gill claims, is 'all sideways, dishonoured, neglected, ridiculed and ridiculous – no longer the virile member' (1937). The poor 'dishonoured penis'! It's certainly ridiculous. Some would laugh while others would feel sorry for Eric Gill and D.H. Lawrence and their cult of the penis, and their plea for the rebirth of the phallus.

With *Lady Chatterley's Lover* it seems as if Lorenzo is trying to redress the trend towards the macho phallicism of *Kangaroo* and *The Plumed Serpent*, his previous novels, to exalt women again. But he ends up exalting women's sexuality only (Mellors effuses over Connie's buttocks and body). Mellors is still a man trying to dominate a woman. The exchange is sexual. This is the really sad thing about the book. *Lady Chatterley's Lover* is a big plea for tenderness, but the means to this tenderness is sex, and only sex. The first time Connie and Mellors make love they have hardly spoken, as in pornography, where people start fucking with barely a word exchanged. Mellors puts his hand on Connie's 'flank' (120) and makes love to her rapidly.

This gesture, the man's hand on the woman's body (typically the breasts), is the prelude to sex. One finds this image everywhere, throughout Eric Gill's art (in, for example, *Woman Asleep*; two illustrations for *The Green Ship* (title page and *Woman Asleep*, 1936); *Dalliance* from *Procreant Hymn* and others), and in much of 'high art' (in Rembrandt van Rijn, for example).[2] It expresses, in blatantly sexual terms, the power relations between men and women. Man is the active one, the doer, the toucher; woman is passive, the acted upon, the touched (in sculpture, too: see Antonio Canova's *Cupid and Venus*).[3]

The second time Connie and Mellors make love in *Lady C* it is similar –

a few words then quick sex on the blanket. Hardly any contact, or tenderness, or sympathy for the other person. The relationship does get tenderer, but Connie's final transformation stems from sodomy in the 'night of sensual passion'.

For some feminists (of the second wave/ Kate Millett persuasion), it's a pity that D.H. Lawrence couldn't show more than just sex here. Sex is part of love but not the whole of it. Lawrence's mistake is to place all the emphasis on sex and Connie's reawakening through sex. The same criticism can be made of Eric Gill's views. Thus *Lady Chatterley's Lover* is depressing as well as exhilarating. Women are degraded, and in unambiguous ways:

> "Cunt! Eh, that's the beauty o' thee, lass!... A woman's a lovely thing, when 'er's deep ter fuck, and cunt's good... Tha's got the nicest arse of anybody... a bit o' cunt an' tenderness... it's cunt-awareness" (185, 221, 232, 256, 290)

The problem is Mellors reduces Connie to mere cunt. She is just a piece of cunt that he pokes occasionally. Eric Gill too reduces women to cunt. Like the Marquis de Sade, Gill relentlessly eroticized women throughout his life. Gill had very sexist views of women artists: he believed that only men could make great art, and 'women have rarely been even mediocre artists'; contemporary female artists were good only at 'making pretty imitations of natural scenes or objects' (*Art-Nonsense*, 54).

Utter rubbish!

We don't need to remind ourselves of a few women artists who can blast Eric Gill out of the water, do we? All right, here are a few: Ana Mendieta – Eva Hesse – Artemisia Gentileschi – Mary Cassatt – Berthe Morisot – Käthe Kollwitz – Frida Kahlo – Paula Modersohn-Becker – Ch'en Shu – Nancy Holt – Dorothea Lange – Donna Dennis – Georgia O'Keeffe – Diane Arbus – Alice Aycock – Leonor Fini – Niki de Sant-Phalle – Barbara Hepworth – Helen Frankenthaler – Alison Wilding – Barbara Kruger – Agnes Martin – Elizabeth Murray – Louise Bourgeois – Nancy Graves – Louise Nevelson – Rebecca Horn – Mary Miss – Judy Pfaff.

Mellors/ Lawrence exalts sex and forgets the rest of it. In pornography the words 'fuck' and 'love' are interchangeable. To be 'loved' by a man is to be 'fucked'. This is what happened in the censored version of *Lady Chatterley's Lover*: instead of '[w]e fucked a flame into being', one finds '[w]e loved a flame into being'.

The 1928 novel is in some ways a hymn to Mellors' penis, as Kate Millett noted (23), much as Eric Gill's art is a hymn to the phallus (as well as his own penis). Mellors praises Connie's cunt in order to exalt his cock. The highpoint of the book, the night of sensual passion, and the burning out of the deepest 'shames', is only made possible by the phallus. This is rubbish, and the more D.H. Lawrence insists on the primacy of the phallus, as with Eric Gill, the more ridiculous he becomes. '"I know it is the penis which connects us with the stars and the sea and everything"', says Connie in *John Thomas and Lady Jane* (312). It's a ludicrous notion. It's boys with their toys, their phallic stand-ins, their phallic fetish objects. Lawrence and Gill, in exalting the phallus and male genitals, seem to ignore the female sexual parts, the energy, creativity and power of the womb, the vulva and the clitoris. (That's the second wave feminist viewpoint, founded partly in biology and the body: postmodern or 'third wave' feminism is suspicious of feminisms found in biology, which can lead to essentialism and a reactionary, even racist stance).

Where D.H. Lawrence goes wrong, for those critics who find his philosophy crude, sexist or just laughable, is to have the woman worshipping the man in the language and manner of the male. Connie worships Mellor's phallus by cooing over it, kneeling before him. It is a symbolic scene, of course, where symbolism usurps genre and naturalism. In a way, it is the most outrageous scene in the book – far more than Connie and Mellors swiving in the rain, or the night of anal sex.

Connie worships Mellor's penis not as a grown woman but as an idiotic child, someone soft in the head. And the man is so flattered! Men are so easily pleased. Mellors demands total submissiveness after this phallic ritual. Few novelists have been so explicit. Having a woman kneel before a phallus, in all seriousness. Lawrence *means* it, beyond the tensions between naturalism and symbolism, genre and mythology.

> *She was startled and afraid.*
> *'How strange!' she said slowly. 'How strange he stands there! So big! and so dark and cock-sure! Is he like that?'*
> *...'So proud!' she murmured, uneasy. 'And so lordly! Now I know why men are so overbearing! But he's lovely, really.'* (218)

Mellors' dick rises out of gold-red hair, again, the Lawrencean colour of phallic, fiery power. D.H. Lawrence puts everything into *Lady Chatterley's Lover*. He is out in the open, he hides nothing. So he sets himself up to be shot down by anyone. Feminists have rightly sprung upon this scene as an example of Lawrence's misogyny. He is at least honest, artistically, in this scene. But it can't work. It is laughable. But it is true: the erect phallus − '"So big! and so dark and so cock-sure!"' (218) − lies behind so much of male power and violence. He gets that right, even if it is ridiculous.

There's another scene of phallic worship in *Lady Chatterley's Lover*, after an orgasm, as Connie wakes up to the 'queer wonder of him' (181). The language here in religious and ecstatic: 'bliss', 'sacrifice', 'newborn thing', 'wonder', 'strange potency', 'utter stillness of potency' and 'mystery'. Terms such as 'awe', 'wonder', and 'mystery' are repeated throughout the sequence. The narrator refers to the *Book of Genesis* ('the sons of god with the daughters of men', 6:2). Connie's feelings as she touches Mellor's body are those of religious veneration: awe and wonder mixed with fear: '[s]he clung to him with a hiss of wonder that was almost awe, terror' (182). When she senses Mellors having another erection − or as the narrator puts it in his awesome way, when she feels 'again the slow momentous, surging rise of the phallus again, the other power' − her heart 'melt[s] out with a kind of awe'. As she explores his body, the adjectives spilling out from the narrator denote passionate praise:

> *How beautiful he felt... How lovely, how lovely... pure and delicate... How beautiful! How beautiful! ...Beauty! What beauty! ...sheer, warm, potent loveliness.*

She feels his buttocks and thinks of his 'unspeakable beauty'; his balls have a 'strange weight' and '[w]hat a mystery!' (182).

Man, you gotta love D.H. Lawrence!

12

HOLY

Like D.H. Lawrence, Eric Gill believed in the holiness of sex and the holiness of art. Sex, art and religion were a continuum for Gill, as for Lawrence and others, such as Gustav Klimt, Michelangelo Buonaroti and Pablo Picasso. Gill saw everything in terms of religion when he became a Catholic, an observer said, and later thought of everything, including religion, in terms of sex (R. Speaight, 167). For Gill, as for so many artists, making art was a holy activity. Eric Gill espoused the tenets of William Morris and the Arts and Crafts movement, maintaining that craftsmanship was sacred. 'The point is that human works should be holy, for holiness is properly their criterion', wrote Gill in a late essay, "Secular and Sacred in Modern Industry":

> All men are sacred persons. All their works are holy which is to say all the works are holy which are done by men in the exercise of their human personality. For that personality is of its very nature holy. (Last Essays, 81)

The point about the industrial era, Eric Gill reckons, is that it has debased work, turned work into mere drudgery, so that work in not enjoyable, not part of the pleasure of life:

This is the fundamental evil of industrialism. It has depersonalized work. It has disintegrated the worker. It has made the work the least interesting, because the least personal part of his life. It has created a state of things in which nothing is expected from work, but the pay for doing it, and all the happiness of living is relegated to the time when we are not working. (Last Essays, 86)

Modern society and modern thinking was out of kilter with a religious conception of life, Eric Gill reckoned; life, work and art were all holy, all religious, in Gill's view. But contemporary thinking was 'odd and unnatural'. Gill continued:

Our boasted enlightenment is, after all, nothing but the cool-headedness of people who don't happen to be in love. Our boasted religious toleration is, after all, only religious indifference. We don't know where we are going and so we don't know a fair wind from a foul one. How can we possibly know the holy from the unholy. (A, 265)

The two things, work and leisure, are the same thing in Eric Gill's view; that is, life itself. D.H. Lawrence said the same things. Work is 'ghastly' Lawrence wrote in Study of Thomas Hardy (32). When the work is done, what then? he asks. One must get on with the real business of life – living (38). Work is nonsense. It's for the machine, it's not real, but it's back-breaking. Lawrence, like Gill, was not against decent work, getting in touch with your body, with the 'flow of warmth, affection and physical unison', he wrote in "Men Must Work and Women As Well" (in A Selection from Phoenix, 421). But work has become debased, Gill and Lawrence said.

So the robotic grind of mass production is hateful to Eric Gill. Instead, he emphasizes the craft of the artist, the loveliness of things made by hand. In this he concurs with many other thinkers, such as Robert Graves, the poet, another English eccentric, like Gill, who would not have ugly mass of objects around him, not when hand-made things could be found.

❧

Eric Gill, too, hated the idea of a pure, lazy leisure time, the 'Leisure State', with endless 'leisure time'. For him, the two things – leisure and work – should be one. These views were also espoused by John Ruskin, D.H. Lawrence and William Morris. Lawrence reviewed Gill's essay Art-

Nonsense (unfavourably), and thought Gill a very bad preacher. Lawrence called Gill 'crude and crass', 'crude and crass amateur: crass is the only word, maddening, like a tiresome uneducated workman arguing in a pub'. Lawrence, though, complemented Eric Gill on producing a philosophy of more worth, in "Slavery and Freedom", than 'in all of Karl Marx or Professor Whitehead or a dozen other philosophers rolled together'.

D.H. Lawrence agreed with Eric Gill, though, on the subject of work, on how so much everyday work is really slave labour, a prostitution of body *and* soul.[3] Gill agreed with Lawrence that he was probably a bad preacher: 'I am indeed an inept and amateurish preacher'.[4] 'I agree with practically all of [Lawrence's] criticism... I hope it didn't spoil his last hours', Gill said (R. Speaight, 231). For Lawrence as for Gill, work must be made holy, because life itself was holy. It must not be degraded, made profane. Similarly with sex: sex was holy because life was holy: this is the view of Gill and Lawrence. But Gill did not wish to be seen as a 'priest of love', in the Lawrencean manner (one suspects that Lawrence, though, rather enjoyed being a sexual mystic).

✳

Eric Gill was much impressed on his visit to Palestine, which he called literally the Holy Land; it was 'like living with the Apostles. It was like living in the *Bible*' (A, 251). In his *Autobiography* Gill said he wouldn't go on and on about the 'beautiful things' he saw in Palestine, but he did mention

> the beauty of the Judean desert, the beauty of Siloam, the beauty of Justinian's church at Bethlehem, not even the beauty of the Haram at Jerusalem, the Moslem holy place, the most beautiful place I have ever seen and the farthest removed from the Bank of England and all its devil worship, the most civilized, the most cultured, the most quiet and serene, the most spacious, the most spiritually pervaded place now remaining in the whole world. (A, 253)

Throughout his essays and letters, Eric Gill debated the relation between industrialism and the mediæval world, where things seemed to be united in an effort of religious worship. So many artists have looked back nostalgically on the mediæval era, calling it the 'Age of Faith', when there seemed to be societal unity and religious fervour. The German poets Novalis and Rainer Maria Rilke looked back to the Middle Ages, Novalis with his unfinished essay on Christendom in Europe, and Rilke with his *Book of Hours* poems. The love of mediævalism of the Victorian era is well known, in the Pre-Raphaelites, for instance, or the Arts and Crafts movement. The whole mediæval/ Gothic worldview was much discussed by John Ruskin, William Morris, Gill and others, and was bound up with socialism, left-wing politics, materialist notions of work, class and power, and other issues. It was a debate that obsessed Gill throughout his life, a subject he returns to again and again in his letters. It is an issue fraught with ambiguities, ambivalence, confusion, diverging goals and questionable morality.

Eric Gill was clear about one æsthetic, though, and that was the function of art. In the first essay of *Beauty Looks After Herself* ("Art and Prudence"), Gill wrote:

Ethics is the science of happiness in oneself.
Aesthetics is the science of pleasure in things. (1933, 14)

André Gide said exactly the same thing, that ethics and æsthetics were part of the same experience, so that good ethics had to mean good æsthetics, and vice versa. The 'good life', then, in the view of Gill and Gide (and many other artists) was one in which 'good art' and 'good morality' were part of the same experience. The end of art becomes pleasure, art is founded on pleasure in the Gillian system of ethics. 'The supplying of pleasure in the business of art', he wrote (in ib., 15).

In Eric Gill's æsthetics, beauty gives pleasure, as in Plato's philosophy, but it is a mental pleasure, mainly, Gill emphasized: 'beautiful things are those which please when seen – and, of course, I mean mentally seen, and therefore pleasing to the mind' he wrote on March 4th, 1931, to *The Architects' Journal* (*Letters*, 259). And again, in this æsthetic statement on sculpture:

That is what the art of sculpture has been in the world since the beginning – it is the business of making materialisations of things formed in the mind. (*Beauty Looks After Herself*, 120)

Like many artists, Eric Gill disliked critics dissecting art. They complicated things, he said, when art was really quite simple. In a letter to Romney Green (of June 10, 1928), Gill wrote:

It's the curse of the literary man, & the art of letters being paramount at the moment they try & impose their literary business on painters & sculptors & musicians. But I don't think it's quite right that it's what the artist has 'seen or felt' either. The registration of what one has seen or felt is simply one of the possible lines of artistic activity − not the very essence of the matter. It seems that the essence of the thing is very simple − art is concerned with making − just that; and a good artist is one who makes things well (a bad one makes them badly). What people like the N. Statesman Johnny seem to miss is the work of art! They don't see it. They don't even ask themselves: what is it? I make a statue & they ask: what does it say? I reply: it doesn't say anything; it just is − it has being. (Letters, 233-4)

13

FLESH

Art and pleasure, beauty and art, beauty and pleasure, all these are bound up together in Eric Gill's religious view of life. For him, art and religion are continuous, and there isn't enough celebration in life. His was a unifying view of life, in which labour and leisure, art and industry, sex and religion were fused. 'It All Goes Together', Gill asserted. There is too much doom and gloom in Catholicism, so, as he wrote to the Reverend Desmond Chute in 1931:

> As to the figure of Christ... I'd rather carve the naked figure but it seems to me: 1, Christ the King is what is wanted to-day — more than Christ the victim. 2, the risen Christ is more the thing for a Christian's grave than the dying or the dead Christ. (Letters, 261)

The Word of God was the first creative act, Eric Gill says, and writers such as André Gide concur with this view. Gill writes:

> What is a work of art? A word made flesh. That is the truth, in the clearest sense of the text. A word, that which emanates from the mind. Made flesh; a thing, a thing seen, a thing known, the immeasurable translated into terms of the measurable.[1]

In many images, Eric Gill depicted sex in sacred ways, either by giving his pictures of copulating couples a religious context – a title, perhaps, as in *Earth Wrestling*, from E. Powys Mathers' *Procreant Hymn*, or he put the hand of God above the lovers, with rays of light emanating from the hand, blessing the sex act, as in *Earth Receiving* (1926).[2] Here the tupping is what critics call 'athletic'; that is, the woman's limbs are bent over, her legs in the air, the lovers' fingers clasped together (why do critics say 'athletic'? Don't critics fuck any other way than the flat-on-flat missionary position?).

The image of the couple making love below the hand of God perfectly summarizes Eric Gill's view of sex, of sex as a religious experience. A giant divine hand blessing lovers also occurs in *With Ritual Chant*, an illustration for *Art & Love* (1927); as in *Approaching Dawn* from *Twenty-Five Nudes*, the bedding is all curving black-and-white stripes, which echo the curves of the lovers' bodies (note that it is the nude woman in these engravings which forms the basis of the patterns and curving shapes of the background).

In most of his religious-erotic images, Eric Gill is wildly phallic and heterosexual. The woman is usually 'passive' and the male is 'active'. The woman, as Earth, 'receives', while the man thrusts. The woman 'gives' herself, gives of herself, in Eric Gill's art, as in his series of erotic prints illustrating the most sensual poem in the *Bible*, the *Song of Songs*, where the woman offers her breasts to the man, her eyes closed (in *Ibi Dabo Tibi*, 1925).[3] According to Marina Warner in her book on the Virgin Mary, the *Song of Songs* is immensely erotic: '[t]here has never been a more intense communication of the experience of desire' (1985, 126). In Solomon's *Song of Songs*, the Queen of Sheba says 'nigra sum sed formosa' ('I am black but comely)':

> The *song of songs*, which is Solomon's. Let him kiss me with the kisses of his mouth: for thy love is better than wine.
>
> ...I am black, but comely, O ye daughters of Jerusalem, as the tents of Kedar, as the curtains of Solomon.
>
> ... I am the rose of Sharon, and the lily of the valleys.
>
> ... Behold, thou art fair, my love; behold, thou art fair; thou hast doves' eyes within thy locks: thy hair is as a flock of goats, that appear from Mount Gilead.
>
> Thy teeth are like a flock of sheep that are even shorn, which came up from the washing; whereof every one bear twins, and none is barren among them.

Thy lips are like a thread of scarlet, and thy speech is comely: thy temples are like a piece of a pomegranate within thy locks.

Thy neck is like the tower of David builded for an armoury, whereon there hang a thousand bucklers, all shields of mighty men.

Thy two breasts are like two young roes that are twins, which feed among the lilies.

The *Cantia Canticarum* allows for depictions of unbridled sensuality. The nuptial imagery encourages artists to be as sensual as they dare in a religious setting. Eric Gill's merging of eroticism with Catholicism operates within the mystical tradition of Catholicism, as espoused by mystics like St Bernard, Jan van Ruysbroeck, St Teresa and St John of the Cross. It is a wild and ecstatic mysticism which describes religious bliss in very sensual terms. In *Drawings From Life* Gill wrote:

> *heaven forbid that I should seem to preach an erotic mysticism. We know what we have seen and touched, both with the body and with the mind — and that these things are inseparable; for it is the man, the whole man, body and soul, who enjoys and not his eye or his hand merely or his mind alone — we know the unnerving loveliness, heart-breaking, tear-bringing, which sometimes, however rarely, shakes the soul of the man and of the draughtsman. We know the sense of contact with God Himself which such moments seem to bring — as though a sort of arrow pierced our heart.*

Beds are prominent in Eric Gill's *Song of Songs* illustrations: the nude woman is shown sleeping alone (in *Wake Not My Beloved, On My Bed By Night* and *Girl Sleeping*). In *The Voice of My Beloved*, the man is shown, looking at the sleeping woman, greeting her. In *The Serenade* he is seen singing outside her room. In *His Left Hand Under My Head*, the love-making begins, the woman beneath the man; the forms of the lovers are seen through the transparent covers. In *Inter Ubera Mea*, the man lies with his head between the woman's breasts, as after orgasm.

Throughout the *Song of Songs* series the woman is continually eroticized, with her breasts visible in nearly every picture. (Not all the pictures in the *Song of Songs* depict love-making: *The Harem, The Serenade, My Love Among the Lilies, The Watchmen, A Garden Enclosed, Let Us Fare Forth Into the Fields, Girl Sleeping* and *Swineherd*).

In the 1930 *Canticum Canticorum*, the eroticism is gentler, more concerned with tender embracing and caresses than penetrative sex. There are still nude images throughout, though, such as in *Nigra Sum Sed Formosai*, *Hortus Conclusus*, *Vadam Ad Montem* and *Dulecti Mei Pulsantis*. Unlike the *Song of Songs* engravings, Eric Gill's versions for *Canticum Canticorum* are in his black, stippled style, with the forms of the human figures indicated by white, feathery outlines. Only in a few places is the eroticism of the *Song of Songs* recalled: in *Ibi Dabo Tibi*, the woman offers he man her breasts; in *In Domum Matris Meae*, the couple embrace in a pose from Gill's *Divine Lovers*.

In Eric Gill's art, eroticism veers from moments of tender affection, as in *Approaching Dawn* (1927),[4] from an illustration of Geoffrey Chaucer's *Troilus and Creseyde*, to undiluted pornography, such as in *The Chinese Maidservant* (1929), which shows a woman bending over, revealing her ass. The aim of such images is to sexualize the female body, to make it available to the (male) gaze. There are many images of copulation in Gill's art. While other (male) artists (Titian, J.M.W. Turner, Rembrandt van Rijn, Henry Fuseli and Francesco Parmigiano) made erotic art depicting penetration that was for centuries kept hidden, Gill's penetrative erotic art is more widely published, as with Hans Bellmer, Egon Schiele and Salvador Dali. Gill ran into problems by showing copulation, but he was not imprisoned, as Egon Schiele was.

The 20th and 21st centuries have seen a 'liberalization', perhaps, of representations of sex, so that more 'realistic' scenes of love-making are found in many places (magazines, TV, cinema, painting, dance, theatre, and so on). Yet, there is no erect penis seen entering a vagina in two of the main media of recent times – cinema and television (except in porn, with its meat shots [penetration] and come shots or money shots [ejaculation shots are called 'money shots' because they are expensive to produce]). Only in 'high art', such as painting and drawing and sculpture, is penetration depicted and accepted by the art establishment. The whole representation of love-making in art is fraught with hypocrisy and ambivalence. You can wander off the street into a New York art gallery and see images of female ejaculation thirty feet wide, giant images of spread thighs and squirting vulvas, but not on mainstream television.

Eric Gill, though, glorifies copulation throughout his work. There are bizarre engravings, such as *The Invisible Man* (1924),[5] which shows a woman – nude of course – standing up, having sex with an invisible man. Standing up is a favoured sexual position in Gill's art (in *Lady C.* for example, or the sculpture *Ecstasy*). Other images of penetration include the *Song of Songs* engravings; the illustrations to E. Powys Mathers' *Procreant Hymn*; *Lot's Daughter*; *Lovers*; and *Approaching Dawn*. The 1924 engravings *Lovers* (P294 in John Skelton's 1990 book) shows a man and woman about to make love, the man's erect wiener very prominent.

Although Eric Gill's famous for depicting plenty of tupping, his art sticks mainly to conventional postures and types of sex – for instance, the missionary position, and occasionally women on top, or standing up. Not much fucking from behind, though, or the side, or in other ways.

Similarly, although Eric Gill's art espouses a passionate love of women, there's not a lot of oral sex – either from men or women. You'd think, knowing Gill's views on sex, that there would be a least a few depictions of blowjobs, if not cunnilingus, in his published works. After all, as with D.H. Lawrence's fiction, there's a good deal of worshipping of the phallus in Gill's theology of love.

Also, there are few portrayals of orgasms, a key element in any erotic art. You'd think that Eric Gill might include a few spraying penises in his work, but no. It's one of the paradoxes of Gill's art – that it seems sexually explicit, but it's also sexually reticent.

As extraordinary as Eric Gill's art is in terms of depicting eroticism, it is often surpassed by contemporary erotic artists, such as Erich von Gotha, Ferocius, Horace Altuna, James Lemay and Hans Kovacq. These artists produce erotica for comicbooks, graphic novels and cartoons. By comparison with von Gotha, Ferocius, Altuna and Lemay, Gill's erotic art can seem tame and homely.

The relief sculpture *Ecstasy* (Tate Gallery) was originally entitled *Fucking* by Eric Gill. It was carved in 1911, and shows two people making love standing up, the man's knees bent, his arms around her head, the woman's legs either side of his, her arms clasping him tightly. The sculpture has a number of details in the limbs – the muscles of the man's legs – but is an idealized portrayal.

The models for *Fucking* were apparently Eric Gill's sister Gladys, and

Ernest Laughton, her spouse. *Ecstasy* was known 'they – large' in Gill's diary, with *Votes For Women*, another image of copulation, known as 'they – small'. *Ecstasy* was probably meant for the open-air temple of love that Gill had planned with Jacob Epstein at one time (that might have been a great place to visit).

In the engravings entitled *Lovers* (1922), the rationalization of the copulating figures is even more pronounced: Eric Gill has drawn just the outlines of their limbs, with just a short line to indicate their waists. In *Fucking/ Ecstasy*, the woman's face is visible, with the man's face behind hers; in the *Lovers*, the man buries his head in the woman's shoulder, so their both their heads are a mass of hair.

Another relief sculpture, entitled *Lovers Relief* (1921, Texas) is also called 'Fucking', and is related to *Ecstasy*. Here, the two standing figures are all entwined limbs, the woman with her left leg raised high, which the man grips under his right arm, his left arm wrapped around her back, their heads pressed together. The genitals are prominent here – the penis and balls especially.

In another 1921 *Lovers Relief*, a stone-incised relief, the woman clings to a standing man, thighs clasping his torso, her buttocks spread to reveal his genitals. In one *Lovers* engraving (of 1932), made for Miriam Rothschild, the woman is fully pregnant. E. Powys Mathers was a connoisseur of pornography; his Lincoln's Inn Fields flat housed his porn collection. Mathers' *Procreant Hymn* was illustrated by Gill in 1926 in his explicit style: one version of *Earth Inviting* showed the man and woman embracing each other but standing slightly apart; another version showed the woman caressing her lover's cock.

E. Powys Mathers translated erotic Middle Eastern Oriental poetry, such as this *ghazal* from 19th century Afghanistan:

To-day I saw Laila's breasts, the hills of a fair city
From which my heart might leap to heaven.

Her breasts are a garden of white roses
Having two drifted hills of fallen rose-leaves.

Her breasts are a garden where doves are singing
And doves are moaning with arrows because of her.

Dalliance featured a classic erotic pose, familiar from the history of art, the man with his arms around the woman, their faces pressed together, his hand on her breasts. The man's erect penis was on display again in *Earth Wrestling*. *Procreant Hymn* also contained the amazing Gill image of a naked, erect Jesus flying down from heaven blessed by God's hand, and the man and woman fucking joyously, again with God's benediction.

In love-making images, such as *Lot's Daughter*, Eric Gill depicted two people tupping in a picture employing plain, unadorned marks,6 as found in Taoist sex manuals.7 Or in the 'acrobatic' fucking of *Lovers in a Tent* (1929) or *Lovers, The Raised Bottom* (1934), which depict two people getting jiggy on a bed, and, as so often in pornography, focuses on the penis and vagina, as if that was all there was to sex (Andrea Dworkin writes that sex means 'penile intromission followed by penile thrusting, or fucking', 1984, 23]). This is clearly often the case in Eric Gill's work, where the phallus is at the centre of pleasure and power. Sex in his works often means penile thrusting. In both *Lovers, The Raised Bottom* and *Lovers in a Tent*, Gill puts the conjoined genitals at the centre of the composition; in the former, the woman has her legs bent double over her torso; Gill makes the vaginal penetration clear, with the penis bisecting the labia, surrounded by Gill's fetishized pubic hair. For *Lovers in a Tent*, Gill again concentrated on what hardcore porn filmmakers call the 'meat shot', the all-important penetration; the man holds the woman up under the shoulders, in a sexual position out of the *Kama Sutra*.

In the engravings *Lovers, Man Kneeling* and *Lovers, Man Lying* (both 1920), the naked couple are etched in fine white lines, making love in a balletic, graceful manner. In *Lovers, Man Kneeling*, the woman sits above the man, his cock just inside her, so that the genitals are clearly displayed. Gill portrayed vaginal penetration many times, but often didn't have the penis embedded fully in the conch, so that the phallus he celebrated so much could be seen.

The sculpture *Lovers* is particularly similar to the carvings on Indian temples (the *maithuna* figures, famously at Khajuraho, which Eric Gill admired). The man is 'on top', the woman is underneath, accepting everything (except in the rare instance, such as the sculpted relief *Votes for Women*, which Fiona MacCarthy describes, oddly, as 'both very pure and very shocking' [M, 104]).

Votes For Women (1910, Leeds City Art Gallery)8 was once owned by Maynard Keynes, who bought it for £5.00. The woman crouches above the man, her body double, with man arching his back, he has his head thrown back and legs buckled under him, clutching her hips. Usually, the woman is underneath; she is the Earth, the soil, 'Earth receiving', as Eric Gill terms it, waiting to absorb the holy seed of the man. Woman is Earth, passive, 'receiving', supine; man is Heaven, holy, active, creative. The typical Gill sex pose is the missionary position in *The Juice of My Pomegranates* (1925),9 where the woman swoons at the man's sexual prowess. Gill draws attention to the copulation by having the sheet covering the lovers transparent, so the man is shown lying between the woman's legs through the folds.

Another image of love-making looks back directly to the lost drawing by Michelangelo Buonaroti of the moment in Greek mythology, where the god Zeus appears to Leda as a swan and sleeps with her. Or as second wave feminists would say: he raped her. Eric Eric Gill's *Leda Loved* (1929)10 is practically a re-run of Michelangelo's highly erotic image. As in Michelangelo's drawing, Gill's swan lies between Leda's thighs, his wings caressing her vulva. Gill's engraving, like Michelangelo's lost drawing, is an exaltation of the fusion of sacred and profane love, where a divine being has sex with a human being.

An earlier, 1924 *Leda* was not much less explicitly erotic; it showed the swan being embraced between the woman's thighs, the two of them kissing. Essentially, this picture of sex's made 'acceptable' to the art establishment because of its 'high art' pretensions, its use of 'high' mythology, the Græco-Roman mythology which is the companion to the Judæo-Christian tradition. Images which draw on Judæo-Christian religion are protected, sanctified, for the Judæo-Christian tradition is at the centre of Western philosophy.

Eric Gill explores this tradition, but, even when he seems to be heretical or blasphemous, he remains within that tradition. The other tradition, Græco-Roman art, is just as exalted in 'high art'. Since Francesco Petrarch inaugurated the Renaissance by recycling Ovid's *Metamorphoses* in his *Canzoniere*, Greek and Roman mythology has been the major alternative to the Judæo-Christian tradition. Since the Renaissance, artists have turned to Græco-Roman mythology when the Judæo-Christian one has become exhausted.

14

MYTHOLOGY

What Eric Gill did, interestingly, was to put the 'secular' and 'profane' (i.e., sexual) aspects of 'pagan' or Greek mythology back into the 'sacred' area of the Judæo-Christian tradition. Gill eroticized Christianity. He put eroticism back into it, where there was hardly any before (there was plenty of eroticism, but it was nearly always highly suppressed and repressed). Gill transplanted the eroticism and wildness of Greek and Roman mythology, which for centuries Christianity regarded as 'secular' or 'pagan' (whereas in fact it was as 'holy' or 'sacred' as Christianity itself), and embedded it in Christianity. For Christianity is extraordinarily humourless and unerotic. In the Renaissance, artists turned to Græco-Roman mythology for images of erotic human love; you could have naked Venuses, cherubs, satyrs and so on. Christianity allowed mother love, in the *Madonna and Child* images, the homoeroticism of the occasionally naked Christ and St Sebastian, but little else. There was Mary Magdalene, the 'holy whore' of Christianity, but she was depicted alone, pathetically penitent, a woman of 'sin' and 'lust' (male projections again).

For mystics of the mediæval and early modern era, God is the ultimate, Divine Lover, much as Christ is regarded as the bridegroom who 'marries' the bride, the Church. The New Jerusalem, in the *Revelations* in the *Bible*, comes down arrayed 'as a bride'. Nuptial imagery – that is, thoroughly erotic imagery – occurs sometimes in Judæo-Christianity, from the very sensual *Song of Songs* onwards (but it is rarely depicted in art). Indeed, the more ascetic and austere the mystic, the more erotic and joyous the mystical outpourings. Burning with the fire of love, pierced hearts bleeding the blood of life, the imagery of mysticism is drenched in eroticism. It is all about, like Tantrism or Taoist sex magic, desire. St John of the Cross wrote in his *The Dark Night of the Soul*: 'love is like fire, which ever rises upward with the desire to be absorbed in the centre of its sphere.'[1] Even seemingly unbudgably ascetic mystics such as the Arabic, Persian and Sufis, Al-Hallaj, Rumi, Jami, Al-Ghazzali, Rab'ia and Hafiz, wrote incredibly erotically of being God-intoxicated, and Allah was seen often as the Divine Lover in whose arms the mystic desired to be extinguished in an excess of rapture that is clearly associated with sex.

The tensions in Eric Gill's art, between flesh and spirit, between the human and the divine, the erotic and the spiritual, are also those between the Christian and the pagan, between West and East. For Gill, spirit and matter, spirit and sex, are one, part of the same mystery. In his letters, often to fellow Catholics, Gill defended his fusion of sex and spirit, and attacked Christian dualism, which separated the two.

At times, Eric Gill's life-philosophy took on the flavour of Aleister Crowley, another quasi-guru who aimed to fuse sex and spirit: in his introduction to his *Engravings by Eric Gill*, Gill wrote 'the proper speech of man to God, as of woman to man, wife to husband, mistress to lover, is 'do with me what thou wilt'', recalling Crowley's 'do what thou wilt' (derived from William Blake and Francois Rabelais). Commenting on Gill's *The Splits* sculpture and the Rossall School War Memorial, J.G. Fletcher wrote:

> The one is ascetic, unworldly; the other is pagan to a degree in which not even the Greeks were pagan. Gill is a standing proof that the soul is not naturally Christian. For fundamentally he is interested in the human body and in all its adventures of birth, love-making, begetting, toiling and death. And against these, the sombre ideas of self-sacrifice, atonement, ascetic denial, which his faith teaches, work like an irritant rather

than an antidote. When he is pagan, in his engraving or his sculpture, he is free to express himself as Eric Gill; when he carves Stations of the Cross or attempts Madonnas, he is curiously hampered by the traditions of the past. (1928, 95)

Some artists did try to eroticize Christianity: Gianlorenzo Bernini made St Teresa orgasmic in his famous statue in Rome, for instance. Instead, what one finds in Christian art is a barely suppressed homoeroticism, where the nearly naked body of Christ is openly displayed everywhere. The heart of Christianity is the extremely brutal suicide of Christ, suicide as sacrifice, an image of supreme sadomasochism if ever there was one. Thus, at the heart of Christianity, the thing which is the holy of holies of Christianity, is an image that could be regarded as hardcore pornography, a man being tortured to death on a Cross.

This is the pornography of religion.

Eric Gill indulges in this 'pornography of Christianity', with his images of Mary Magdalene making love to Christ on the Cross (*Nuptials of God*), with his images of Christ looking sexually 'virile', as critics say (the critics really mean Gill drew a big penis on Jesus); with his images of Christ and the Church as copulating men and women; with his images of people fucking blessed by the hand of God. All this is part of the eroticization of religion, which can easily be seen as pornography.

Nuptials of God (1922) was originally designed for the Reverend Gerald Vann's ordination card, and was used to illustrate *The Game* (1923). The eroticism of *Nuptials of God* is expressed in the blasphemous kiss, and in the conjunction of the two nude bodies. The Magdalene is eroticized through her body – the swell of her naked hips, for example, and her very long hair, a standard image of eroticism, spreading all over her body. Note how both figures sport haloes. (A more restrained depiction of Jesus and Mary Magdalene occurred in Eric Gill's illustration for *The Four Gospels* [1931], where the holy whore is shown washing the Saviour's feet, with the sepulchre seen in the distance, below a cross).

15

PAIN

Eric Gill celebrates love, but love is also pain, death, sin, vice and fornication in the Christian view. Love poets transform the pain into art, as do creators of erotic art. The masochism at the heart of Western art, as at the core of Christianity, Christ on the Cross, the supreme example of masochistic agony in the West, is the most painted image in the West, apart from the Madonna and Child. There is a link here, between the Crucifixion and the Madonna and Child images: the Crucifixion is the end of life, the painful letting go, while the child in the Madonna's arms is the beginning of life, swathed in the softness and care of the mother figure. The two images, Virgin and Child and the Crucifixion, form the twin poles of Western art. Both images are dominated by the feminine, for the Cross in the Crucifixion is the Mother, the Goddess, the Cross being part of the Earth from which Christ is later reborn – the second, spiritual birth echoing his first, earthly birth, depicted in so many Nativity scenes and Madonna and Child images.

Eric Gill produced many *Madonna and Child* images, and many *Crucifixions*, just like a jobbing Renaissance painter, and, significantly, he eroticizes both images, making the suckling of the Virgin's breast an erotic experience, and making Jesus an erotic figure (in sculptures such as

Deposition). 'After all, since in his physical nature he was every inch a man, Jesus must have had proper genitals', Gill remarked (in R. Heppenstall, 99). The drawings entitled Deposition show the naked dead Jesus turned towards the viewer, his genitals and pubic hair clearly visible. Eric Gill has made Christ what some critics coyly refer to as 'well-endowed'. If Gill was going to give Christ a penis, it might as well be large (contrary to the images of Jesus in the Renaissance where, if the pecker was shown at all, which was rare, it was small and unobtrusive). However, in the Deposition sculpture (1924, black Hoptonwood stone, King's School, Canterbury),[1] Christ's manhood is somewhat shorter than in the engravings.

The mother-child dyad is a recurring theme in Eric Gill's work; not only are there many Madonna and Childs, there are many images of secular, domestic mothers and children. Often these feature the mother suckling the child (as in Mother and Child, 1923). Some of Gill's images of the Virgin and Child depict the mother offering her breasts to the baby (as in Madonna and Child, 1914 and Madonna and Child, 1925).

In a 1922 Christmas card (Madonna and Child: The Shrimp) and a 1923 Madonna and Child, the two are embracing closely, and kissing each other. Eric Gill's Madonna and Child images of course recall many Renaissance images; the simplicity and clarity of many of his Madonnas resemble those of the Italian Early Renaissance painters, such as Fra Filippo Lippi and Fra Angelico. Some of Gill's engravings, such as Madonna and Child With Chalice (1916), Madonna and Child, With Gallows (1916) and Madonna and Child, With Crucifix (1917), very much recall Fra Angelico's quiet, passive Virgins, such as in Angelico's Annunciation paintings in the San Marco monastery in Florence.

One imagines that Eric Gill would relish the peaceful atmosphere of the Florentine monastery, with its whitewashed monks' cells and Angelico frescoes. In his letters he hankered after bare white rooms where one could paint books of songs or prayers.[2]

The San Marco Museum in Florence is really extraordinary. The monks' cells are marvellous, not at all oppressive or cloyingly monastic or 'religious' in the traditional sense. It is not dusty and fusty as so many churches are. The cells are simple, sparse, washed with a creamy white paint. Fra Angelico's frescoes fit perfectly. Seen together, all at once, they are overwhelming. Each cell contains a mystery. Each cell is made for a meditation on mystery.

The sequence of Fra Angelico's paintings follows the story of the Passion, but roughly. *The Crucifixion* appears most often. The sequence is punctuated by a variety of *Crucifixions*. These are torturous – truly anguished. Angelico's art is seemingly so simple, yet capable of such spiritual heights.

The kneeling Madonnas in Eric Gill's drawings also recall those of the Early Netherlandish painters: the Virgin praying in silence and awe before the Christ Child was a motif particular to the Northern European artists (it was later taken up in Italy by painters such as Fra Filippo Lippi).

Another Christian sadomasochistic image which Eric Gill drew and sculpted is St Sebastian being shot with arrows. This is a sublime piece of sadomasochism, where the greater the pain means the greater the martyrdom and the greater the final hagiographic holiness. Depictions of St Sebastian, like those of Jesus, have dwelt lovingly on the lusciousness of the nude male. With the martyrdom of St Sebastian, there is opportunity to exploit the voluptuousness of penetration and pain, where the arrows enter the skin, recalling too the painful metaphor of falling in love, where Cupid's arrow literally enters the bewitched one's eyes and heart. Gill's sculpture of St Sebastian, like his drawings of the subject, emphasize the erotic beauty of the male nude, reclining back languidly, eyes closed, against a pillar.[3]

16

ORIENT

Eric Gill took inspiration from Eastern forms of love and the depictions of love. Hindu, Tantric, Taoist and Chinese erotic art is founded in religions quite different in some key areas from Western religion. There is less guilt, sin, body-hating and suppression in Indian, Japanese and Chinese erotic art. The cosmic energy of life has a sexual dimension which is gloriously celebrated. Indian, Japanese and Chinese erotic art may be just as sexist and misogynist and patriarchal as Western erotic art, but it is also freer, more exuberant, more joyous. Gill often advocates the necessity of joy in love-making, something lacking in Western religion, except in the *Song of Songs* and some of the mystics, as he noted (see "Indian Sculpture", in *Art-Nonsense*).

Eric Gill was impressed by the writings of Ananda Coomaraswamy (1877-1947) on Indian art, in particular on erotic Eastern art (painter William Rothenstein also introduced Gill to Indian erotic sculptures). Gill met with Coomaraswamy and discussed the subject at the Art Workers' Guild meeting hall in London. Coomaraswamy's dictum that 'the artist is not a special kind of man, but every man is a special kind of artist' became one of Gill's key tenets. Coomaraswamy's philosophizing helped Gill to rationalize his thoughts on erotic art. Gill gushed in his

Autobiography:

> I dare not confess myself his disciple; that would only embarrass him. I can only say that I believe that no other living writer has written the truth in matters of art and life and religion and piety with such wisdom and understanding. (174).

Like other thinkers in the first half of the 20th century, Ananda Coomaraswamy brought together many strands of world religion, in a perennial philosophy which united elements of Christianity with Buddhism, Hinduism and Islam; Eric Gill and Coomaraswamy also shared an interest in Friedrich Nietzsche, William Blake, Thomas Aquinas, John Ruskin and socialism (Y, 69).

In Oriental erotic art, sexuality is a cosmic energy, an essential part of an authentic religious worldview, but it is gendered into heterosexual components, as *shiva* and *shakti*, and the symbols of the *lingam* and *yoni* are, yet again, the penis and vagina. Eric Gill had planned an edition of *Ananga-Ranga*, an Indian erotic book. Gill's sculpture *Lovers* recalls the *maithuna* figures, where idealized figures tup away blissfully and anonymously.[1] *Maithuna*, the carvings of love-making couples, are found on Indian temples, and Gill's erotic sculptures have the same idealized view of the human form.

The mytho-cosmic view of sexuality of the Orient is that of Eric Gill's art: in Indian religion there is *shiva* and *shakti* as the cosmic forces; in China it is the *yin* and *yang*. Always there is an emphasis on the masculine and the feminine, and the union of the two, as there is in Gill's art. As the *I Ching* puts it: the '[s]exual union of man and woman gives life to all things.'[2]

What one notices, though, is the sense of humour and joy in Oriental erotic art. People *smile*, and *laugh*. This sense of fun is what is missing from so much of Occidental erotic art, which is shot through with Judæo-Christian feelings of sin, guilt, shame and death-awareness.

Those figures on the temples of Khajuraho or in Rajasthan, they look like they're having a great time. They make love and they *smile*. Sex is fun! – and those carvings on the Indian temples show love-making as intimate, sensual pleasure, unblemished by death-consciousness or sin or guilt.[3] It is the effect Eric Gill desired in his erotic creations. One sees those Oriental smiles on the faces of his lovers in the *Song of Songs* engravings, in *Earth Receiving*, or in the *Troilus and Criseyde* illustrations. For Gill, the body was a humorous as well as a beautiful thing. Not for him the eternally solemn response to the body of the academic or 'high art' critic. He wrote in his preface to *Twenty-Five Nudes*:

> *Don't let's be too solemn about it (drawing the nude). Hair on the belly is certainly as amusing as hair on the head. Man is matter and spirit, both real and both good, and the funny is certainly part of the good. The human body is in fact a good joke — let us take it so.* (1938, 3)

Oriental erotic art is famous for its more unusual sexual positions, as propounded in texts such as *The Perfumed Garden*, *Ananga-Ranga*, or the *Kama Sutra*, which demonstrates 64 ways (the *Ananga-Ranga* contained '34 ways of doing it', as Eric Gill put it). Gill produced a number of sketches of Oriental love-making. The positions themselves have a religious aspect, being associated with yoga, with meditation and sex magic.

In Indian, Japanese and Chinese erotic art, people are shown gleefully and gymnastically contorting and entwining around one another. On hammocks, swinging from trees, on balconies, beds, cushions, tables, beside lakes, they copulate anywhere and everywhere. The depictions, by many anonymous artists, and also by people such as Katsushika Hokusai, Utagawa Kunisada, Kitagawa Utamaro, Nishikawa Sukenobu and Torii Kiyonobu, show all manner of sexual activities. Chinese erotic drawings and Japanese *shunga* prints, especially, depict love-making as an innocent, pleasurable activity. The couples tup amidst serene Eastern landscapes, with vases filled with flowers, little fences, beautiful gardens, bo trees, lakes and streams. It all seems so pastoral and sublimely tranquil.[4]

In Indian erotic art, the participants have a wonderfully serene temperament: in sets of miniatures and paintings, the couples go through every variety of sexual position, while calmly smiling to themselves or to each other. It's explicitly erotic art, with the genitals on display: the thighs of men and women are bent right back, to reveal the penis entering the vagina.

The other striking thing about Indian, Chinese and Japanese erotic art is how *decorative* it is, how much the artists are concentrating on patterns, on shapes, on the props and furniture in the pictures. The world of Oriental erotic art is certainly visually stunning, and luxurious, with its couches and hangings, its large windows opening onto pleasure gardens, its rich carpets and furnishings, and the lavish costumes (the patterned kimonos, for instance). There is little modelling: rather, the pictures, prints and scrolls are flattened visually, with line and colour doing all of the work (shadows, textures, and modelling are dispensed with).

The goal is immortality, oneness, meditation. Sperm, associated with *yang* energy, is believed to rise up the spine to the brain in Chinese sex magic, as in Indian *kundalini* yoga. The imagery and meanings are masculinized: jade, the petrified sperm of the celestial dragon, is associated with the phallus, while *yang* energy is thoroughly phallic. In Japanese Shinto religion there was a gigantic Phallus of heaven, a celestial pillar; giant phalluses were carried in processions, as in ancient Greece.

17

VULVA

Oriental sex magic is, as in Western sex mysticism, and Eric Gill's own cult of eroticism, a male-made construct, built around masculine notions of sexuality. The emphasis on not ejaculating is but one indication of the male-favoured slant of sex magic. Philip Rawson writes in his classic book on Tantrism: '[t]o every Oriental mind, mere orgasm is never the goal of love' (1973b, 29). Oriental eroticism is founded not on the female orgasm, but more on male non-ejaculation. The vulva or *yoni* is glorified: there are images of *yonis* everywhere in India – in Hyderabad, as a woman lying back with her legs spread wide open, in holy water containers, in coco-de-mer shells split open to serve as a *yoni* image, and so on.[1]

Although the vulva is revered – there is a sculpture showing a man worshipping the *yoni* of the Yogini as Goddess (at Madura, South India, 17th century) – the phallus is also the essential component in sex magic. The central image – of the *yoni* and *lingam* – requires the fiery, creative spirit of the male phallic element to set the cosmic, divine energies alight. In the art of Eric Gill, there are few images of the vulva, and even less of the clit. He drew the pudenda often, with or without pubic hair, but not the vulva itself. Sometimes the labia is shown in copulation imagery, but rarely. There is nothing like the vagina art or 'cunt art' of feminists such as Judy Chicago or Carolee Schneemann in Gill's work. And no clitoral art. Instead, he draws the penis countless times.

Everything, it seems, reverts back to the male in Eric Gill's sex cult and in Oriental sex magic. Tantric and Taoist sex magic, which aims for multi-orgasmic sex for both partners, reverts back in the end to the man. It is the same with Gill. The goals of Western sex mysticism are similar to those of Oriental sex magic, as found in Taoism and Tantrism, and they are (largely) Gill's goals as well: to harness the energies of the orgasm, to make life 'cosmic', to unite macro and microcosm, inner and outer, near and far, above and below, Heaven and Earth, to reintroduce the sacred into life, to turn profane time and space into sacred time and space. Ritualized sex has a mythic, religious component, which in Tantrism and Taoism, is uppermost. Mircea Eliade writes that

> in the case of ceremonial sexual union, the individual ceases to live in profane and meaningless time, since he is imitating a divine archetype ("I am heaven, thou art Earth," and so on).[2]

This is clearly Eric Gill's view of love-making, where the man, on top, is clearly Heaven, and the woman is 'Earth receiving'.

✻

Tantrism is a life-affirming cult, with pleasure as a goal. But sexual practice is always contextualized within a cosmic, religious, philosophical framework. It is never pleasure for pleasure's sake, never simply a series of multiple orgasms, so the text books insist. As John Mumford commented in Ecstasy Through Tantra: '[s]ex magic operates upon the premise that whatever is held in the imagination at the moment of orgasm will come to pass.' (93) Orgasm is that prime mystical state, the jouissance at the heart of mysticism. As Mumford wrote: '[o]rgasm is the only spontan-eous, natural experience of a deathless, breathless, timeless, sorrowless dimension.' (33)

Hindu Tantric sex magic is very sensual, with its rites using meat, wine, butter, etc. There is an 'extreme' version of Tantric sex magic, the so-called 'left hand' ritual, where sex is practised when the woman menstruates. The aim, again, is to harness and channel wild sexual energies. The 'left hand' paths of Eastern sex magic were fascinating for groups of Western artists and writers, who were interested in gaining power over the world.

18

POWER

Eric Gill's art reveals the same power relations as depicted in high art, low art, pornography, advertizing, TV and the media: male power is dominant, and sex revolves the phallus. There is no female equivalent, no clitoris in Gill's art. The yoni, yes, but not much else. Similarly, D.H. Lawrence condemned those 'cocksure' women who took control and employed 'clitoral sex', the clitoral, frothing white sex of Aphrodite as found in his The Plumed Serpent. But emphasizing this or that body part shows how the whole thing is very silly.

For Eric Gill, the phallus is the 'transcendent signifier', as in the print Eve (1926) which shows a female nude with a snake between her legs, curling towards her groin; clearly the snake here is the phallic lust, as so often in patriarchal art.[1] The connection is made, explicitly, between women and sexuality, so that, as God said in Genesis, women have to bear the terror and horror and pain of sexuality, of bearing children (that's how the deity speaks sometimes in the Bible). True, God expelled Adam as well as Eve from Paradise. But it is the woman, Eve, who gets the rawer deal. Gill's Eve simply extends the woman-hating philosophy of early Judæo-Christianity (if you think 'woman-hating' is too strong a term, go and look at early Xian theologians like Tertullian, Origen and St

Augustine).

Often, Eric Gill's ithyphallic imagery is laughable, as in his engraving *God Sending* (1926),[2] which shows Jesus flying towards the Earth with an erection, his head beaming with light, with God's hand behind him, in Heaven, sending Christ on his way. The first version of the *Procreant Hymn* illustration showed Christ without an erection; but the other elements remained similar: God's blessing hand, the beams of heavenly light, the tree on earth and the naked, exultant body of Christ. In both pictures, however, Jesus's genitals are the optical centre of the composition. Here is that most blasphemous of images: not only an erotic Christ, but Christ with a hard-on! Gill, Fiona MacCarthy reckoned, 'felt almost propriet-orial about Christ's genitals' (M, 212).

In Eric Gill's art this ithyphallicism can be very silly, but D.H. Lawrence was deadly serious about his ithyphallic Christ, when he wrote of the resurrected Saviour making love with a priestess of the Goddess Isis in *The Escaped Cock*. D.H. Lawrence's novella argued for a regeneration of the world through a full 'awakening' of the body.[3] Gill proposed the same thing.

The first part of *The Escaped Cock* deals with the man's reawakening to 'the astonishing place the phenomenal world is', D.H. Lawrence wrote.[4] 'It is for the Lord thus to rise', Lawrence wrote in an article "Resurrection" (*Phoenix*, 737). The yearning is for a new touch, a new, tender touch to bring the soul and body back to life ('[a]h, lay one little touch | To start my heart afresh', wrote Lawrence in the poem 'Resurrection of the Flesh' (*Complete Poems*, 738).

Christ is seen as a corn god, a fertility deity who must be sacrificed at Midsummer. Robert Briffault, Robert Graves and J.G. Frazer have written in detail of this myth. In D.H. Lawrence's hands, mythology becomes sexualized. The awakening in *The Escaped Cock* is sexualized. The crowning point of the story, just as the phallus is the crowning point in Lawrence's sexual mythopœia, is the moment when Christ/ Osiris makes love with the priestess/ Isis:

Himself bending over powerful and new like dawn.
He crouched to her, and he felt the blaze of his manhood, his power rise up in his loins,

magnificent.

'I am risen!'

Magnificent, blazing indomitable in the depths of his loins, his own sun dawned and sent its fire running along his limbs, so that his face shone unconsciously.

He untied the string on the linen tunic, and slipped the garment down, till he saw the white glow of her white-gold breasts. And he touched them, and he felt his life go molten. — Father! he said, — why did you hide this from me? — And he touched her with the poignancy of wonder, he said. — This is beyond prayer. — It was deep, interfold warmth, warmth living and penetrable, the woman, the heart of the rose!5

19

MARRIAGE

Another seemingly 'blasphemous' image in the art of Arthur Eric Rowton Gill shows two people fucking in a wood engraving which was intended to be used for a sculpture entitled Christ and his Church. Here is another blasphemy: not the Saviour with an erection this time, but Christ making love to his Church. But, again, Gill is not being as heretical as it might seem at first. For, in the last book of the Bible, Revelations, the narrator speaks of Jerusalem coming down out of the clouds like a bride arrayed for a bridegroom. Similarly, Christ was thought of as 'wedded' to the Church. 'Mother' Church was 'married' to the Son of Man, Christians said, so an image of a naked Christ making love to a naked Church is not too blasphemous after all.

What Eric Gill does is, simply, to extend the metaphor a little further, to make concrete what theologians hint at, to render the sexual metaphors of Catholicism in figurative depictions. If Christianity speaks of Christ and the Church as being like a Bride and Groom, then Gill simply portrays what brides and grooms supposedly get up to: making the beast with two backs. Sex, as feminists argue, is the basis of Western bourgeois marriage. It is what marriage is found upon. What Gill did was to cut through the veils of hypocrisy that surround theology and

Christianity, to show the metaphors as actualities. He had, aside from his depictions of Christ in erotic scenarios, the notion of 'being fucked by Christ':

> I wish I could get you to see the point about Xtianity [Gill wrote to Rayner Heppenstall] – e.g. when we 'Marry' we don't say to a girl: madam you realise what we are is the embodiment of an idea (or do you?). We say, darling, we two persons are now one flesh – or words to that effect. It's a love affair first and last. Joining the Church is not like joining the I.L.P. or the 3rd International. It's like getting married and, speaking analogically, we are fucked by Christ, and bear children to him – or we don't. The Church is the whole body of Christians – the bride.[1]

Eric Gill's general views on marriage were conventional: marriage was for having children, otherwise, there was no point getting married. Despite what he preached in his letters and essays, and despite going to suffrage meetings (such as at Hyde Park in 1908), in his private, domestic life Gill's views and practices were often conventional and traditional. For him the woman's place seemed to be at the centre of the home and children.

※

Some of Eric Gill's best works are sculptures: in Divine Lovers and Ecstasy he produced an image of two people clasping each other in an embrace of complete closeness. There is no space between the lovers: Constantin Brancusi had done the same thing in his Kiss sculptures, which flattened the two bodies so they could be merged together completely. Brancusi recognized the anatomical problem, saying that kissing upright is difficult, because of the nose. His lovers are noseless: they simply kiss, eternally joined together, veritably an expression in stone of the Platonic concept of two-as-one, of twin souls joined as one.[4]

The key element of Eric Gill's Divine Lovers is the emphasis on divine. Gill draws attention to this in the 1922 and 1926 engravings by putting haloes above the lovers. Like Gill's drawing of a nude woman embracing Christ on the Cross (Nuptials of God), Divine Lovers is a blasphemous image, fusing flesh and spirit, showing that an act deemed profane and even sinful in Christianity can be holy. The 1922 Divine Lovers is a beautiful boxwood double relief, an image of ecstatic union: like so many of Gill's images of sexual and spiritual unity, it is all intertwining limbs, the slender arms and hands prominent, with the nipples of both the man and the woman visible between the shape of the arms. Another version of the theme occurs in the Portland stone sculpture *Tobias and Sara* (1926, Oxford), in which the swooning couple have their arms clasped tightly around each other. This powerful image derives from the *Book of Tobit*, one of the apocryphal books.

20

CRITICISM

It seems, then, that there is nothing 'blasphemous' about Eric Gill's art, no matter how erotic it seems. All he does is juxtapose sex and religion in a way that people have been doing for millennia. What's astonishing is that anybody thinks Gill's erotic art is 'shocking' or even mildly offensive (his art, that is, not his life). For Gill clearly creates establishment art that only mildly questions patriarchal notions of the erotic and the mystical. Besides, Gill's fusion of the mystic and the erotic is sanctioned in high or intellectual art in artists such as Hans Bellmer, Georges Bataille, the Marquis de Sade, Charles Baudelaire, and Egon Schiele.

Eric Gill's depictions of erotic experiences can be seen as tender and affectionate, but, just as easily, they can be seen as detached, even cold, unemotional, sex without love. Donald Attawater wrote:

> Gill's engravings, drawings and carvings of naked men and women are characterized by a marked detachment, an objective vision sometimes almost amounting to coldness... (110)

Robert Speaight remarked:

> Indeed he was not very interested in personality, And the reason why his eroticism — for all its careful definitions and theological warrant — was distasteful to many people was because it left the personal and psychological out of account. (118)

What's limiting about Eric Gill's art, as about some pornography, is that it continually emphasizes cocks and cunts, and seeming to ignore socio-political considerations, for example, or issues of race, class, economy, homosexuality, and so on. It's the same with Gill's sculptures — his acrobats, for example, are women holding their legs wide open, exposing their vulvas (as in Splits II, 1923).3

For detractors, it's a self-obsessed and sexually obsessed art with no basis in so-called 'reality' (whatever that is). Some critics want their art tackling a range of social issues, not only celebrating things like love and sex. That misses the point of Gill's art, of course: it's not meant to be about everything in the social realm. An artist can't take on everything and every level of the social world. It's just that in Gill's art the emphasis on sex and genitals can seem a little blinkered and compulsive. At the same time, that's one of the elements that makes his work appealing, and powerful.

But I do think Arthur Eric Rowton Gill's art was full of feeling — the coldness derived perhaps from the abstraction. Gill's art remains important, though, despite its sexism, macho posturing, reductionism and depersonalization. It remains a lyrical art, in love with line, the body and ascetic, religious, and sensual pleasures.

Illustrations

Works by Eric Gill, and some of his contemporaries

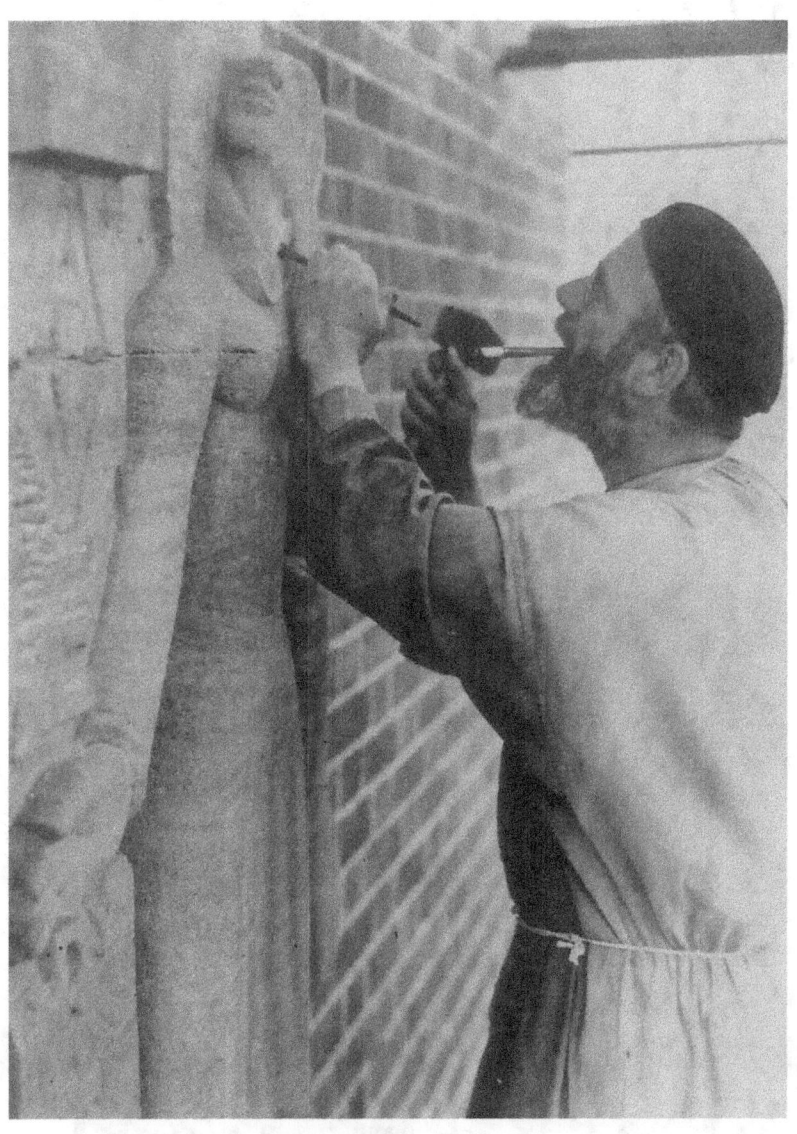

Eric Gill

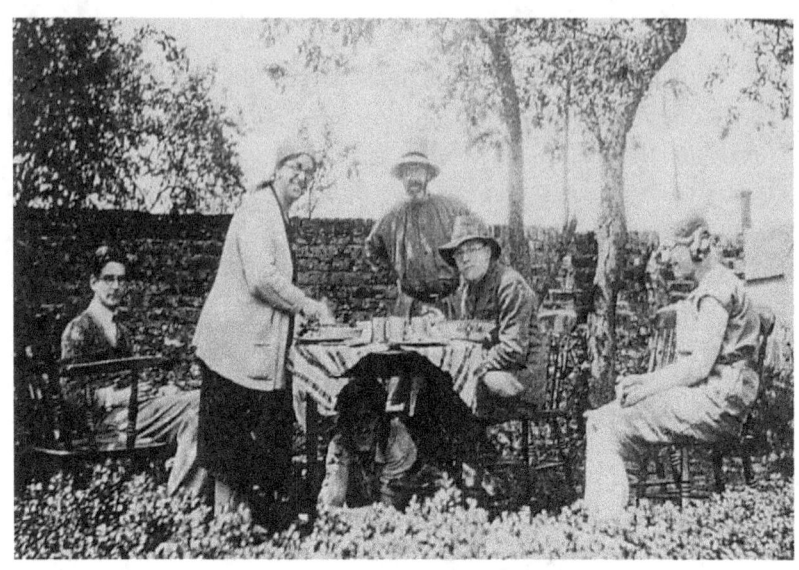

Erric Gill at work on his Creation sculpture in 1937, below.
At Pigotts with friends in the early 930s, above.

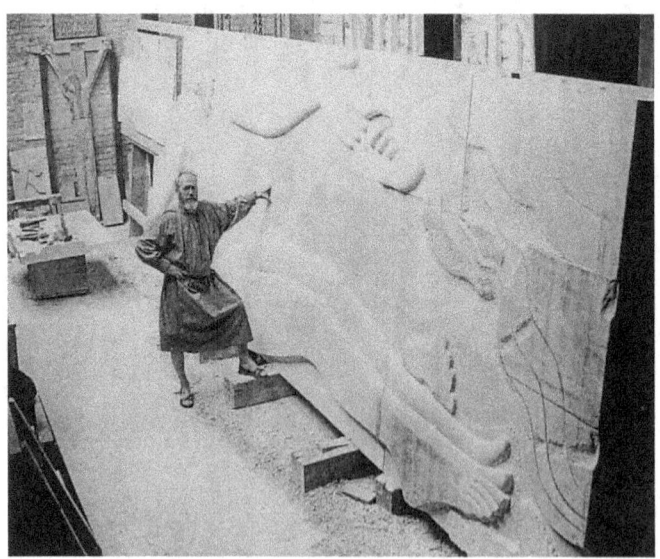

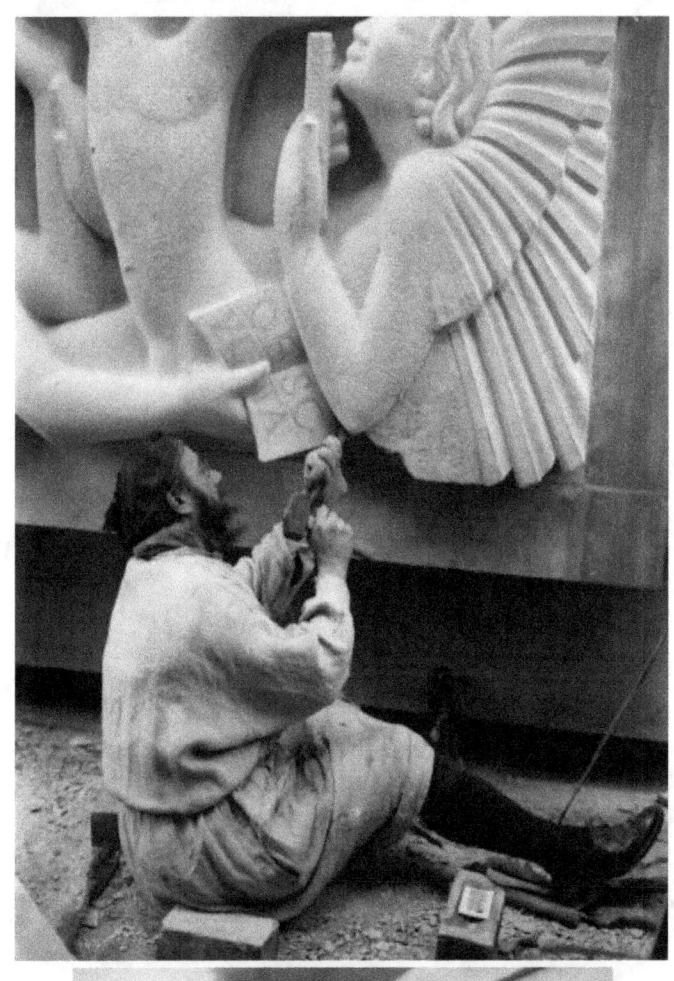

Eric Gill at work

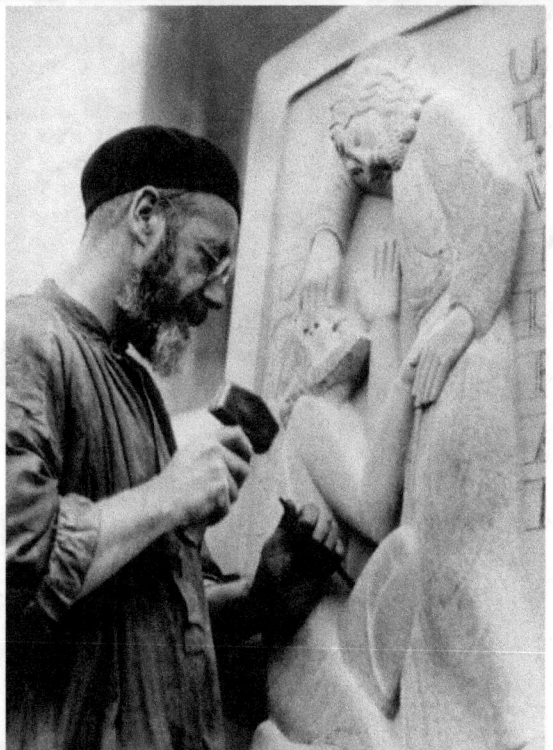

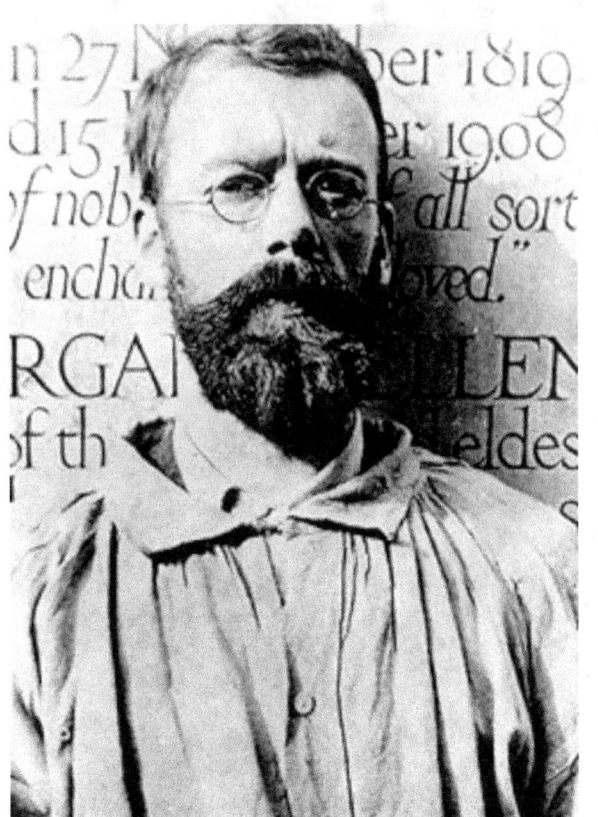

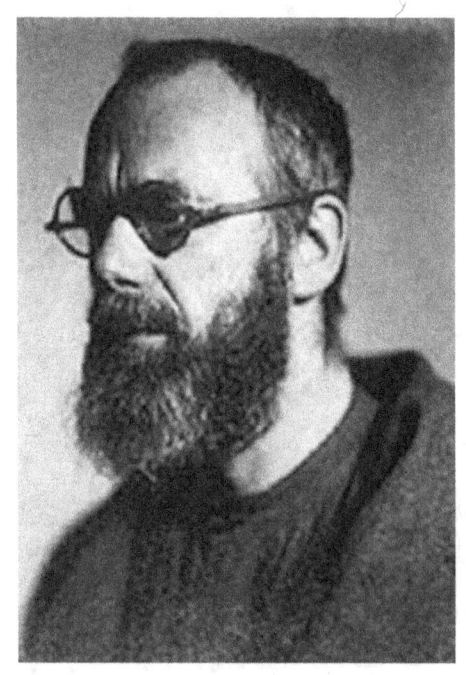

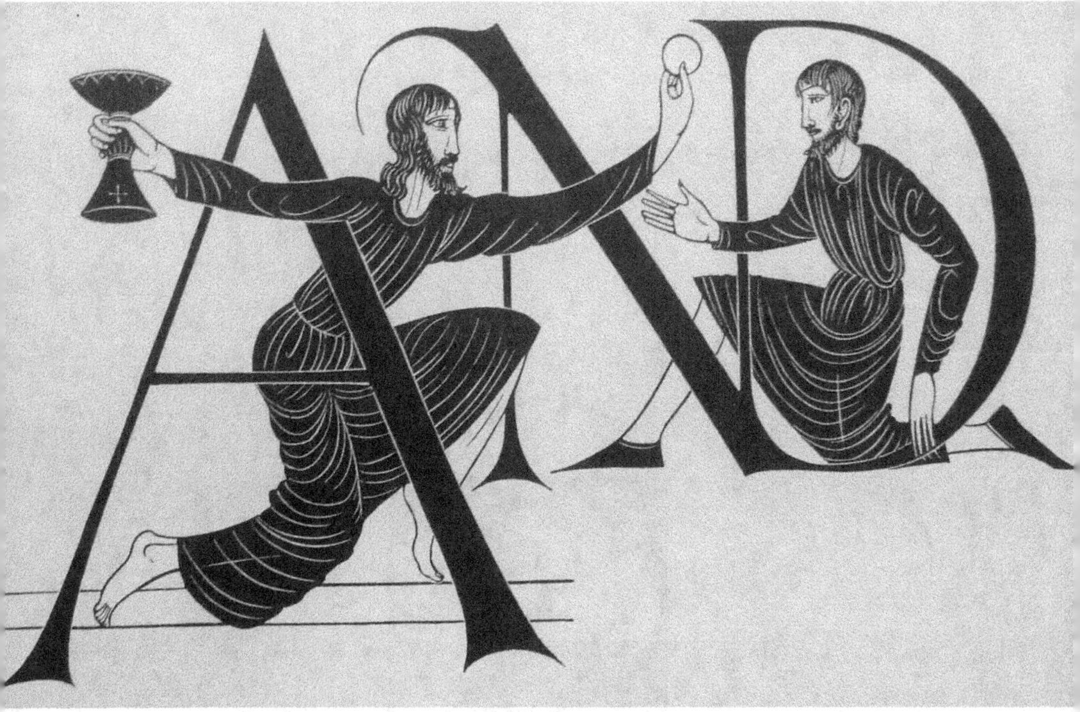

Eric Gill, Woman Asleep, 1936, below, and The Last Supper, 1931, above.

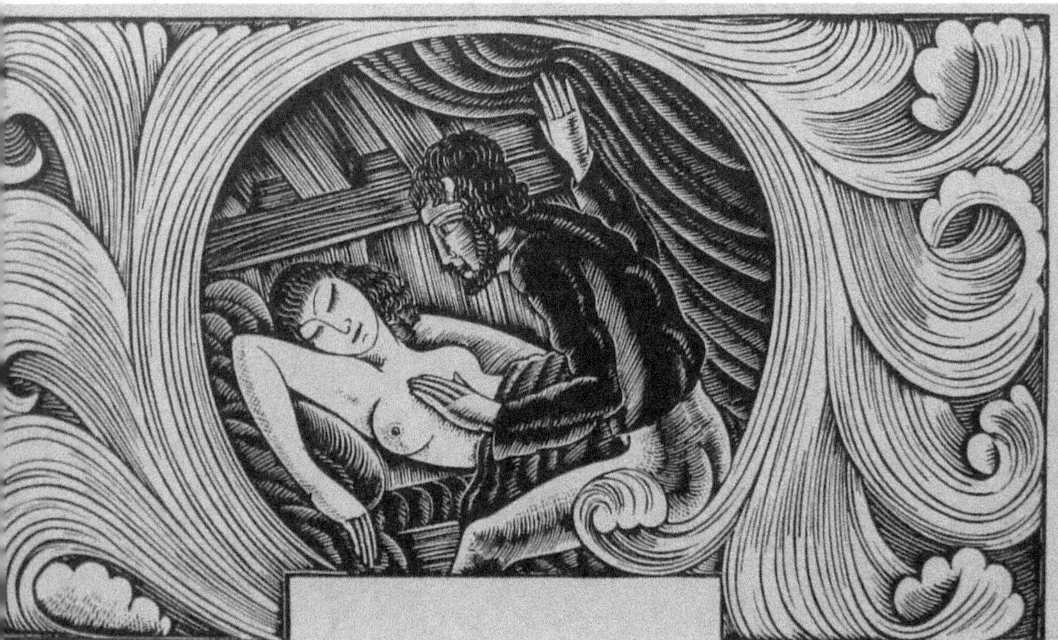

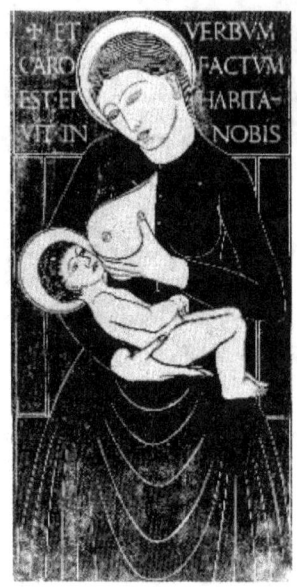

Eric Gill, Madonna and Child

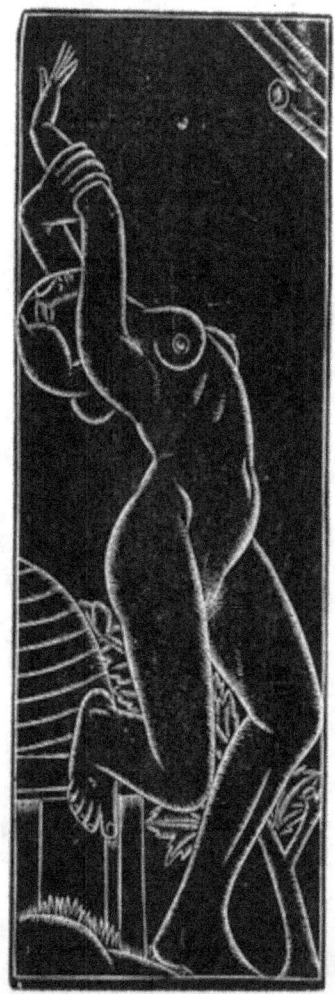

Eric Gill,
The Bee Sting,
1924

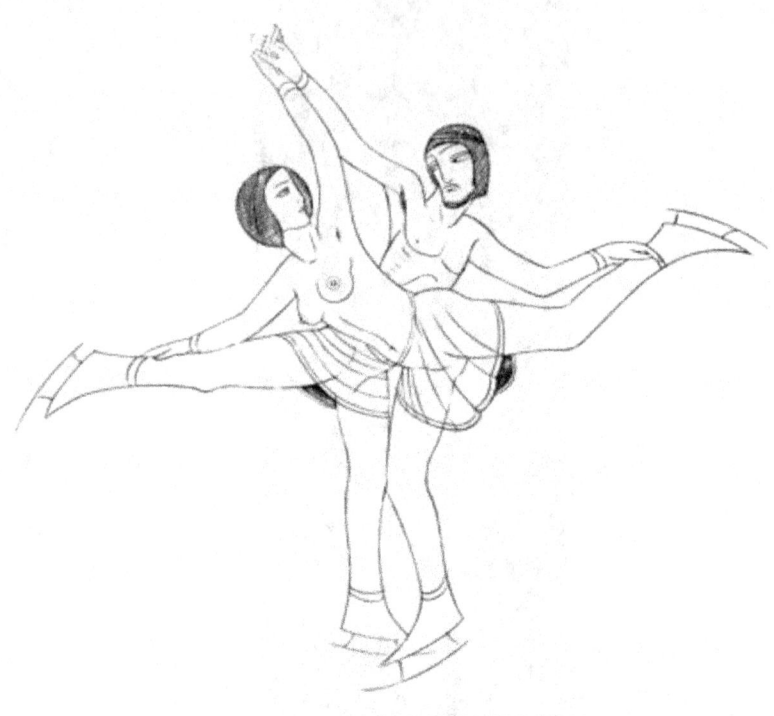

Eric Gill, Skaters, 1929

Some of Eric Gill's engravings and drawings show different versions
of the same subject, often portraying clothed and unclothed
variants: in The Skaters (1929), for example, taken from a Daily
Mirror photograph, Gill depicts them nearly nude,
clad in see-through skirts; in a variant, the male and female skaters
form a cross with their limbs, but are now naked, their genitals at
the optical centre of the picture.

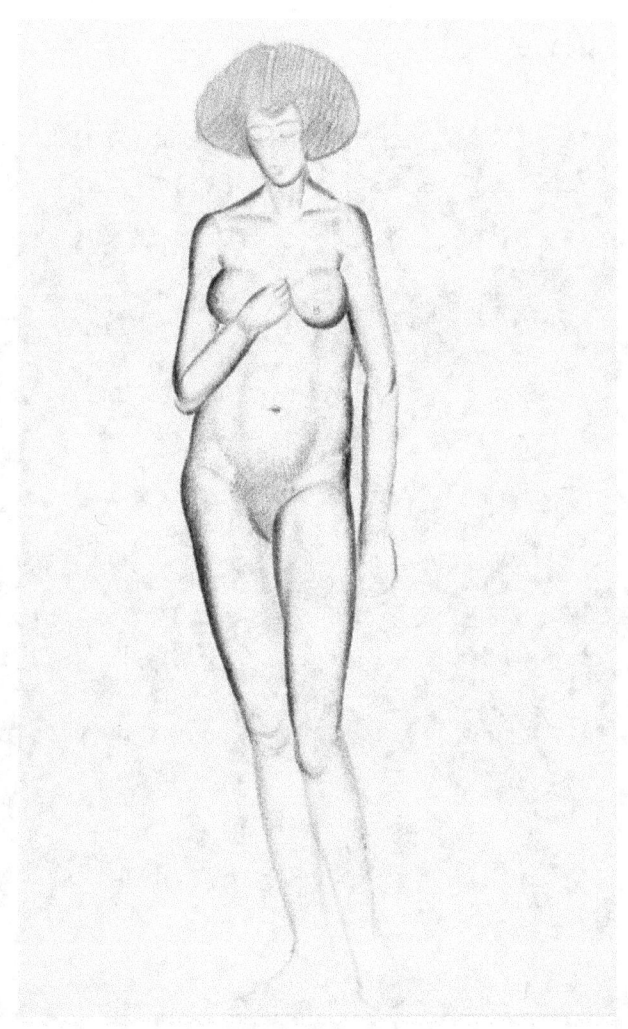

Eric Gill, from First Nudes, 1926

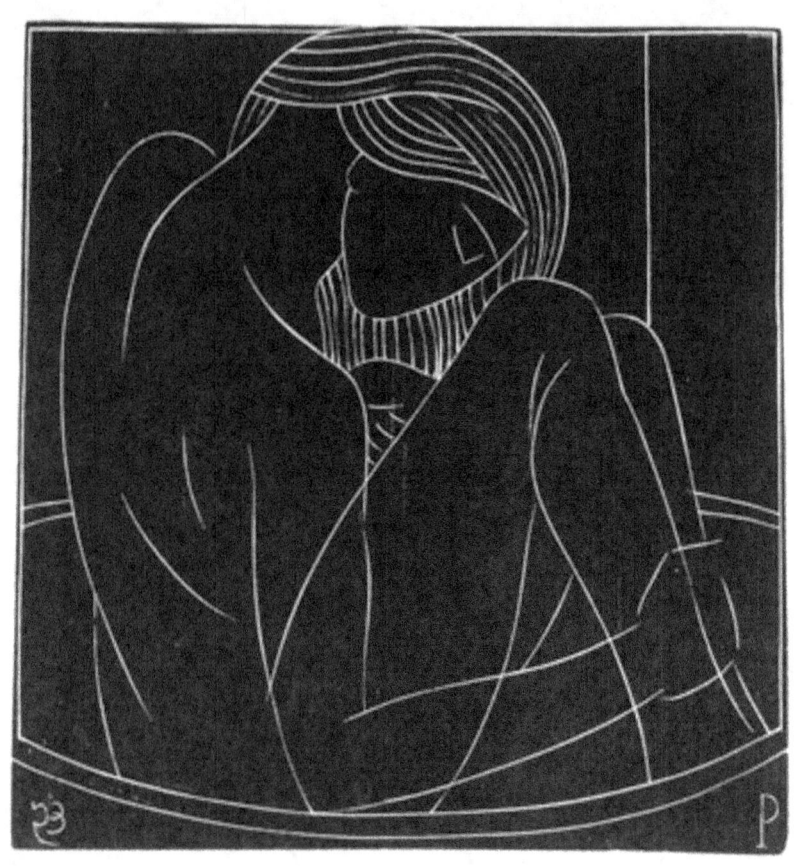

Eric Gill, Girl In Bath, 1929

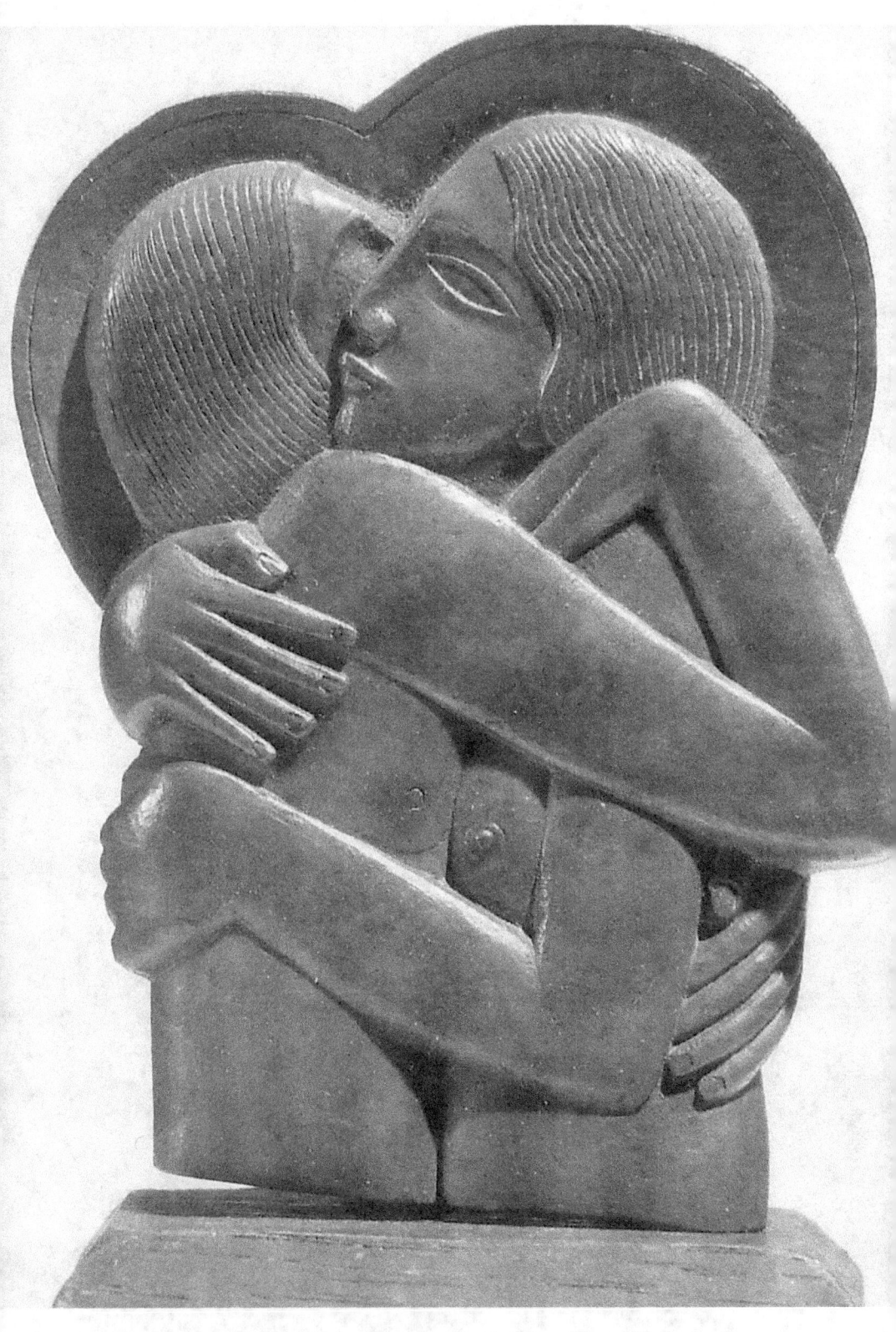

Eric Gill, Divine Lovers, 1922, Fogg Art Museum, Cambridge, MA

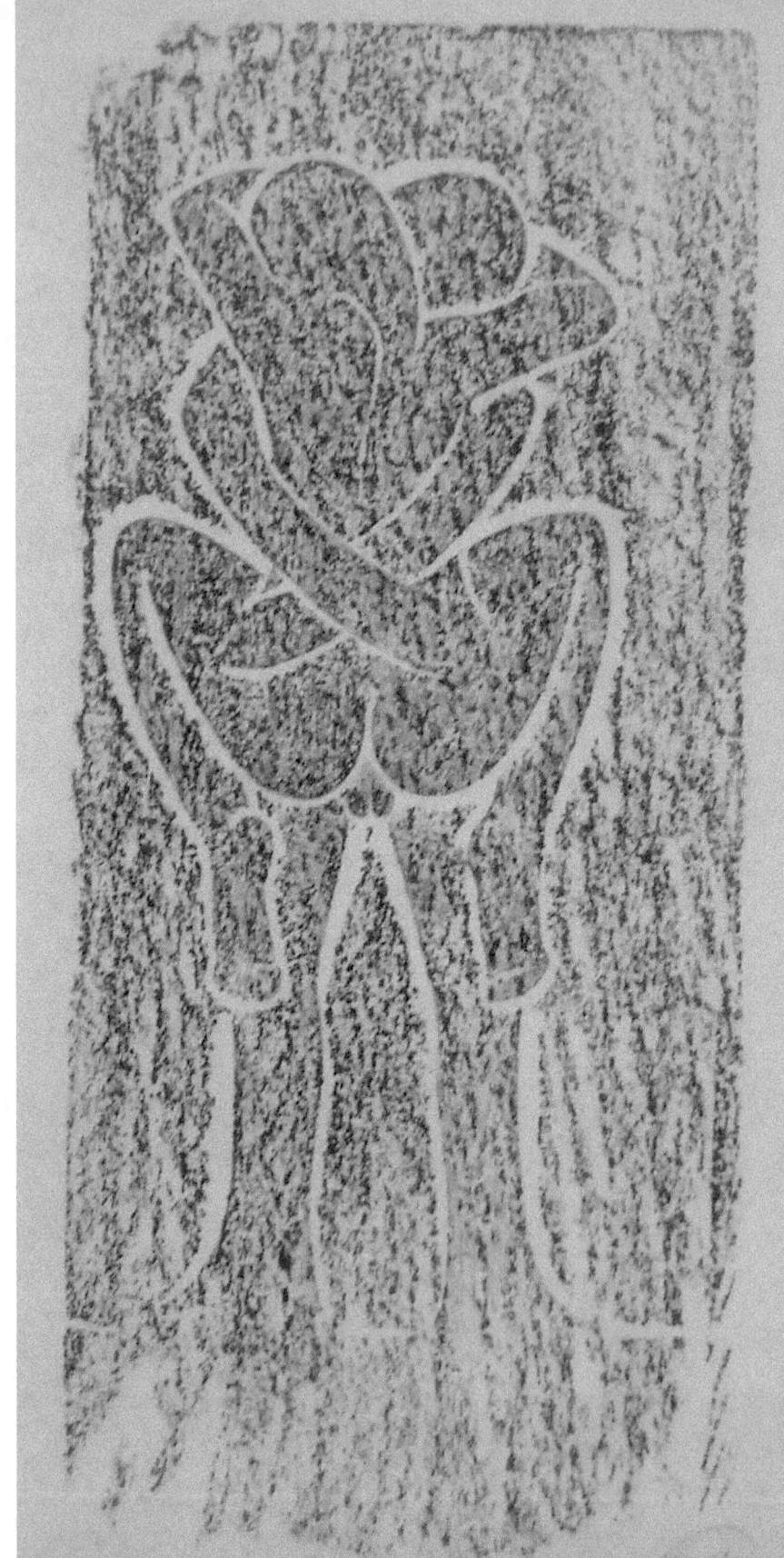

Eric Gill,
rubbing of
Lovers Relief,
1921
(whereabouts
unknown)

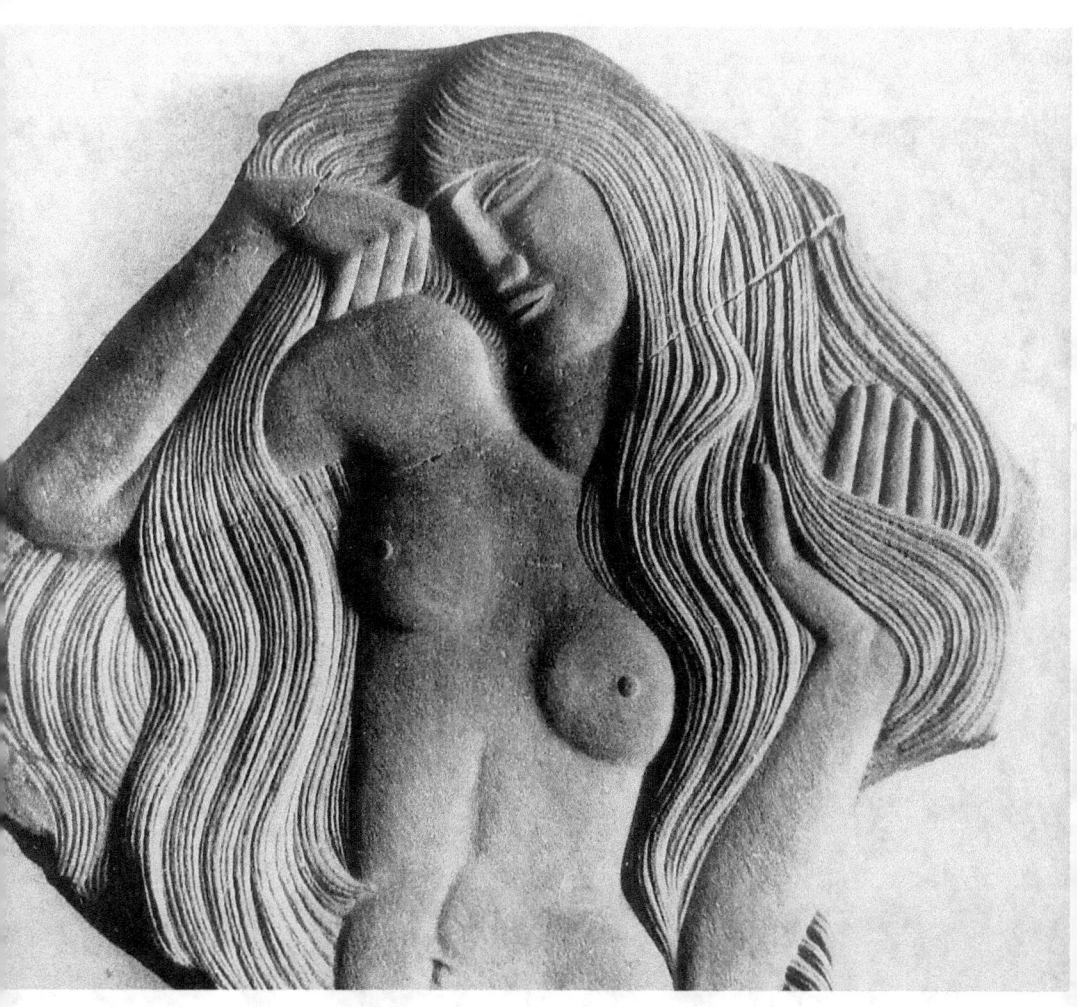

Eric Gill, Nude Girl With Hair, 1925

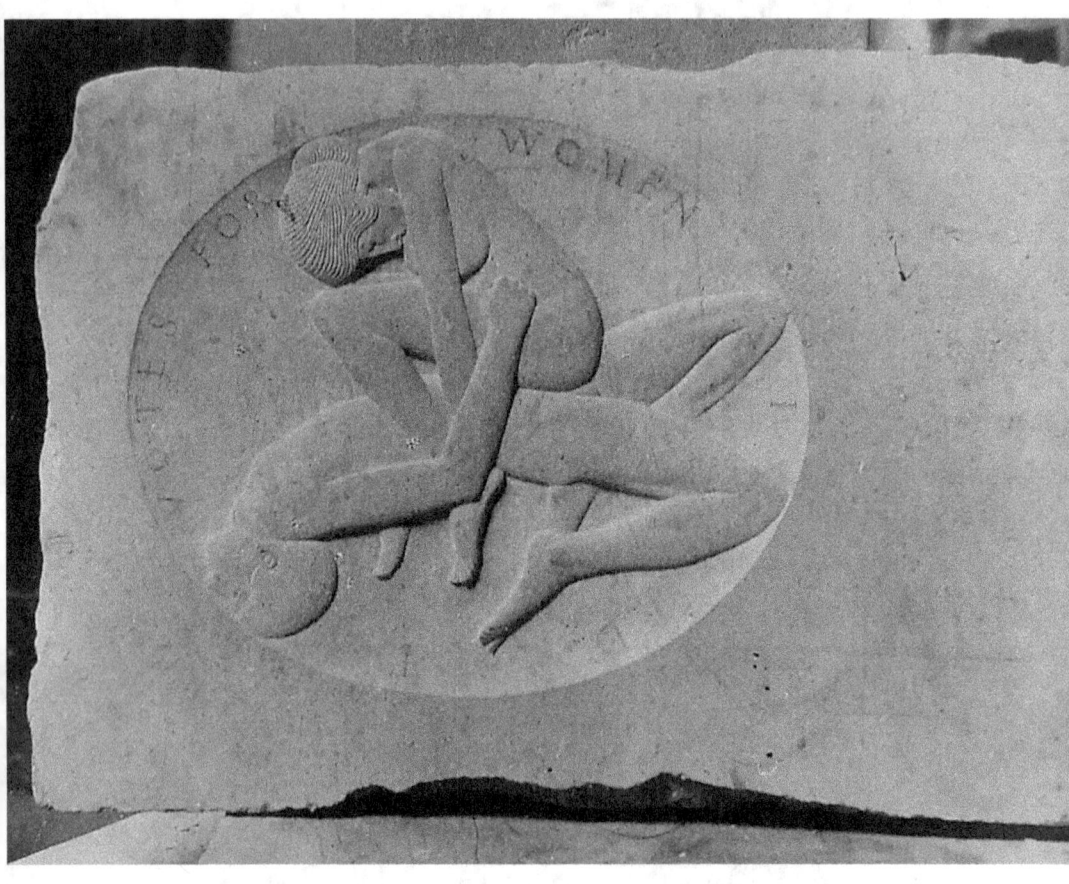

Eric Gill, Votes For Women, 1911 (whereabouts unknown)

Votes for Women (which Fiona MacCarthy described, oddly, as 'both very pure and very shocking' [M, 104]), was once owned by Maynard Keynes, who bought it for £5.00. Usually, the woman is underneath in Gill's art; she is the Earth, the soil, 'Earth receiving', as Gill terms it, waiting to absorb the holy seed of the man. Woman is Earth, passive, 'receiving', supine; man is Heaven, holy, active, creative. But it's the title, Votes For Women, which helps to make this carving especially impressive.

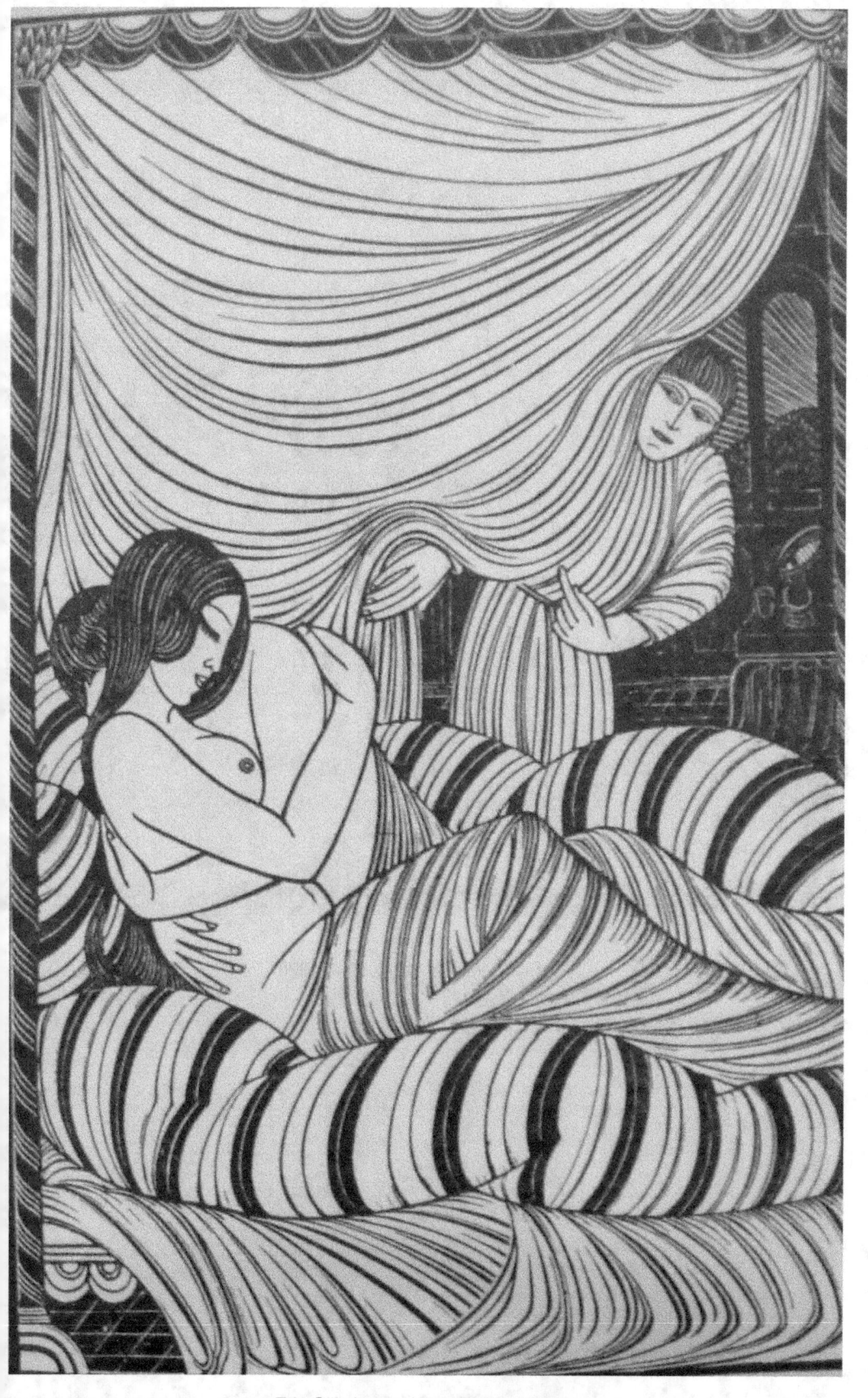

Eric Gill, Approaching Dawn, 1927

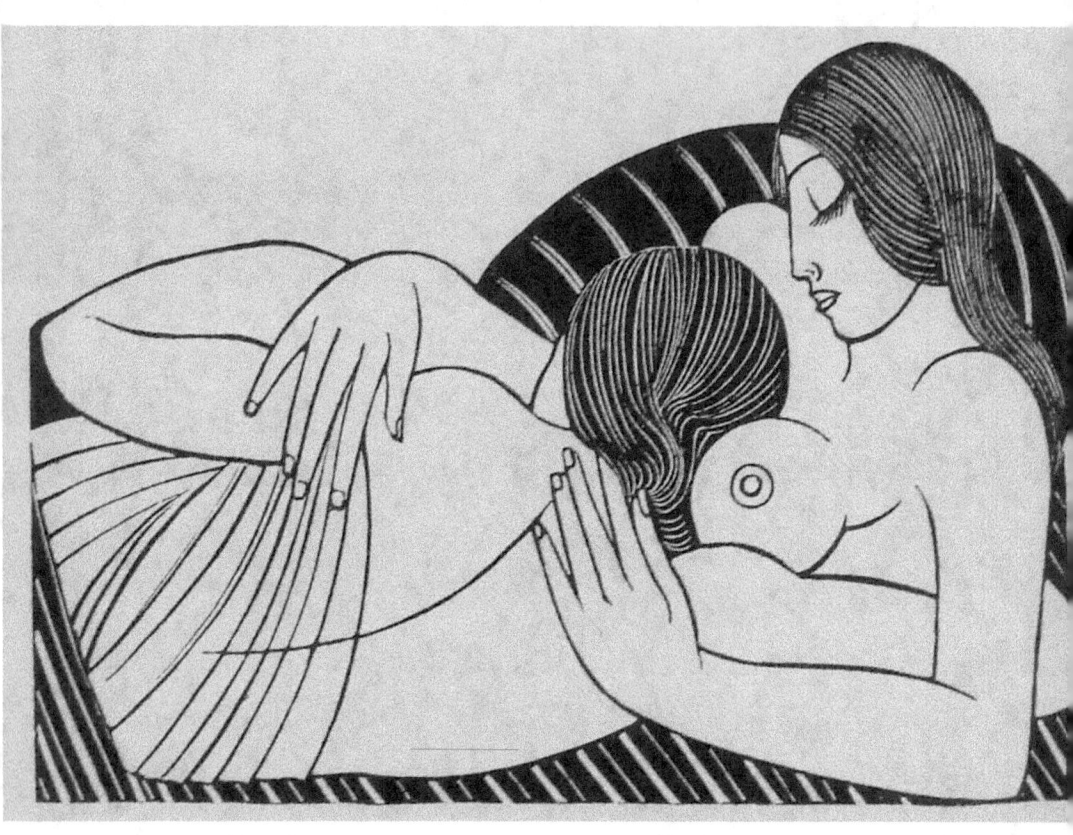

Eric Gill, Inter Ubera Mea, 1925

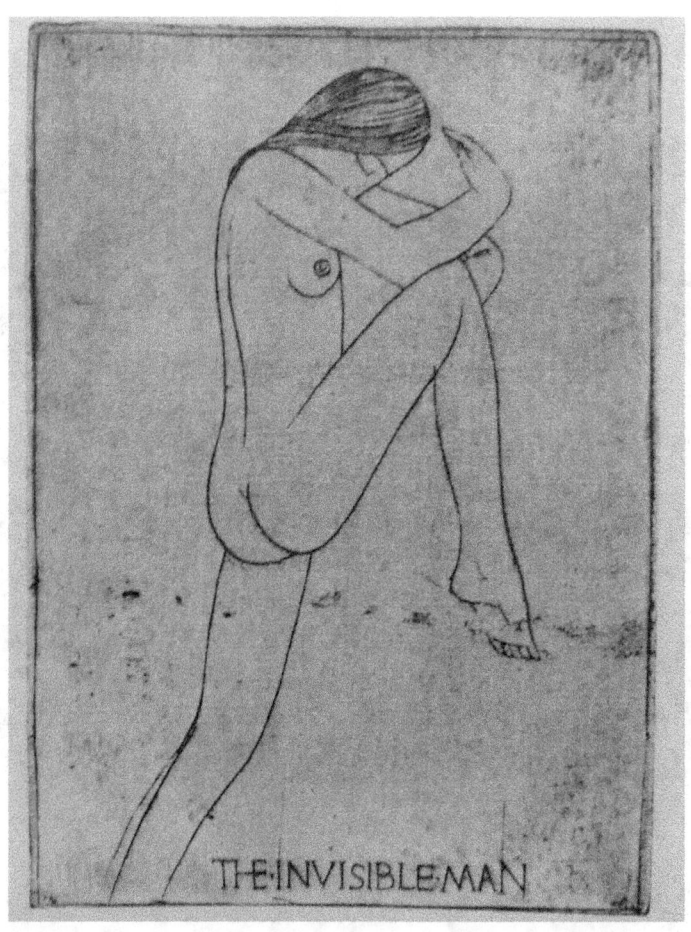

Eric Gill, The Invisible Man, 1924

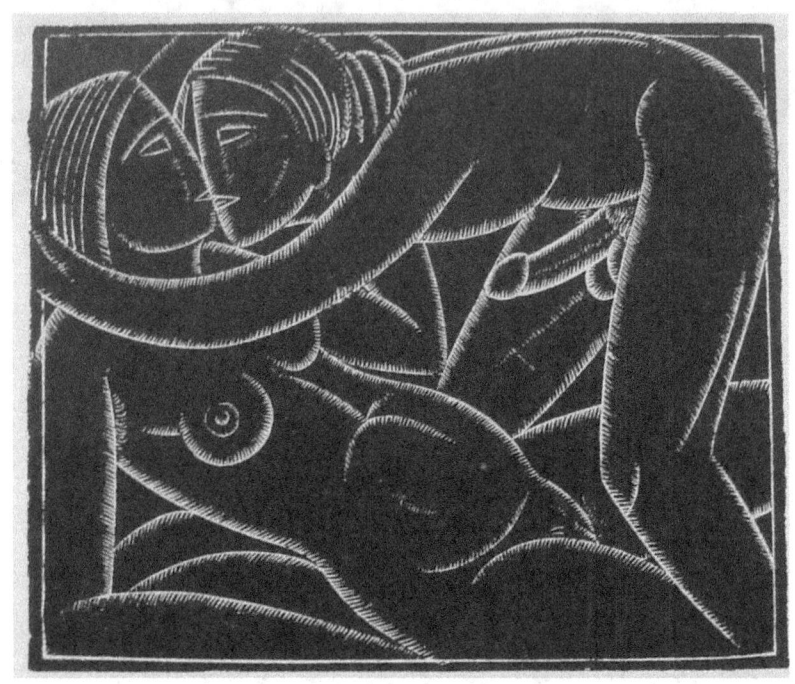

Eric Gill, Lovers, 1924

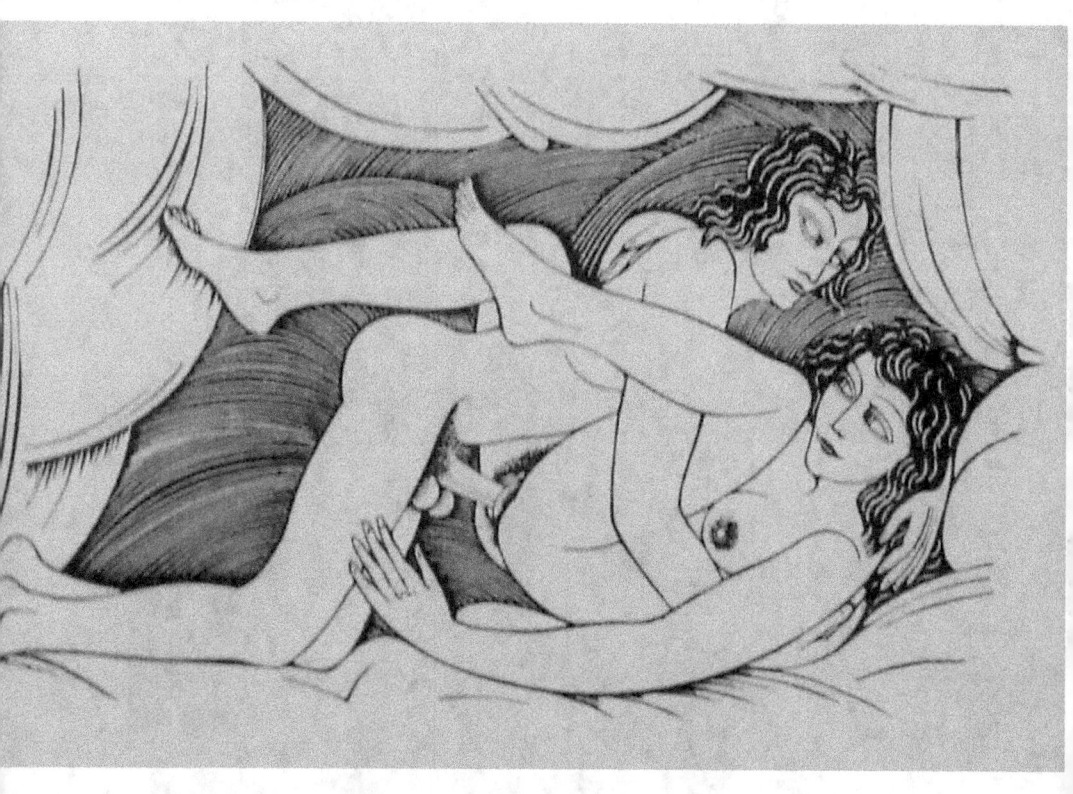

Eric Gill, Lovers (The Raised Bottom), 1934

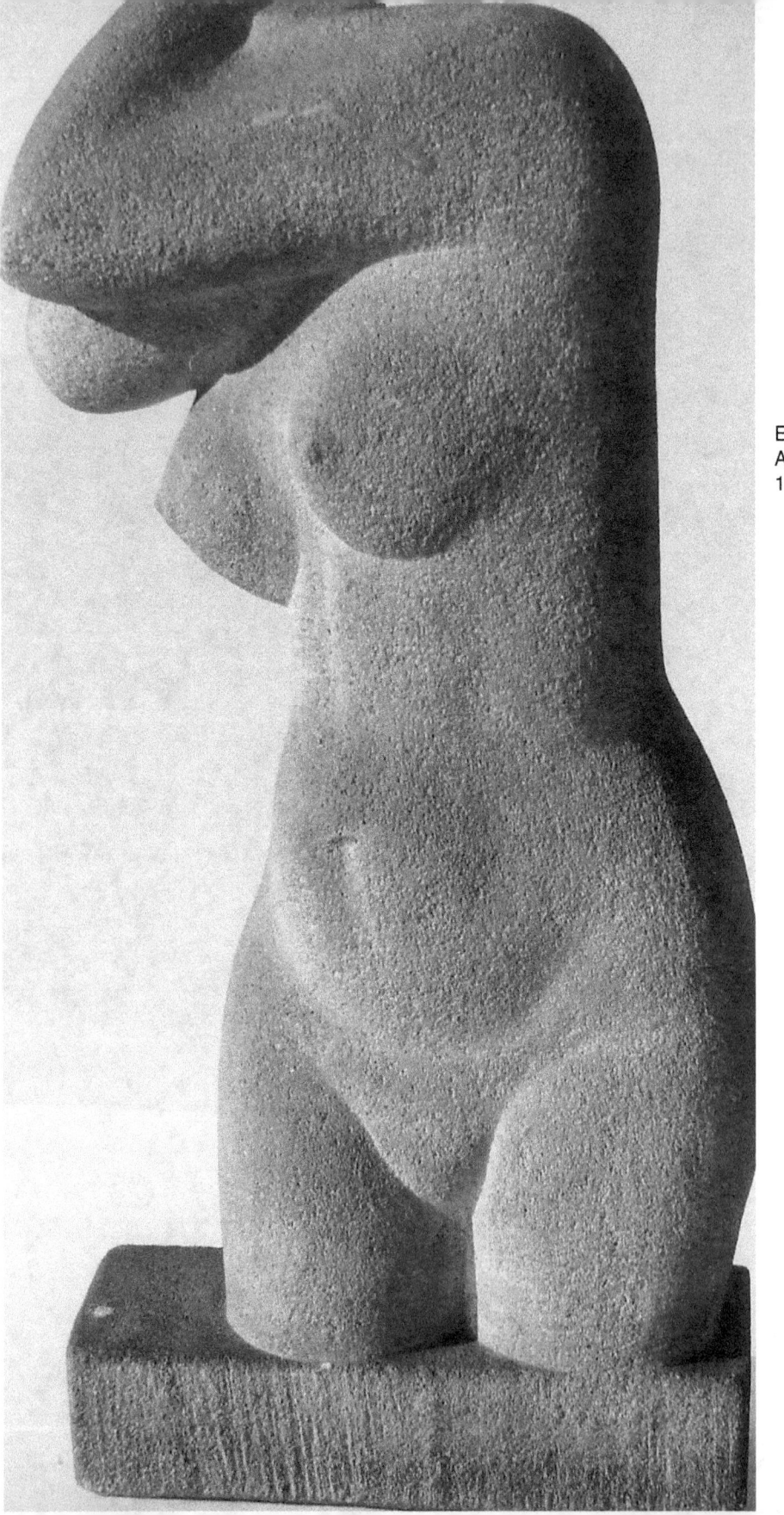

Eric Gill,
Anadyome
1920

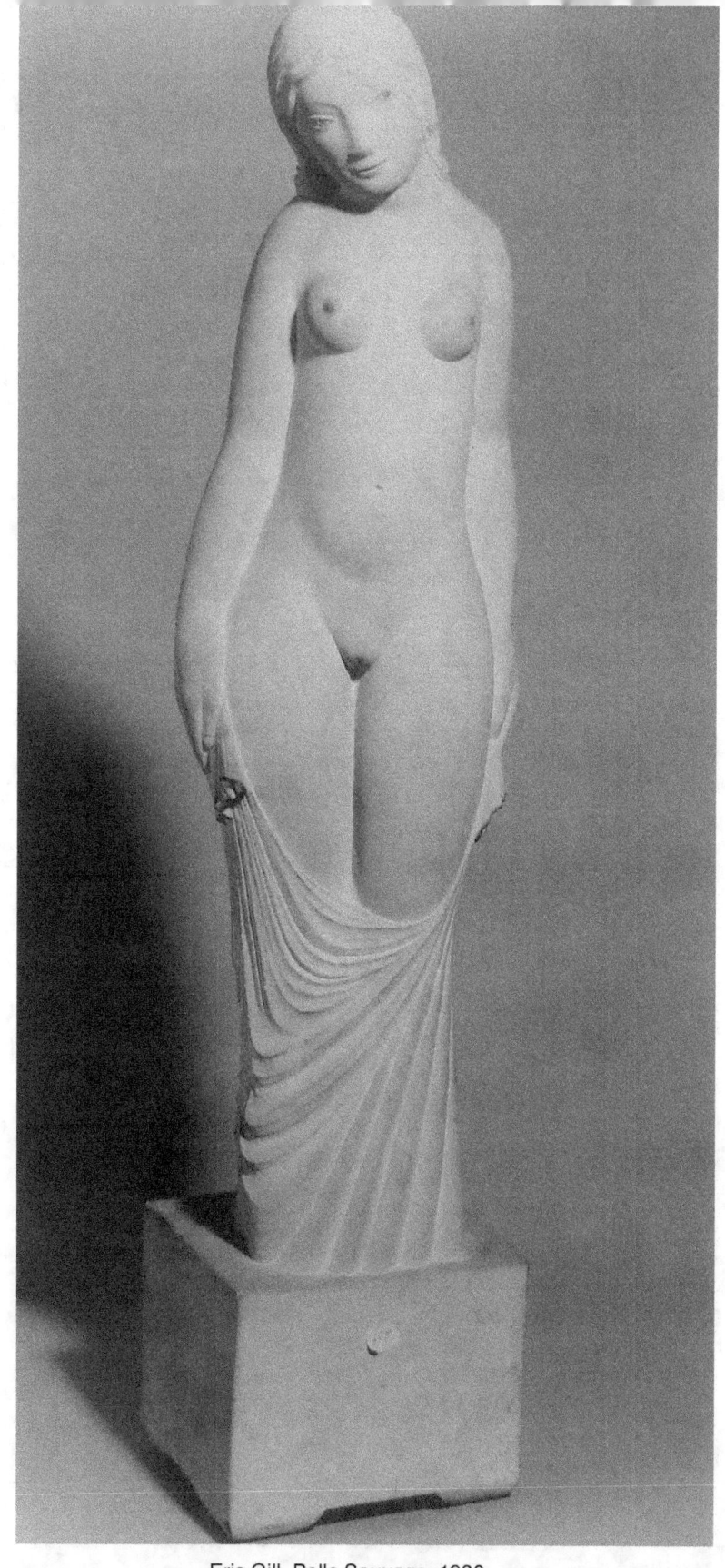

Eric Gill, Belle Sauvage, 1930

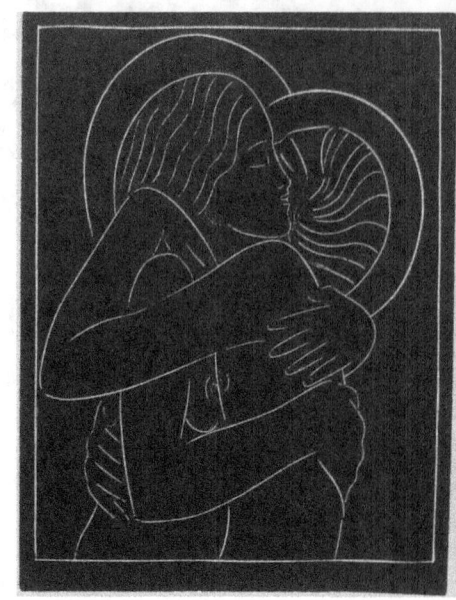

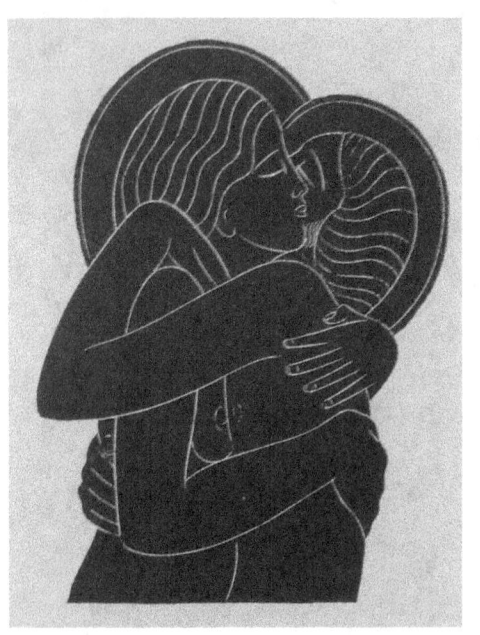

Eric Gill, Divine Lovers, from 1922 above
and left, and 1936, below.

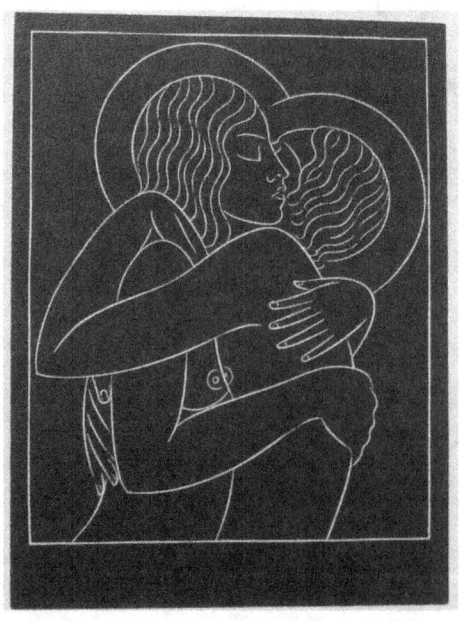

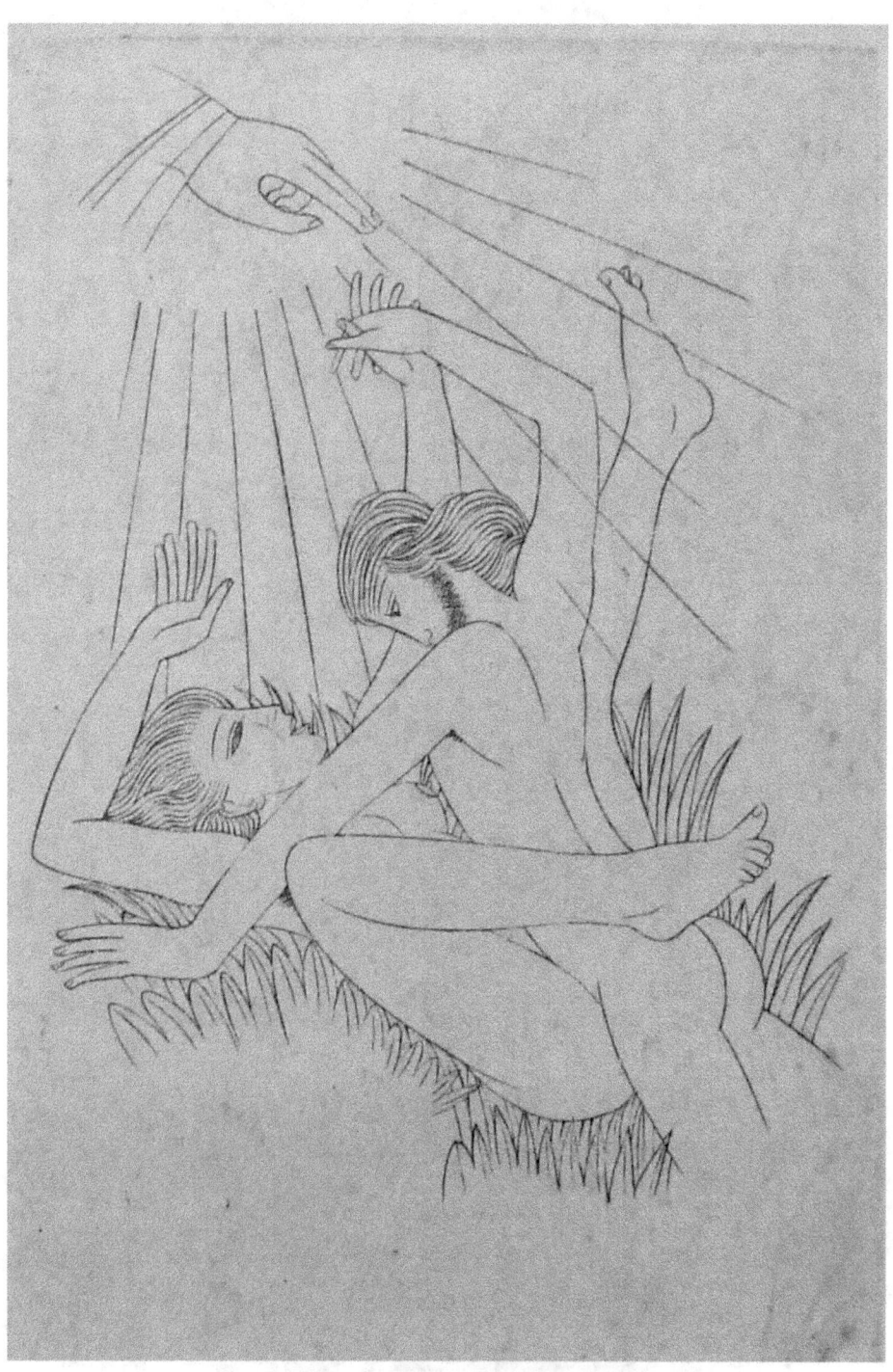

Eric Gill, Earth Receiving, 1926

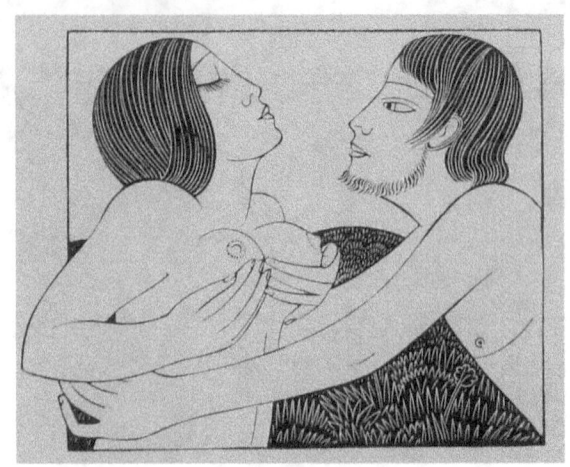

Eric Gill, Ibi Dabo Tibi, from 1930, below, and 1925, above.

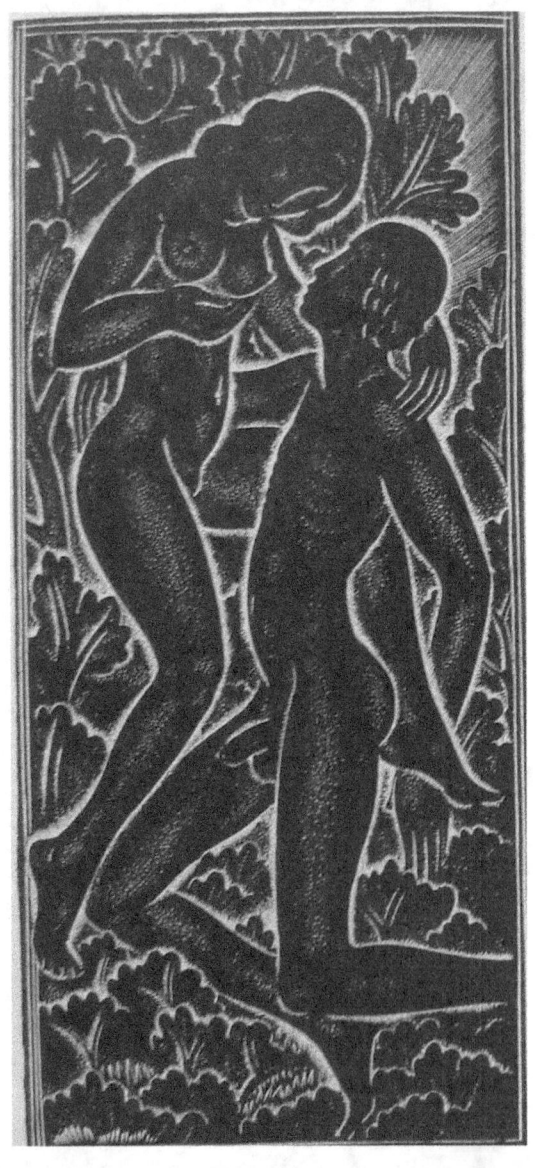

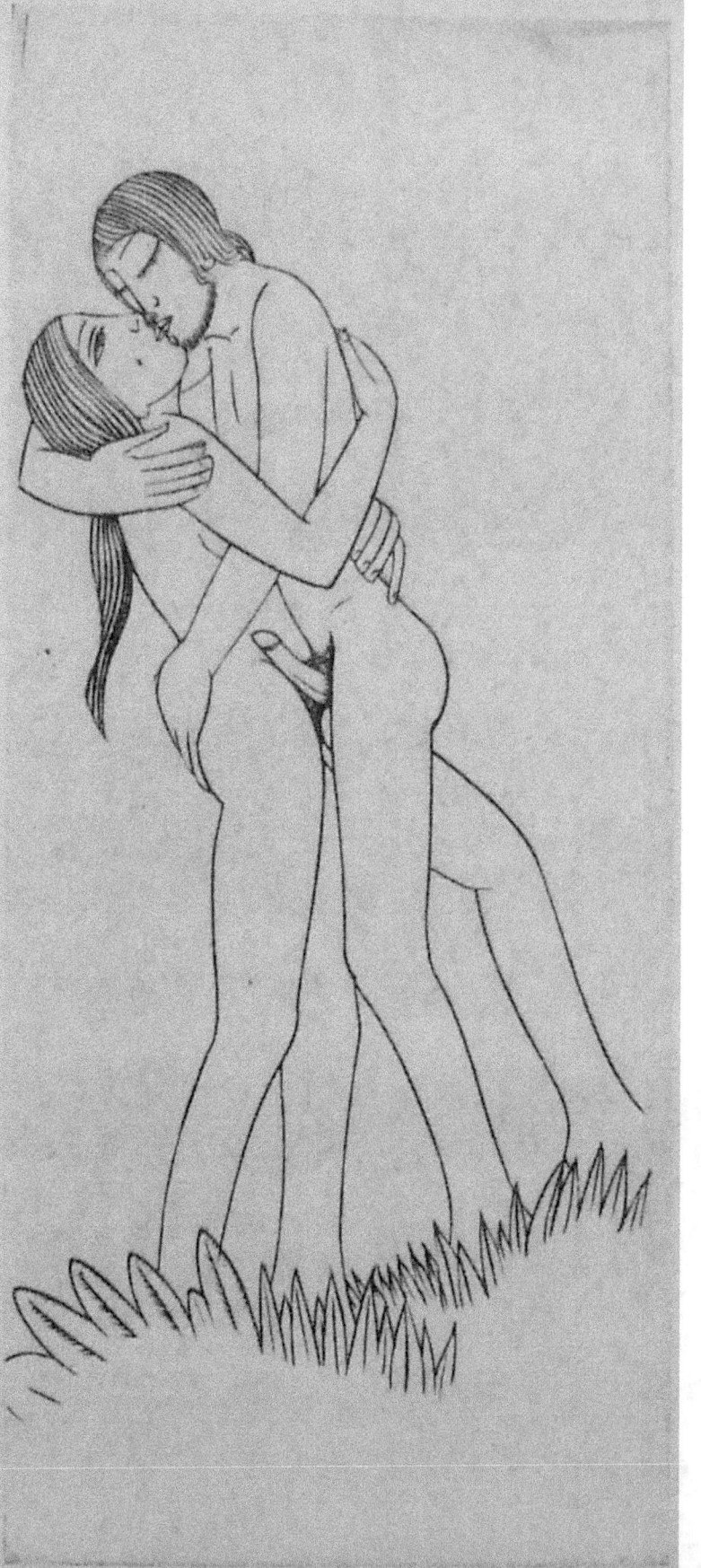

Eric Gill,
Earth Wrestling,
1926

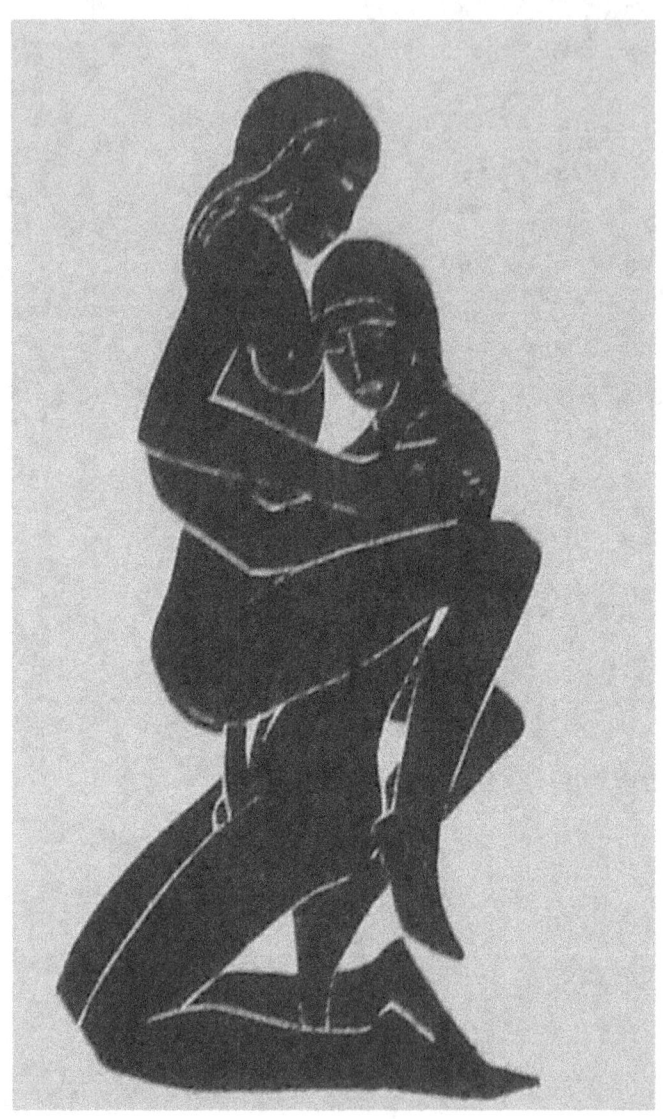

Eric Gill, Lovers, Kneeling, 1920

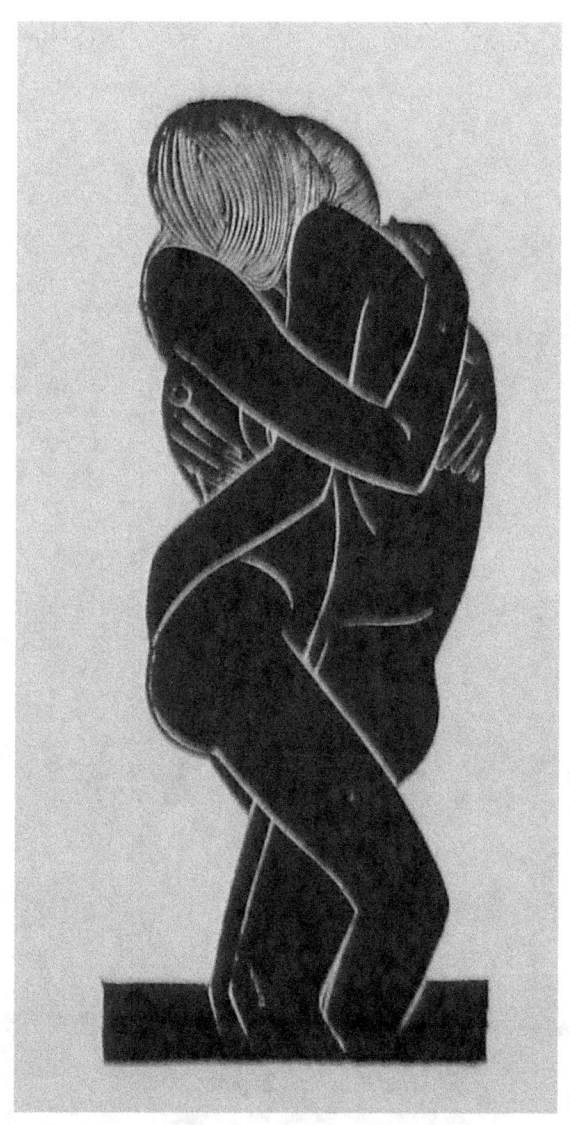

Eric Gill, Lovers, Standing, 1924

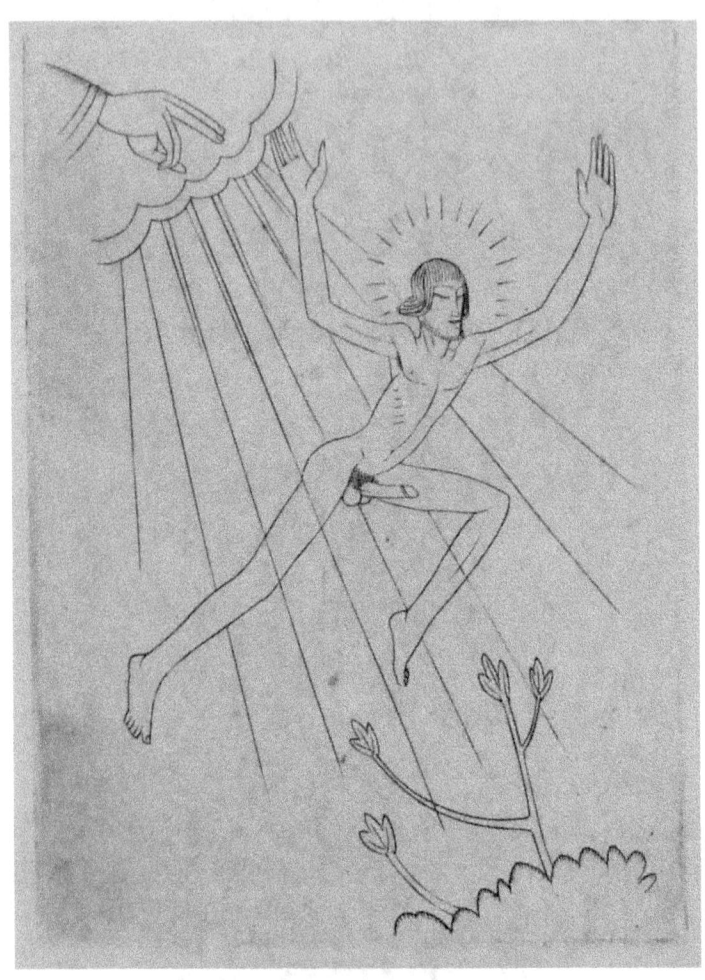

Eric Gill, God Sending, 1926

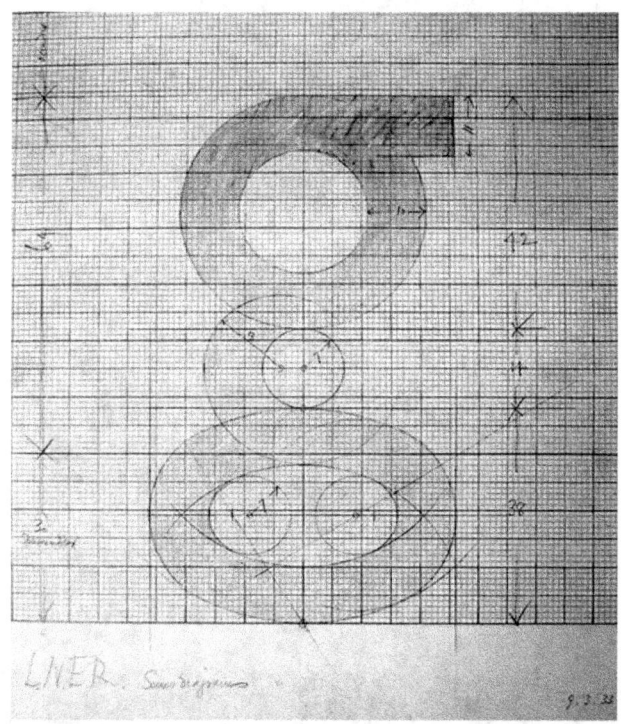

Designing fonts and letters was very important for Eric Gill, as any look at his art shows: there are letters and words everywhere in his art, carved into stone, cut into engravings, sketched in pencil, drawn in ink, printed as posters. His engravings show his love for designing decorative capital letters and monograms, as well as alphabets.

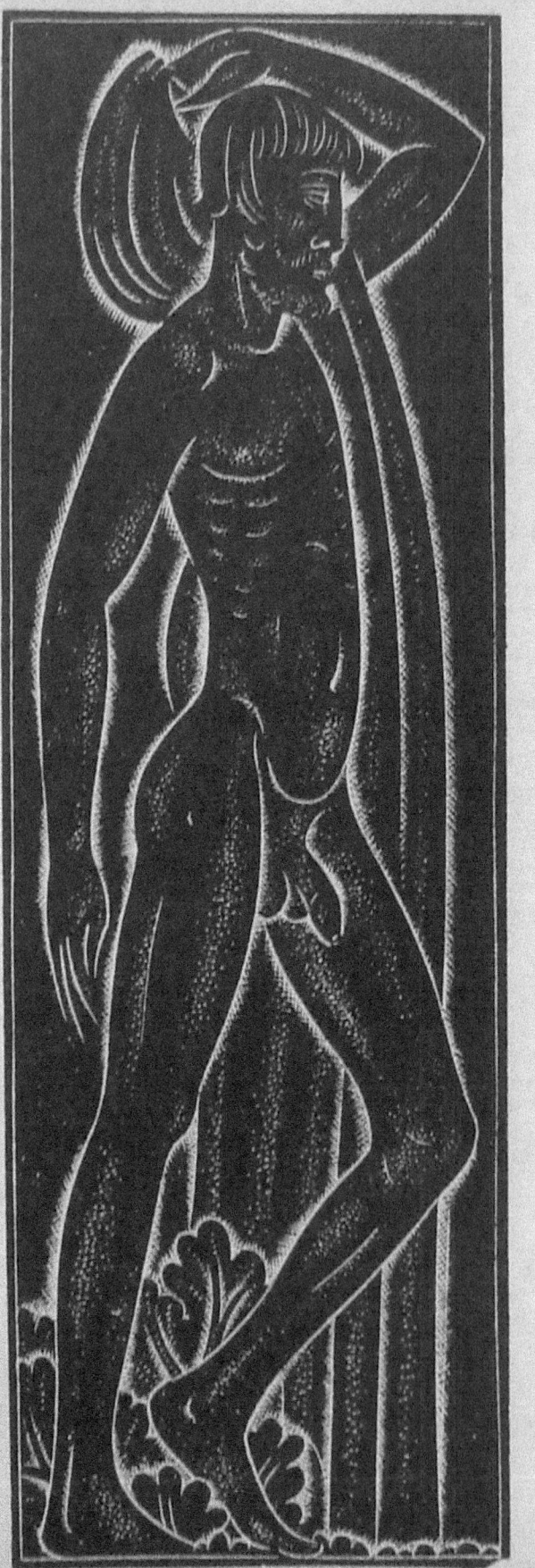

Eric Gill,
Mellors, 1930

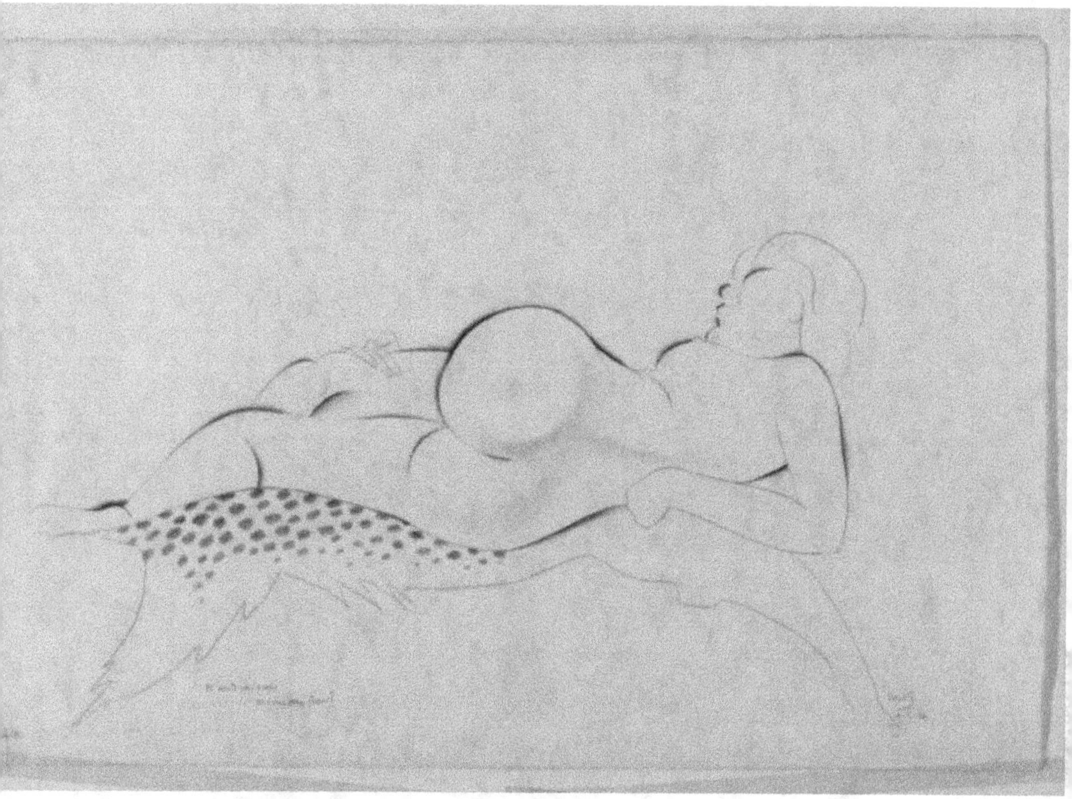

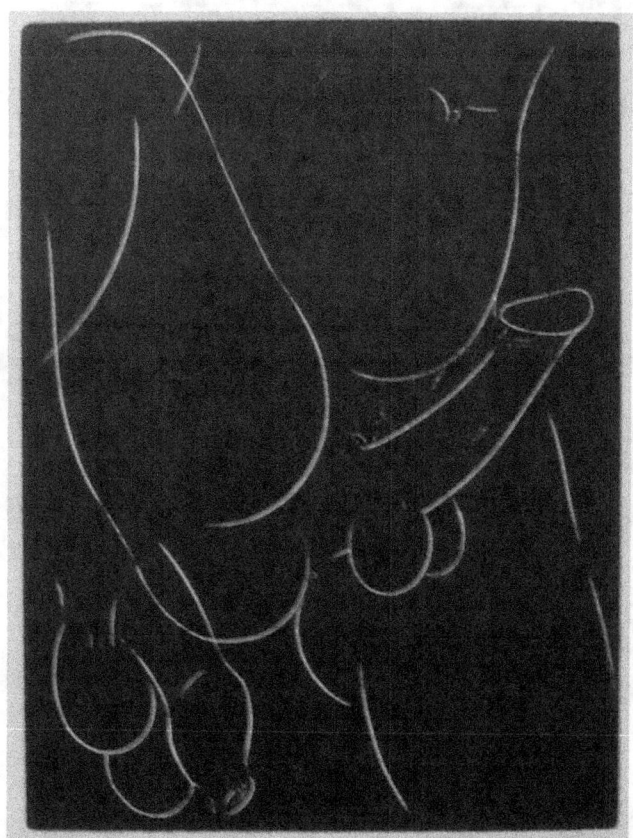

Eric Gill, Cari Naked, 1928 (above).
The Most Precious Ornament,
1937 (left).

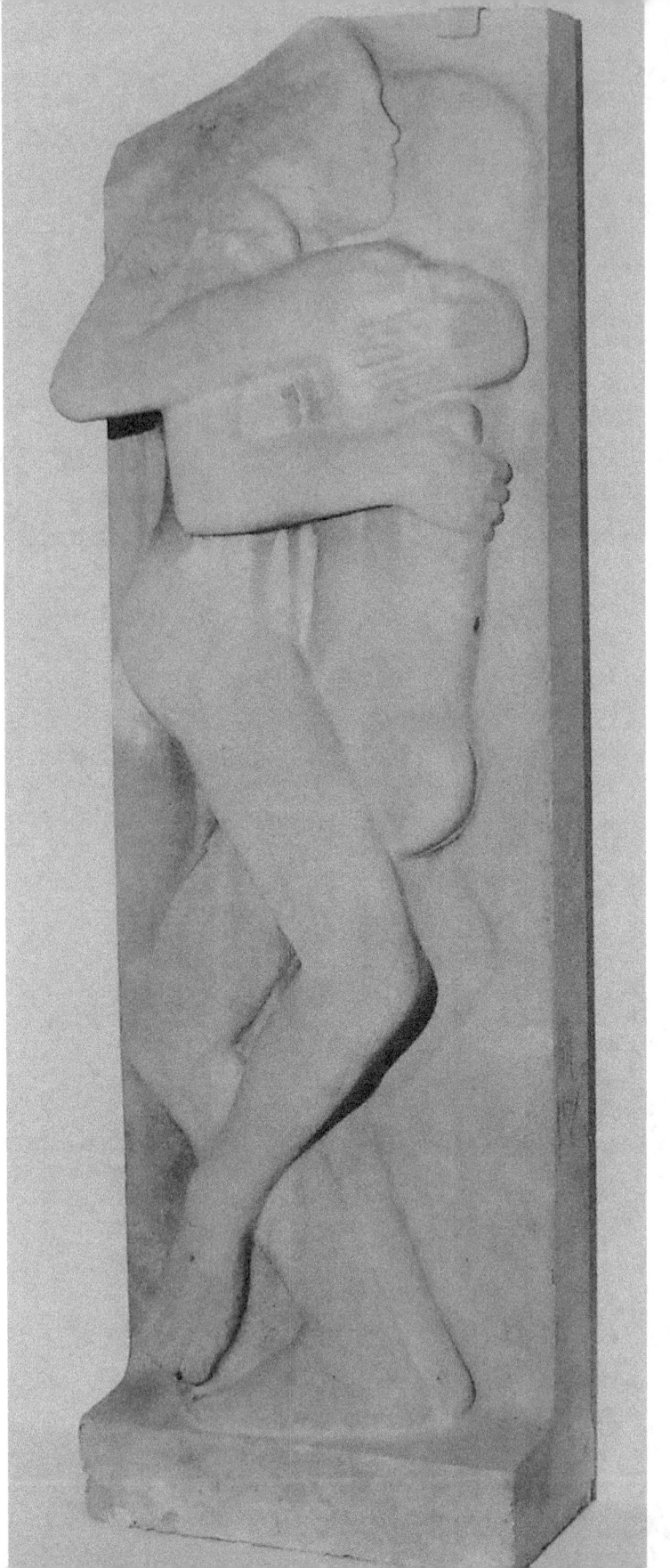

Eric Gill, Ecstasy,
1911, Portland
stone

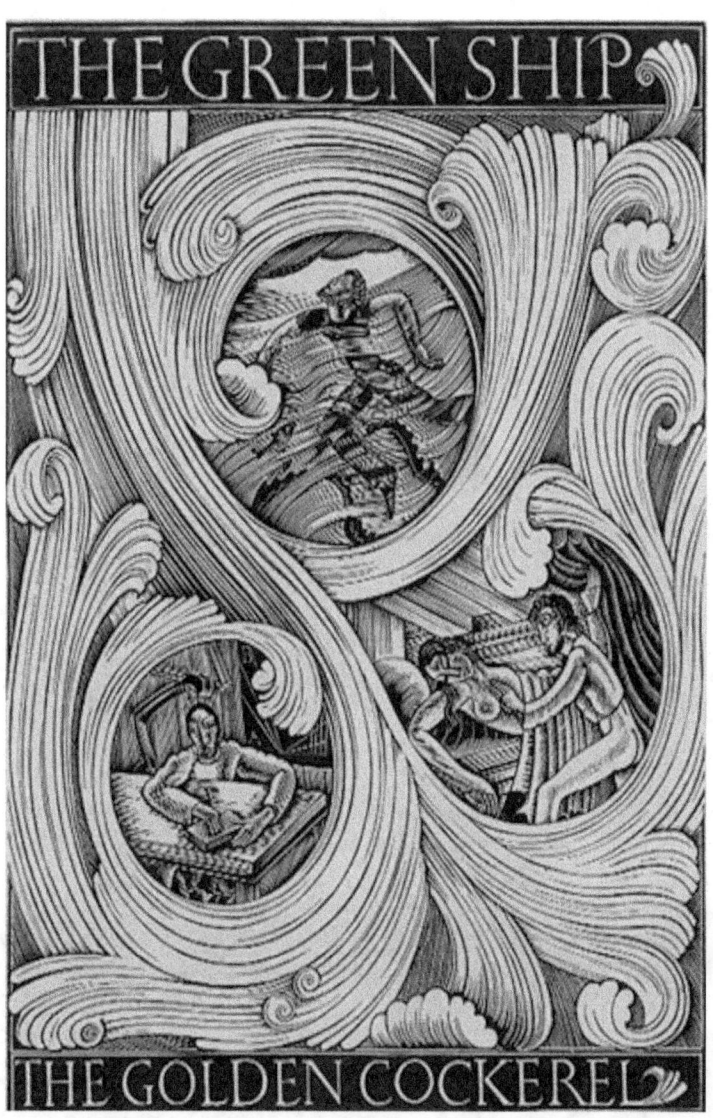

Eric Gill, The Green Ship

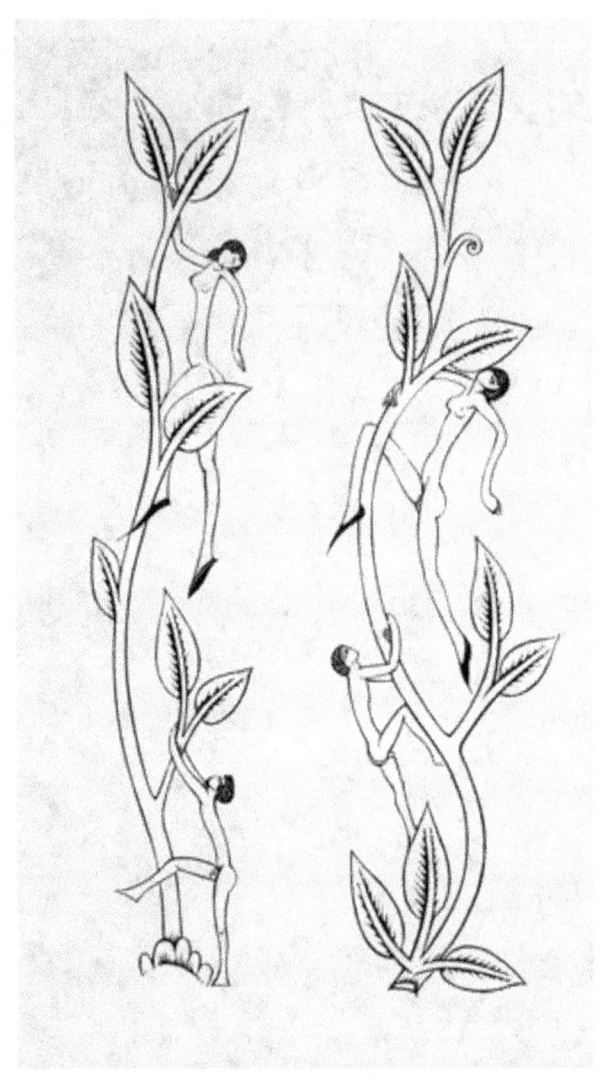

Eric Gill, Naked Boy, Girl, Hermaphrodite, 1930

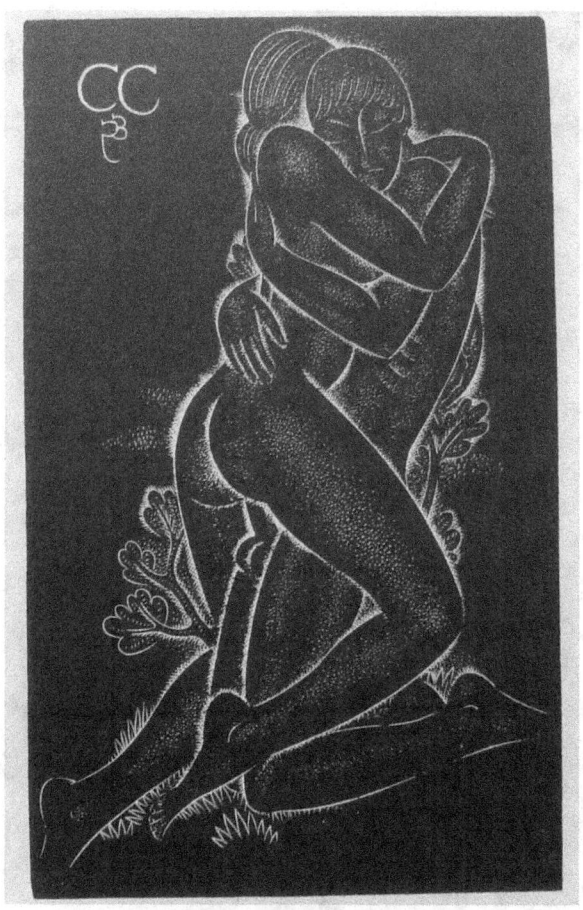

Fucking a flame into being: one of
Eric Gill's illustrations for D.H. Lawrence's book

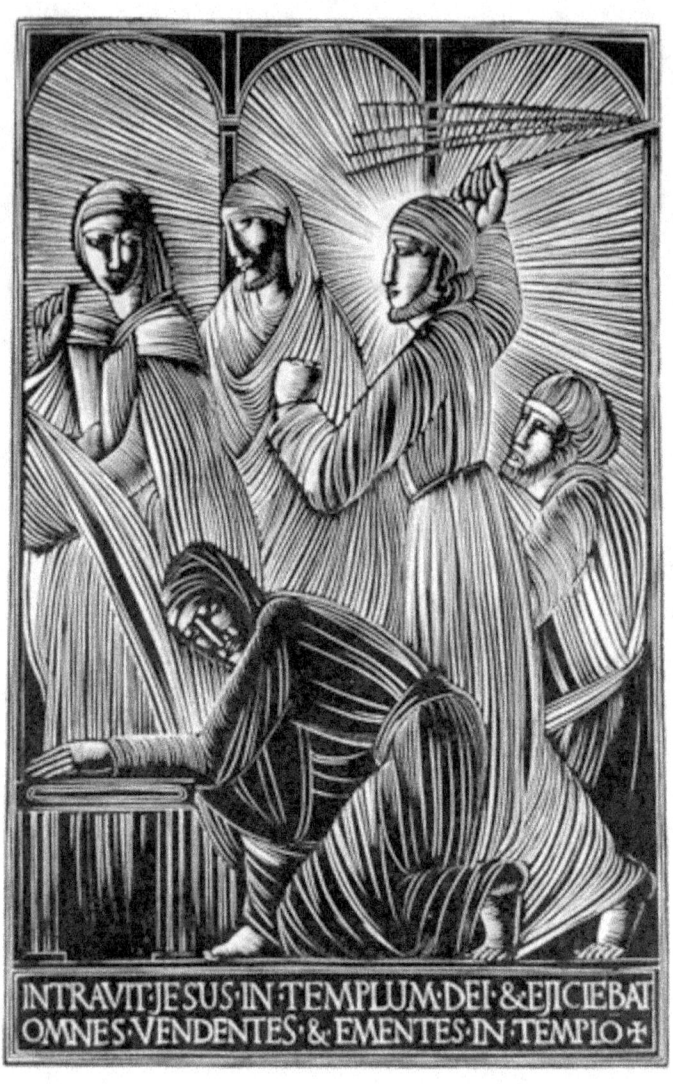

INTRAVIT·JESUS·IN·TEMPLUM·DEI·&·EJICIEBAT
OMNES·VENDENTES·&·EMENTES·IN·TEMPLO✠

Eric Gill, Christ and the Money-Changers

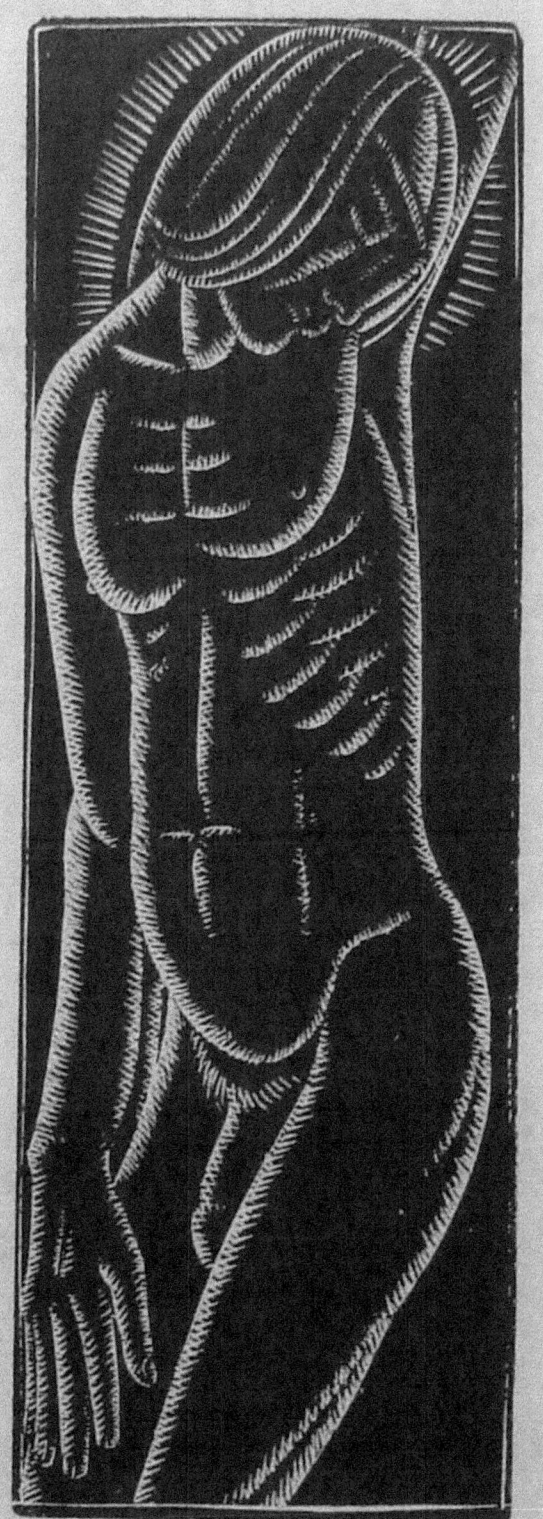

Eric Gill, Deposition, 1924

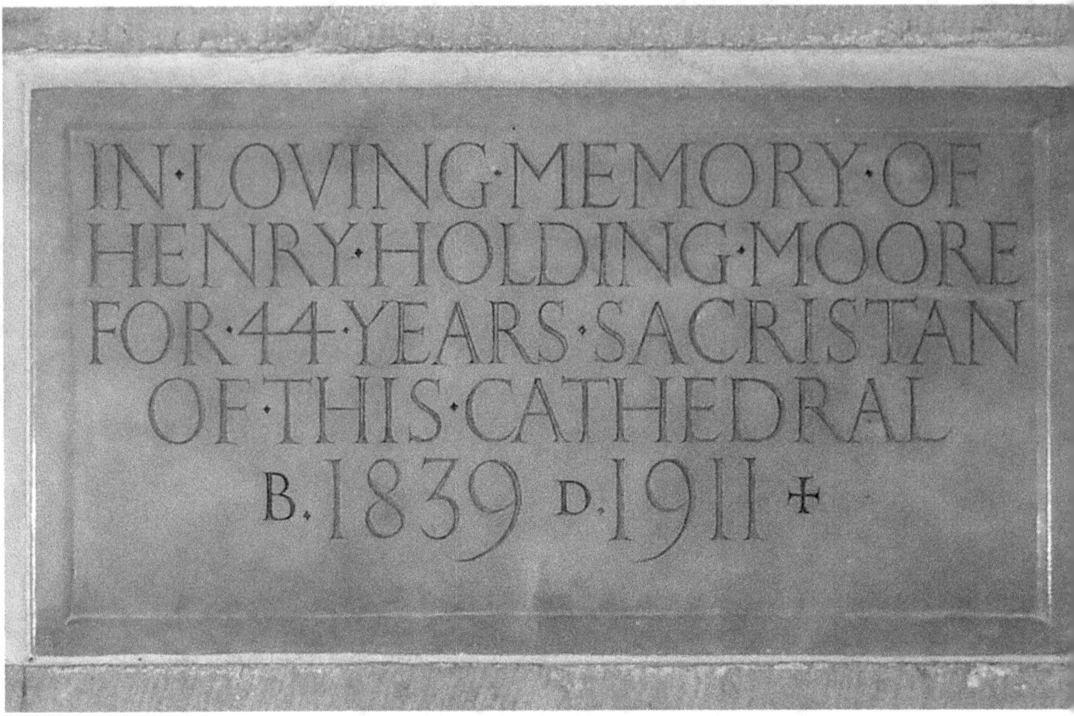

Examples of Eric Gill's lettering in stone

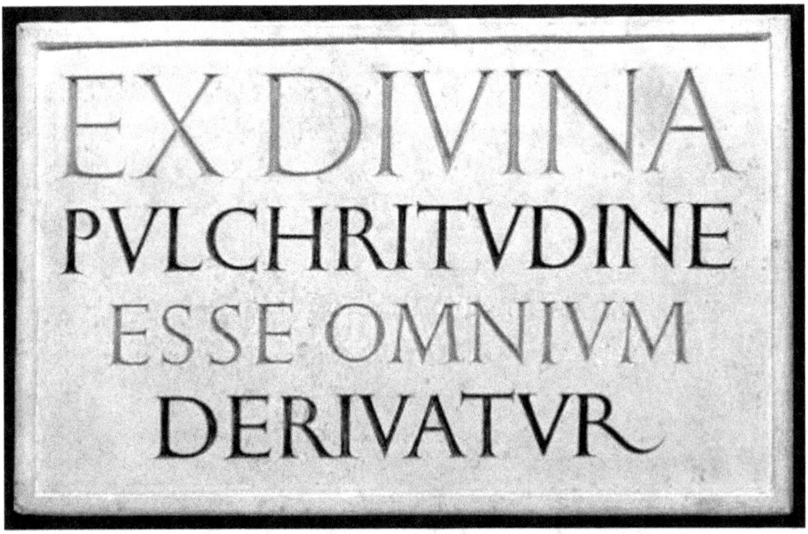

IN·LOVING·MEMORY·OF
HENRY·HOLDING·MOORE
FOR·44·YEARS·SACRISTAN
OF·THIS·CATHEDRAL
B.1839 D.1911 +

EX DIVINA
PVLCHRITVDINE
ESSE·OMNIVM
DERIVATVR

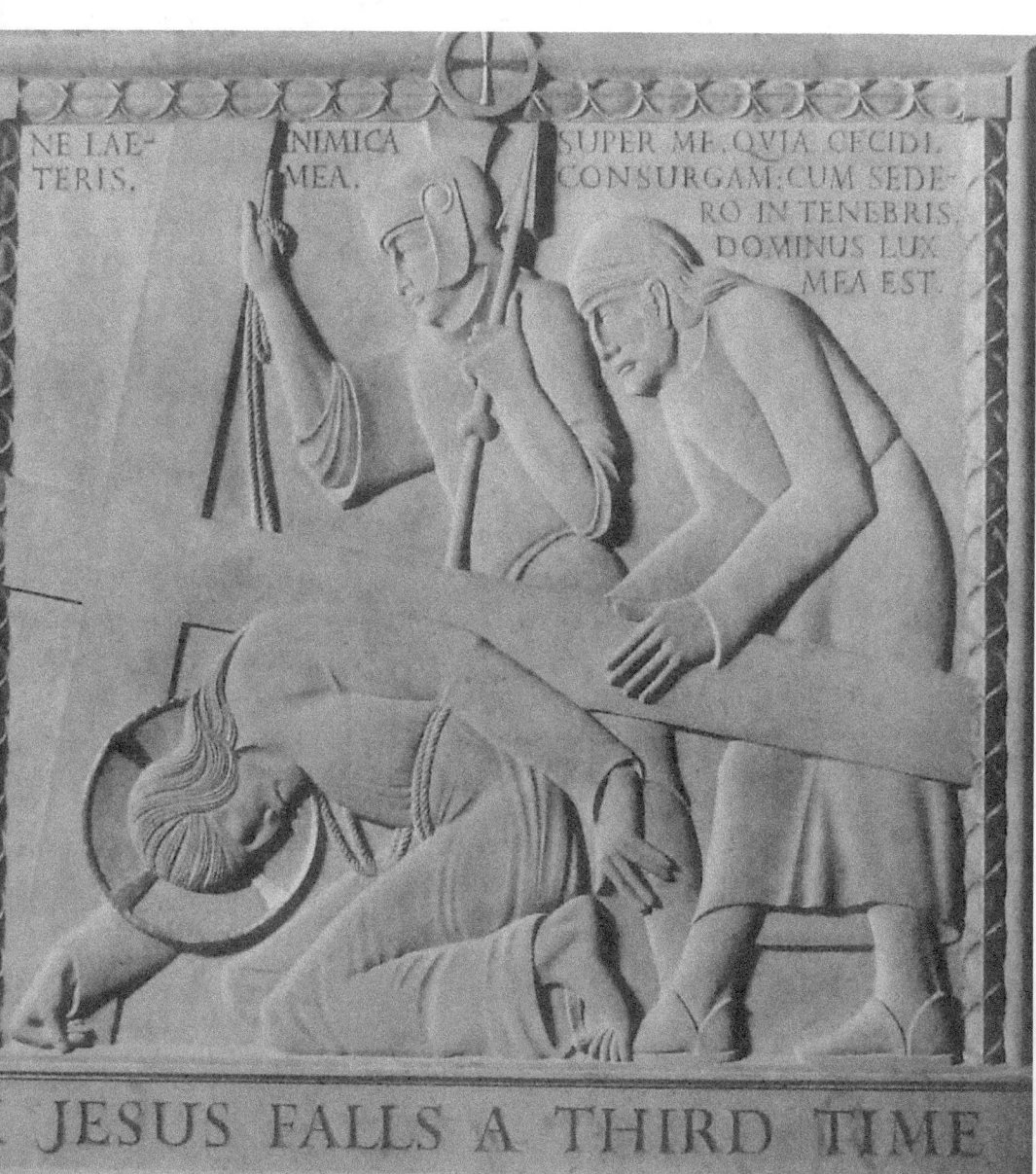

NE LAE- TERIS, NIMICA MEA. SUPER ME, QVIA CECIDI. CONSURGAM; CUM SEDE- RO IN TENEBRIS, DOMINUS LUX MEA EST.

JESUS FALLS A THIRD TIME

Eric Gill, Stations of the Cross, 9, Westminster Cathedral

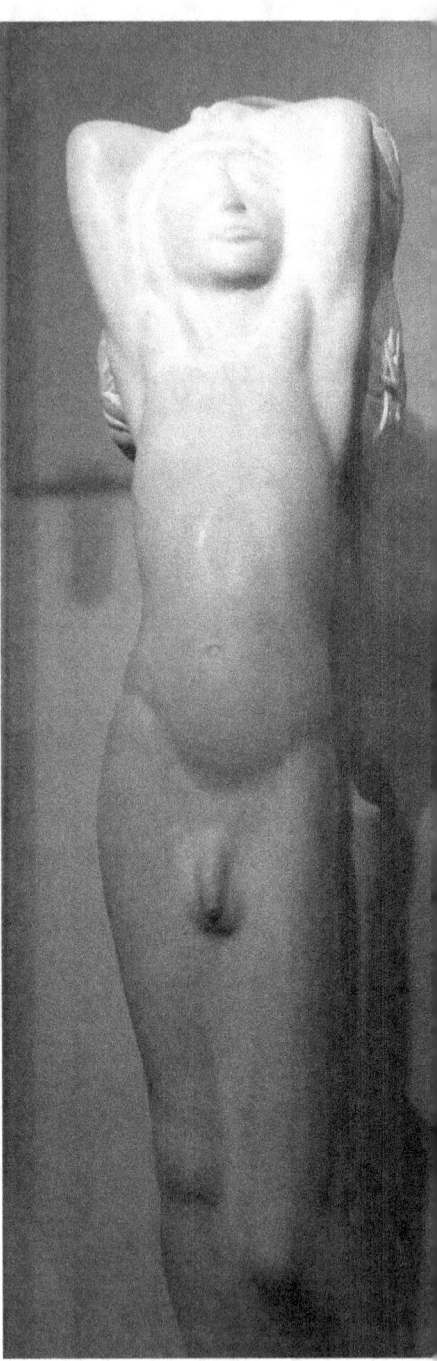

Eric Gill, St Sebastian,
1920, Victoria & Albert Museum,
London

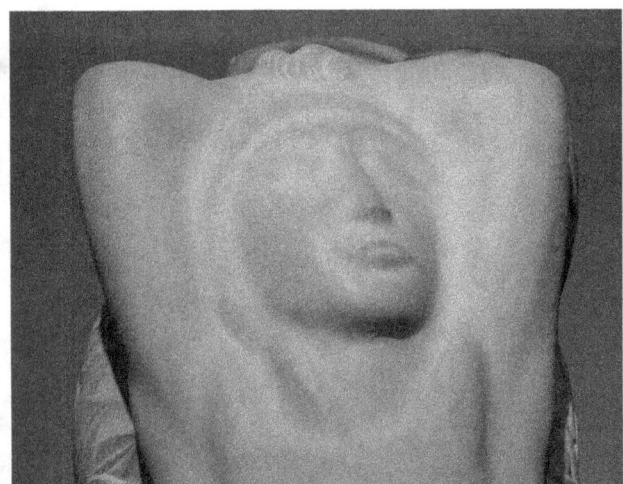

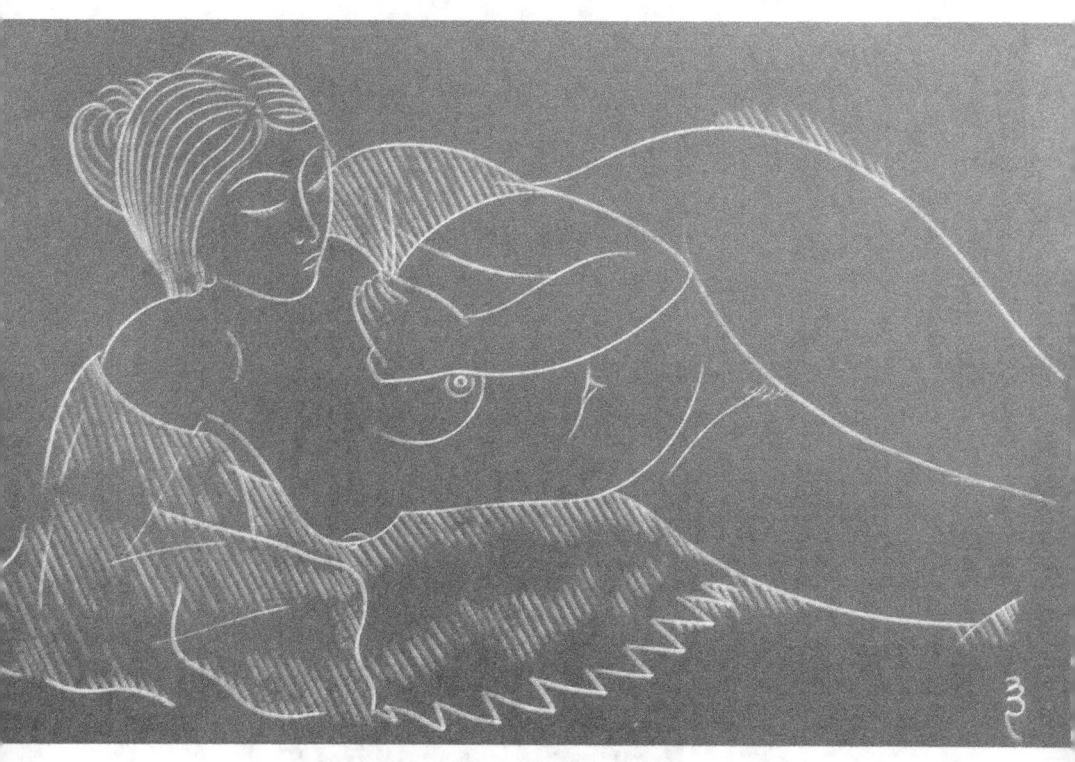

Eric Gill, Female Nude, Lying, 1937

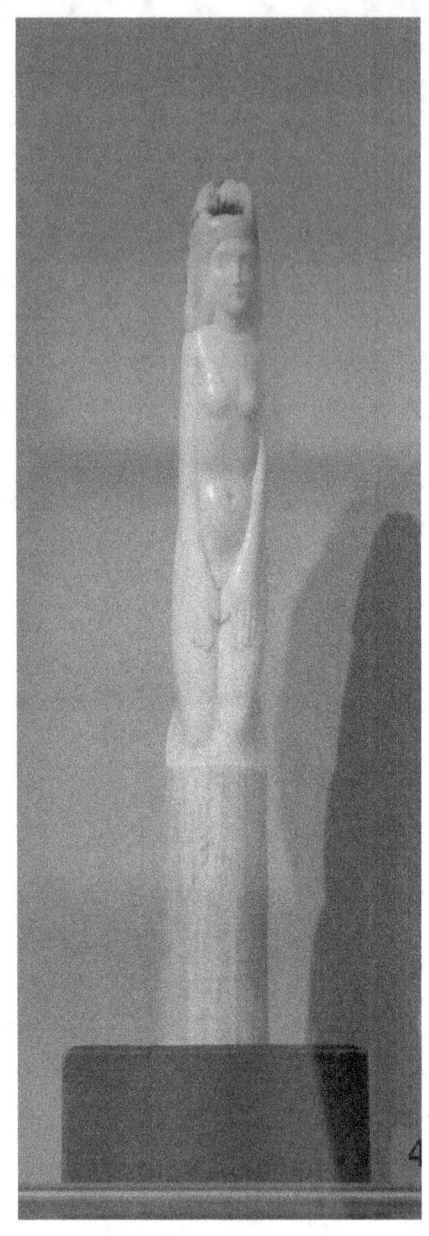

Eric Gill, Female Nude, 1928,
Victoria & Albert Museum, London

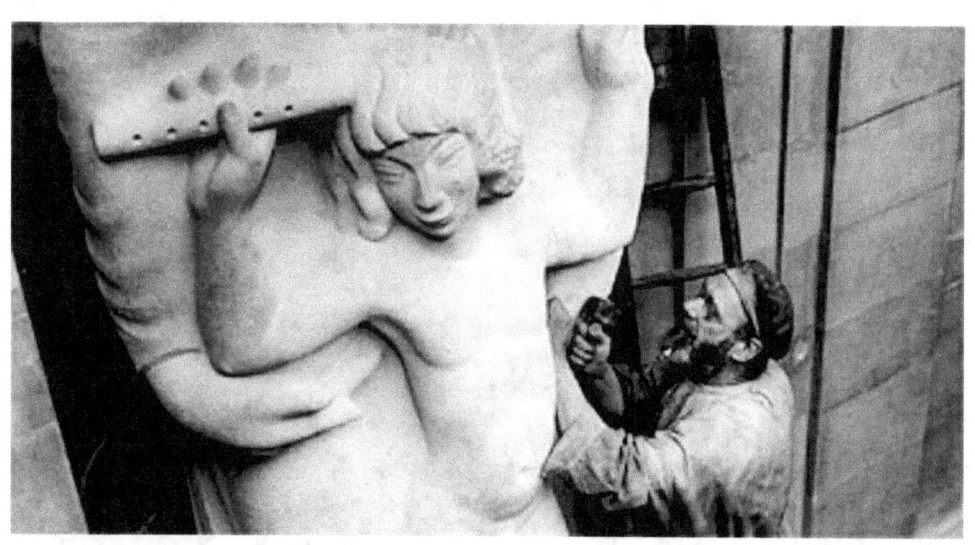

One of Eric Gill's important commissions:
Prospero and Ariel for the BBC.

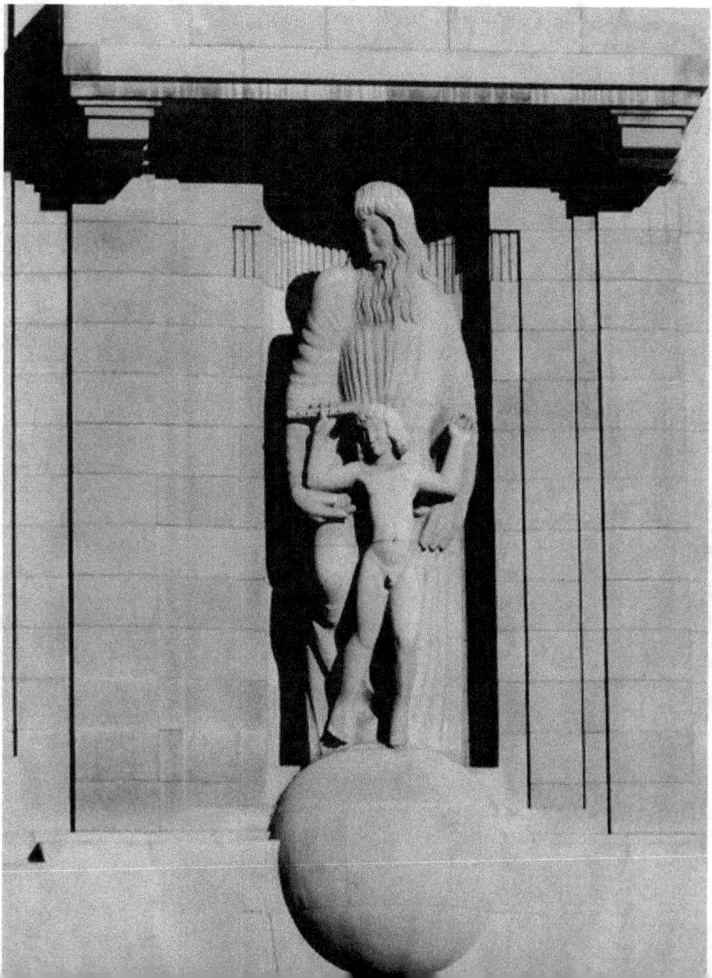

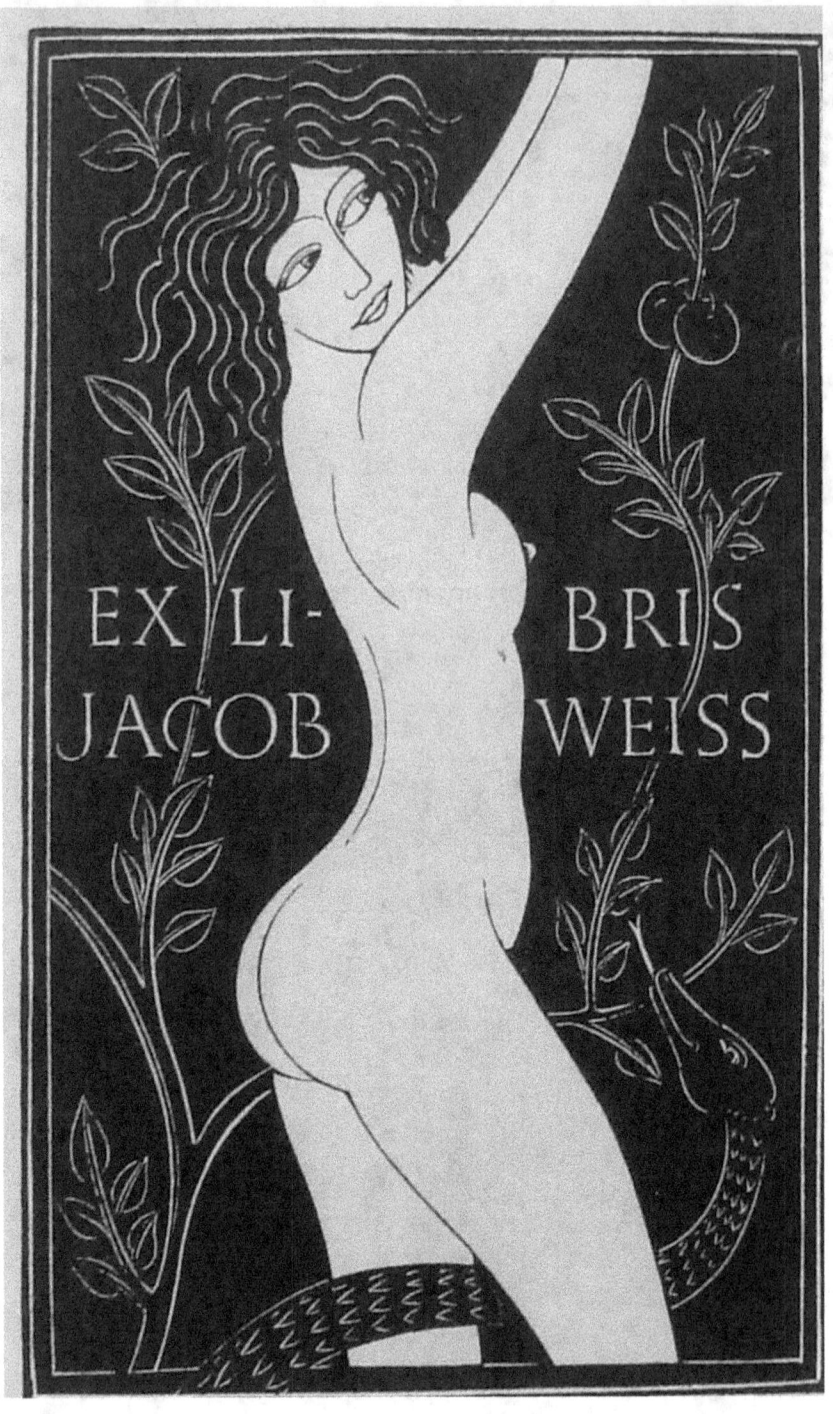

EX LI- BRIS
JACOB WEISS

Eric Gill, Eve, 1935

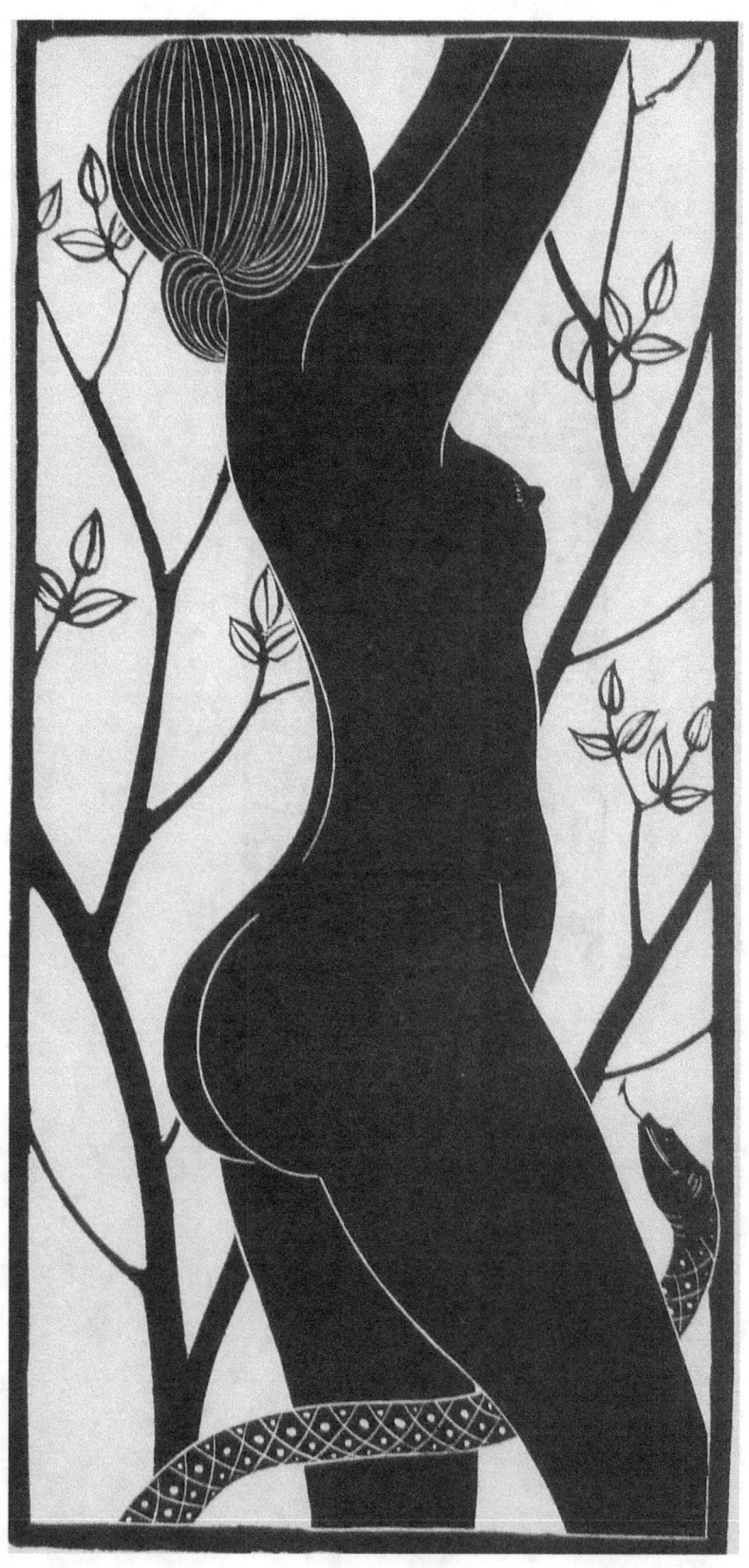

Eric Gill, Eve, 1926

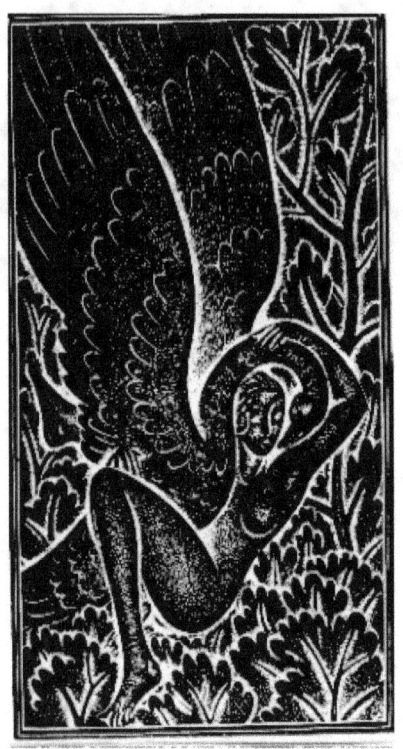

Eric Gill, Leda Loved, 1931

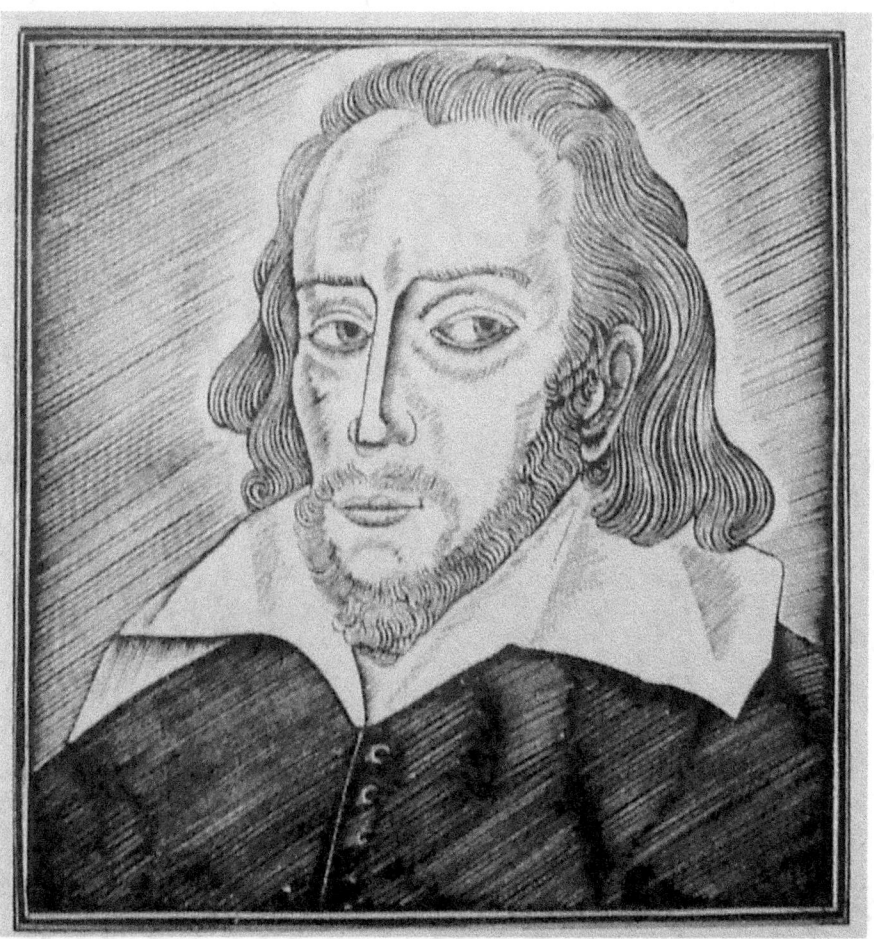

Eric Gill, portrait of Shakespeare, 1936

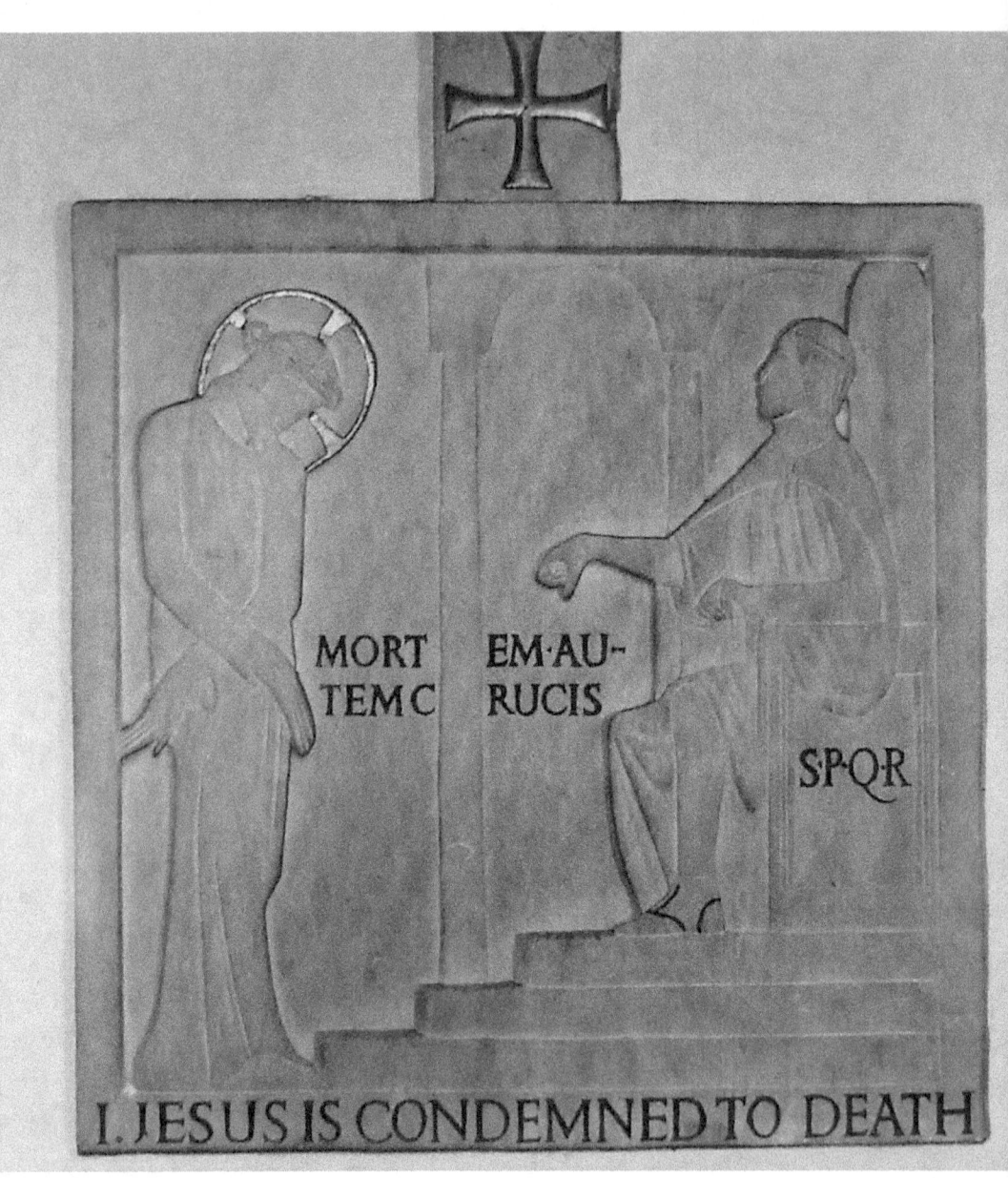

Eric Gill, Stations of the Cross, 1, St Cuthbert's Catholic Church,
Heaton, Bradford, U.K.

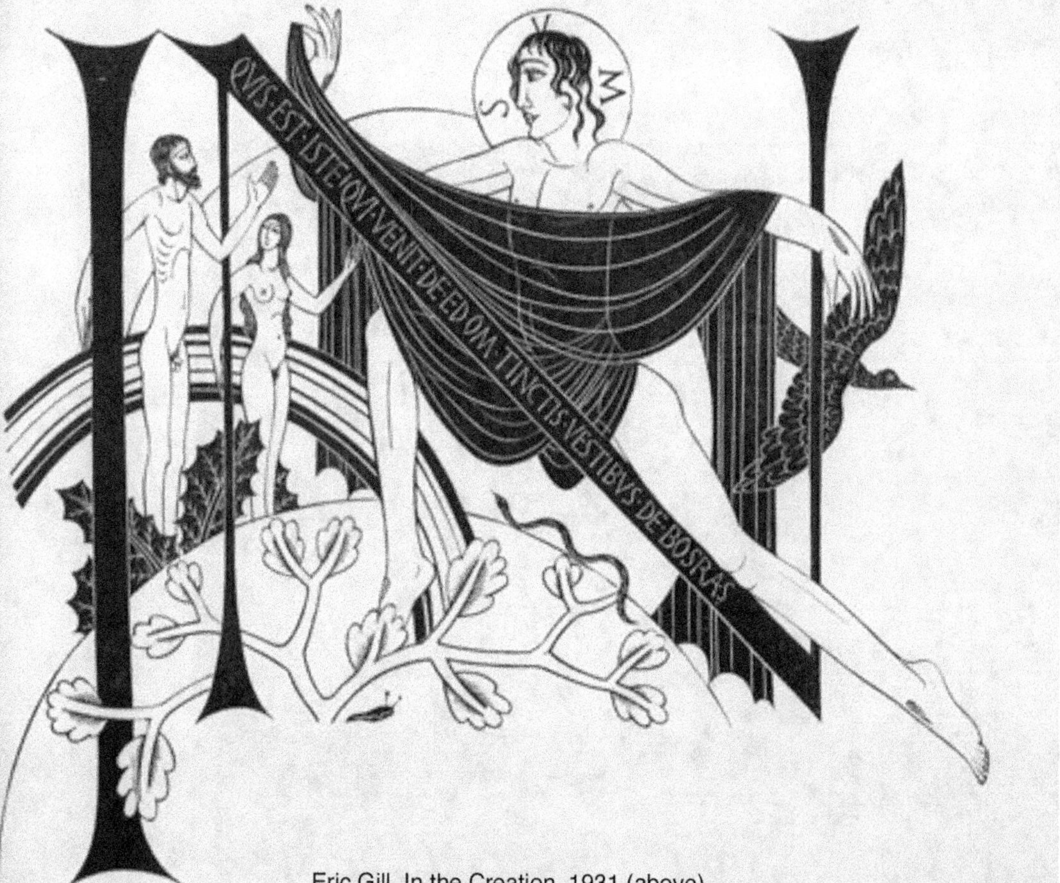

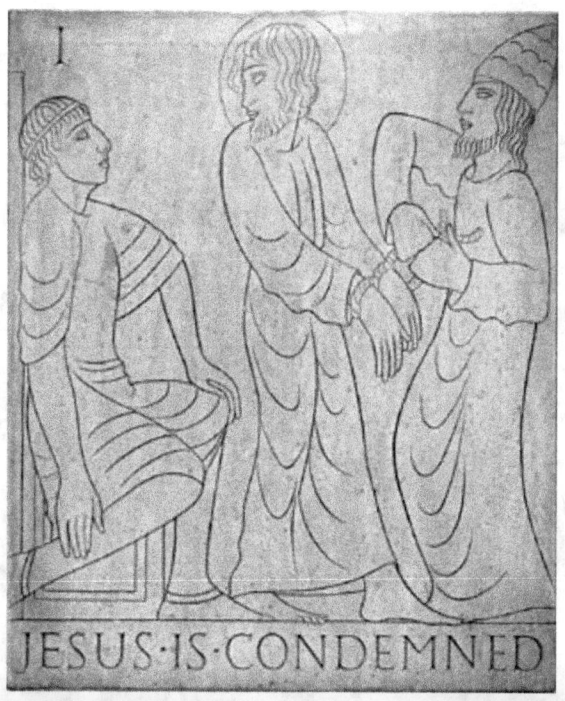

Eric Gill, In the Creation, 1931 (above).
A drawing for the Stations of the Cross (below).

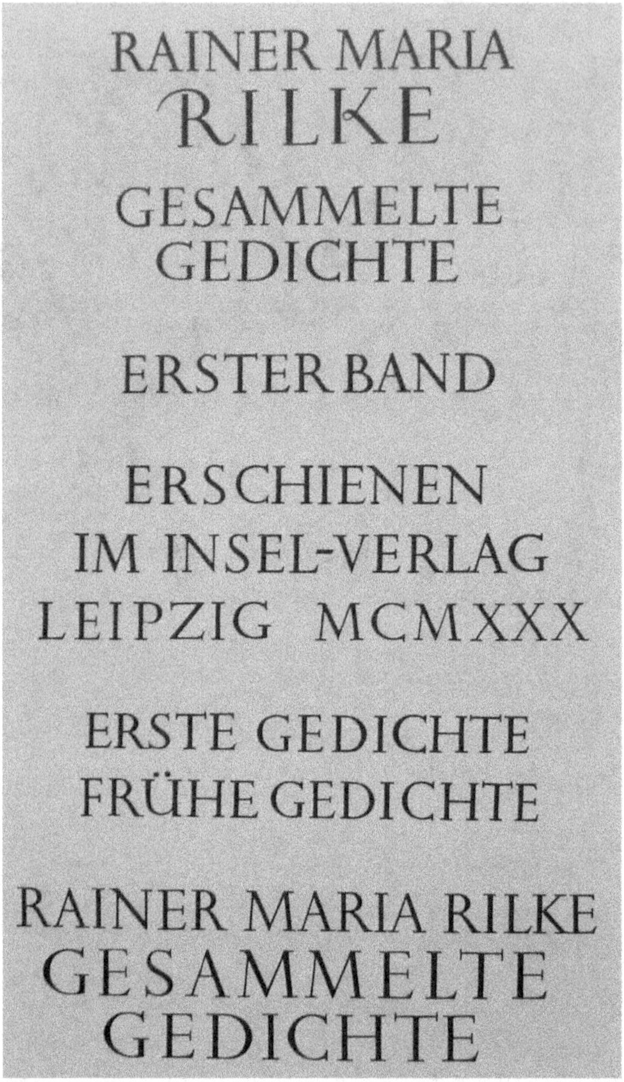

RAINER MARIA
RILKE
GESAMMELTE
GEDICHTE

ERSTER BAND

ERSCHIENEN
IM INSEL-VERLAG
LEIPZIG MCMXXX

ERSTE GEDICHTE
FRÜHE GEDICHTE

RAINER MARIA RILKE
GESAMMELTE
GEDICHTE

Eric Gill, example of lettering for a book by Rainer Maria Rilke

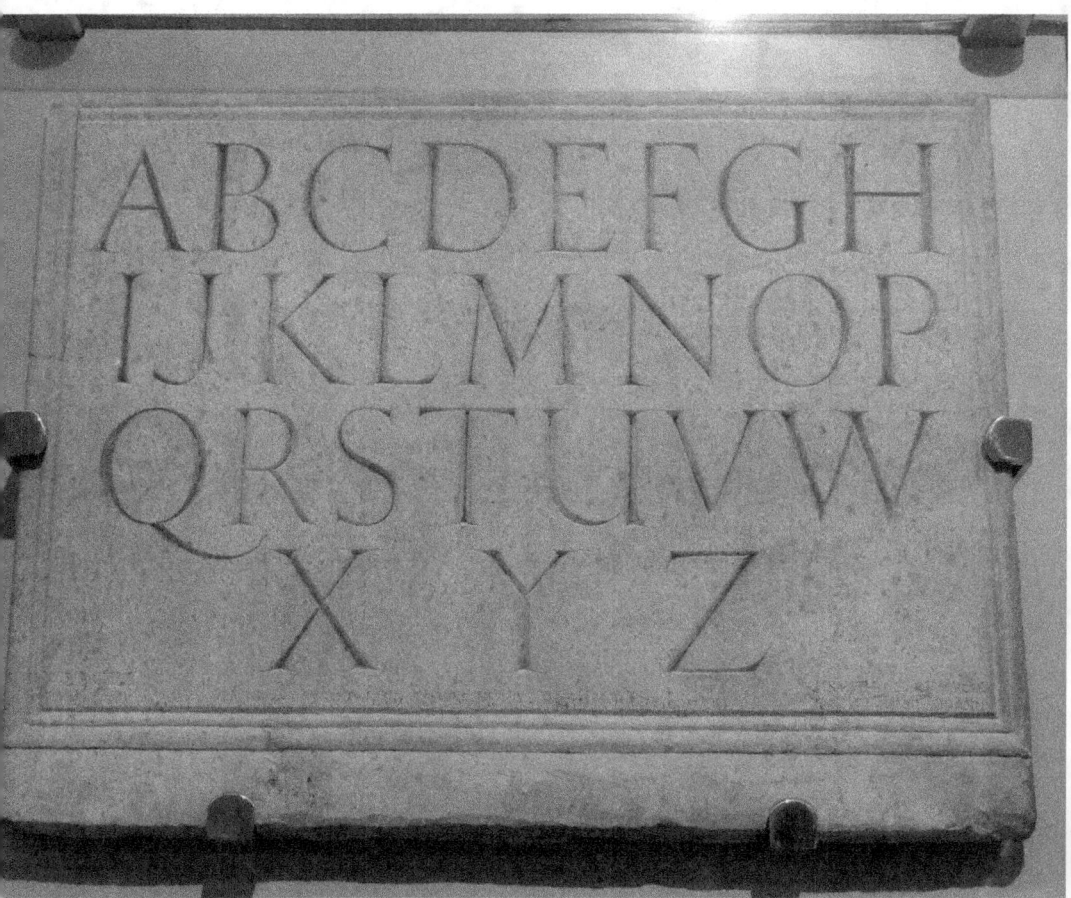

Eric Gill, stone, Victoria & Albert Museum, London

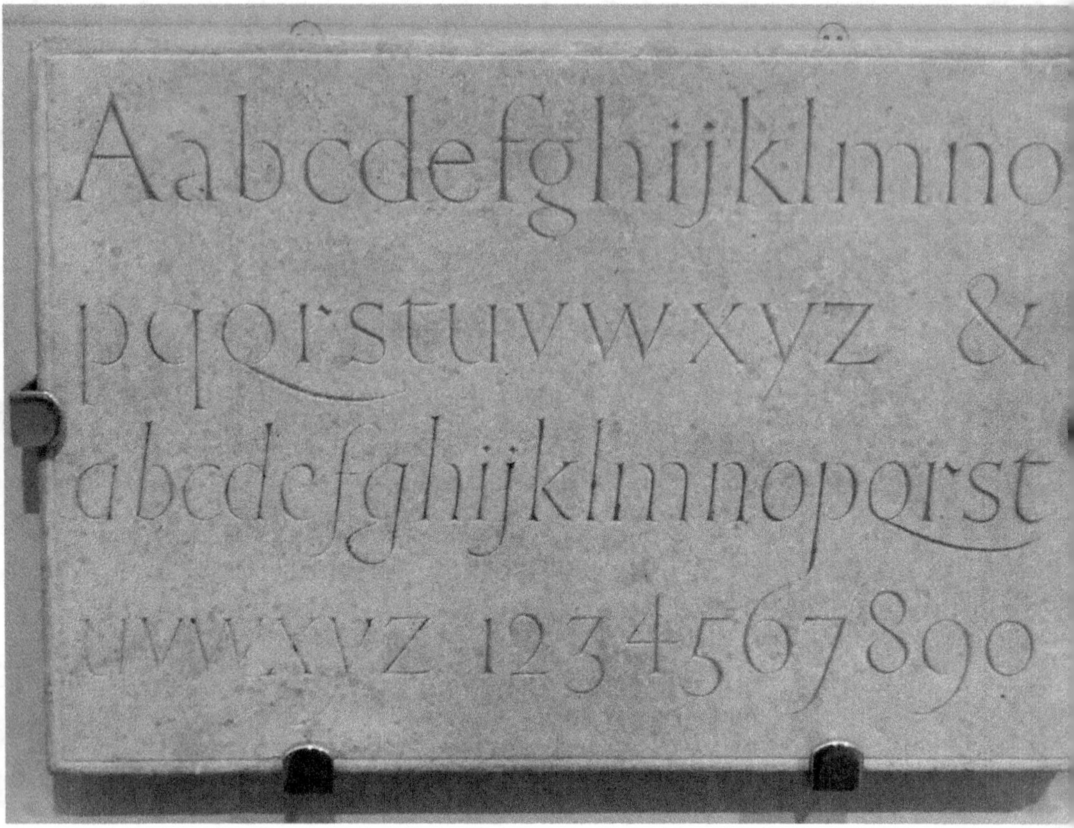

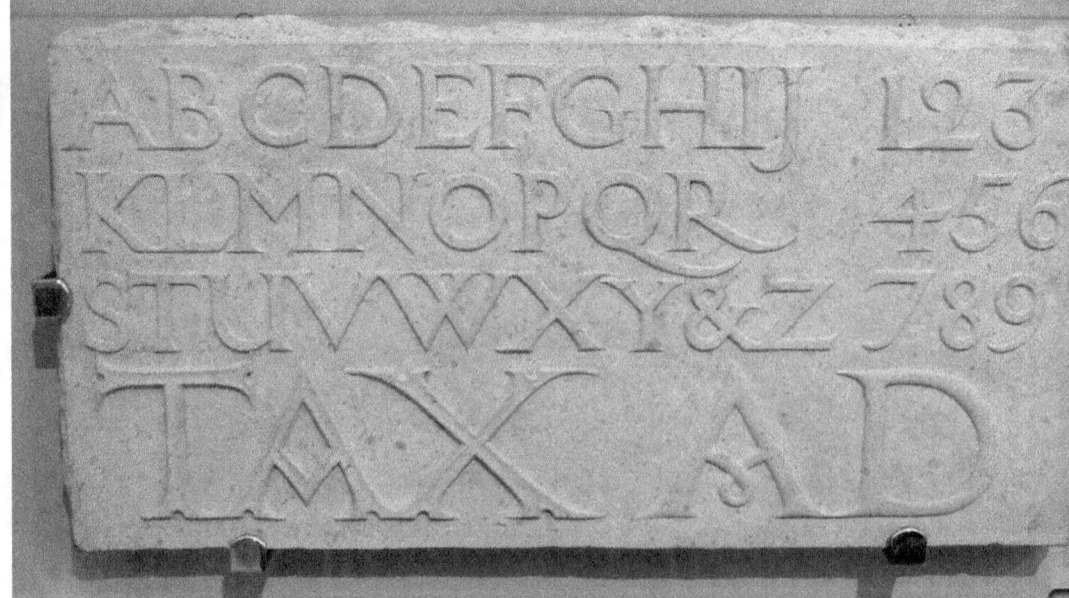

Examples of Eric Gill's stone carving,
Victoria & Albert Museum, London

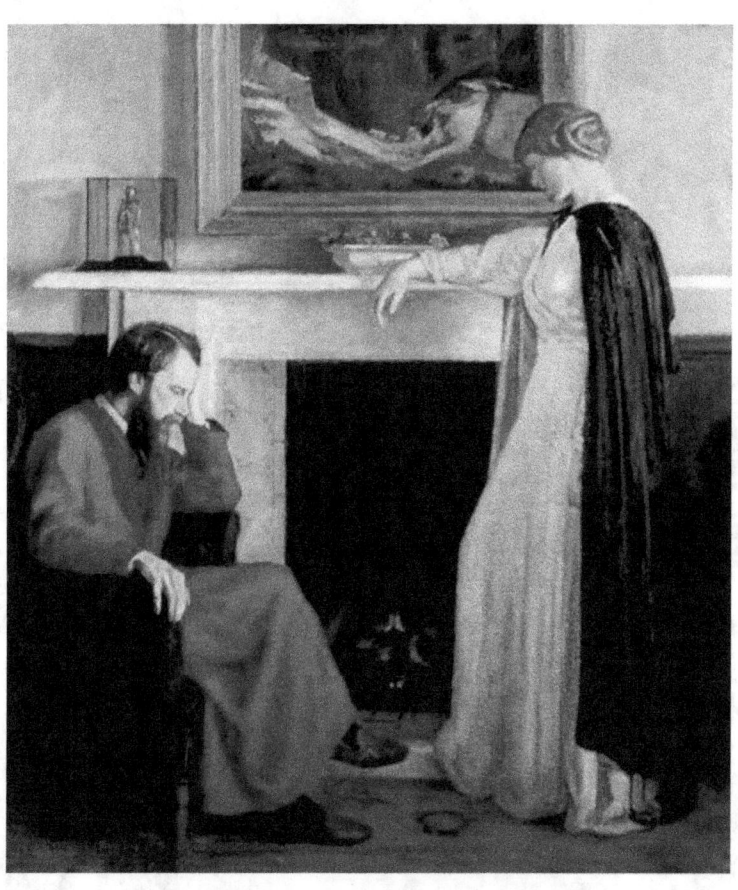

Eric Gill by William Rothenstein, 1914 (above).
The Bath, 1920, Fine Art Society (below).

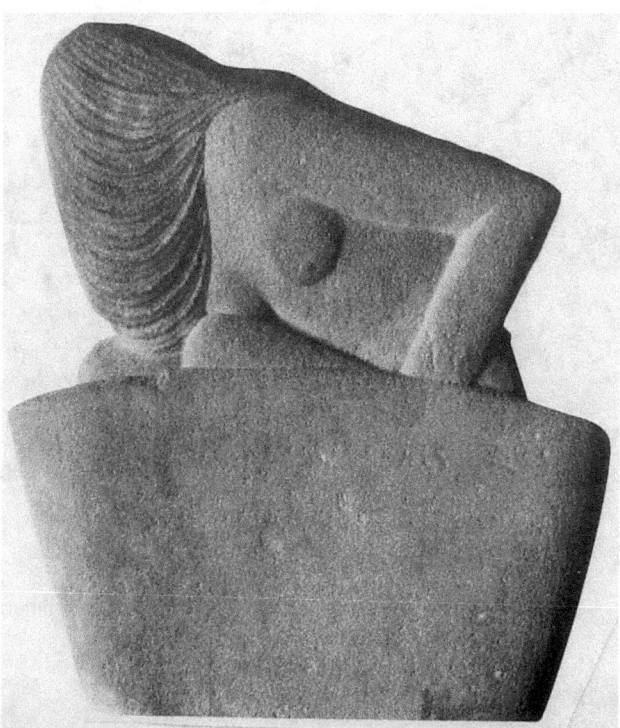

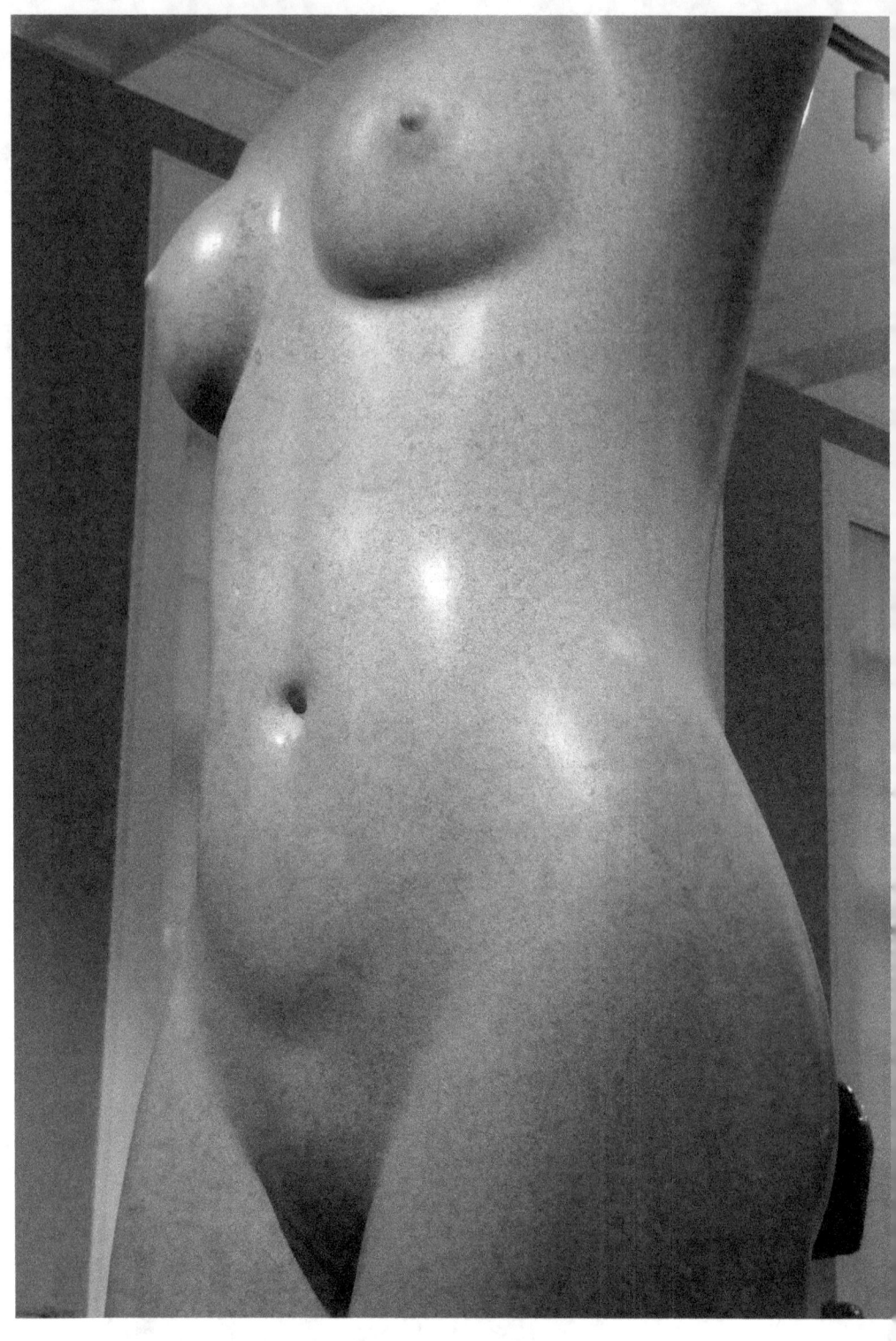

Erig Gill, Mankind, 1928, Victoria & Albert Museum, London.

The photos on the following pages were taken
by Jeremy Robinson in 2008.

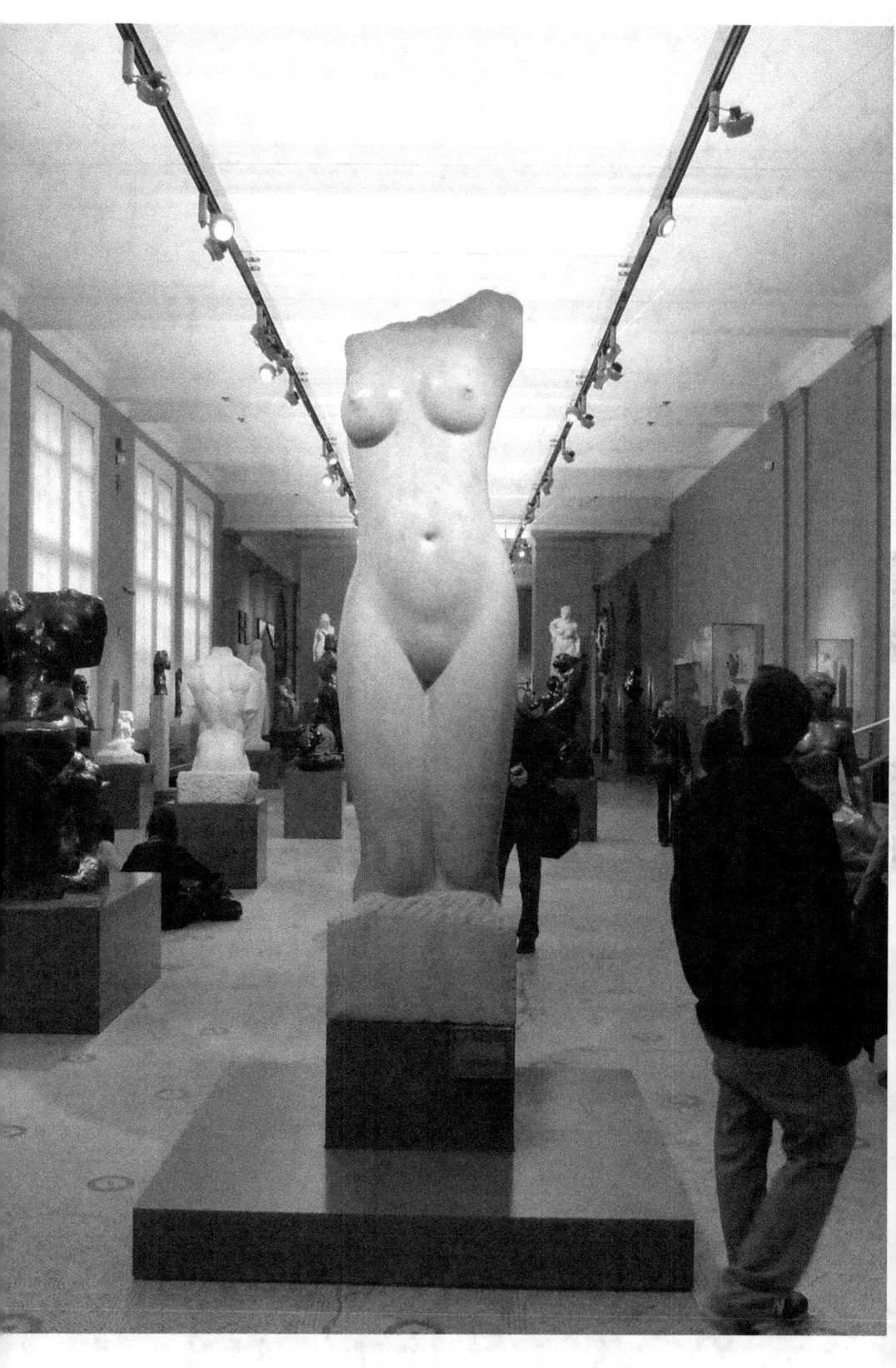

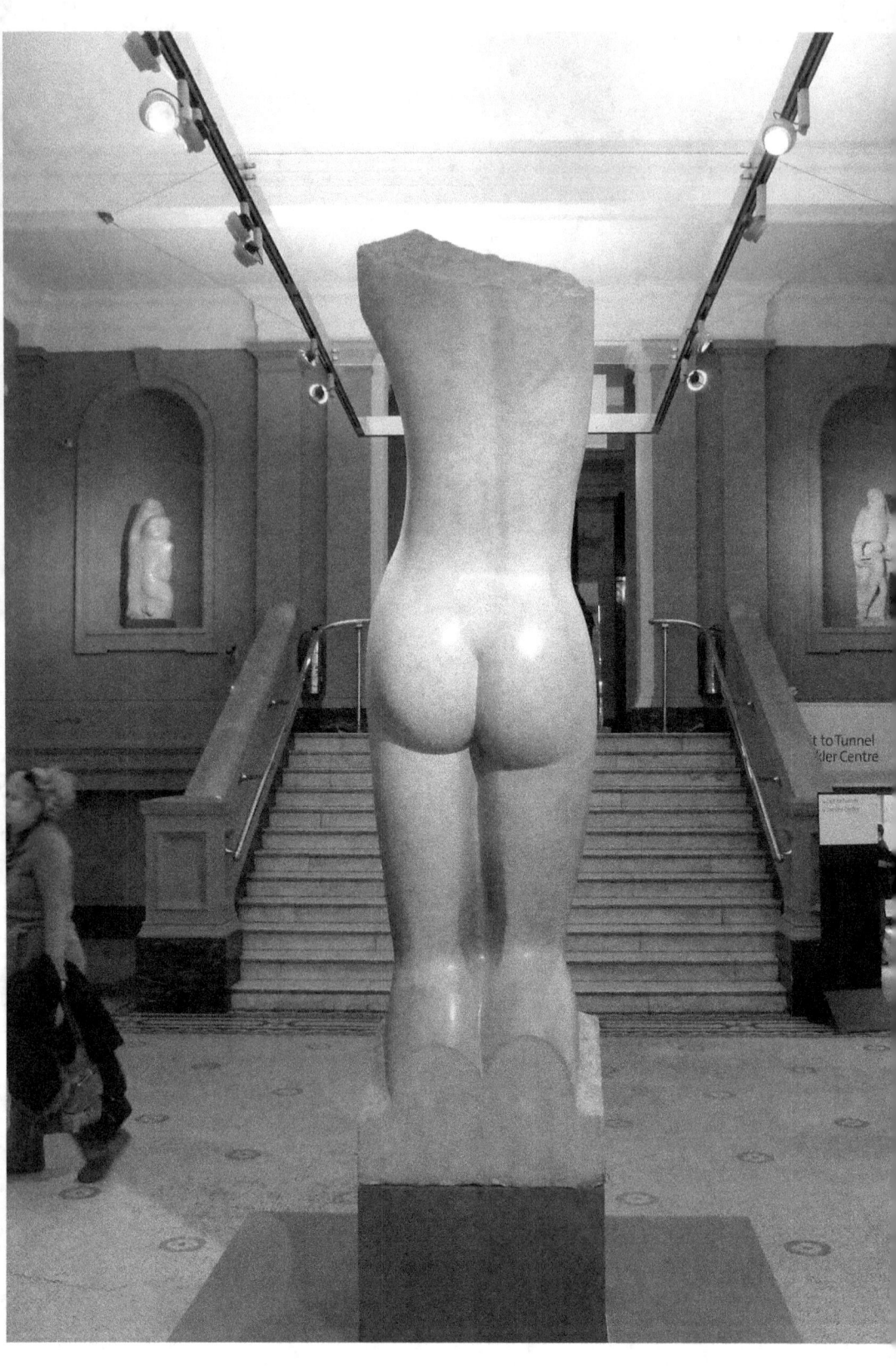

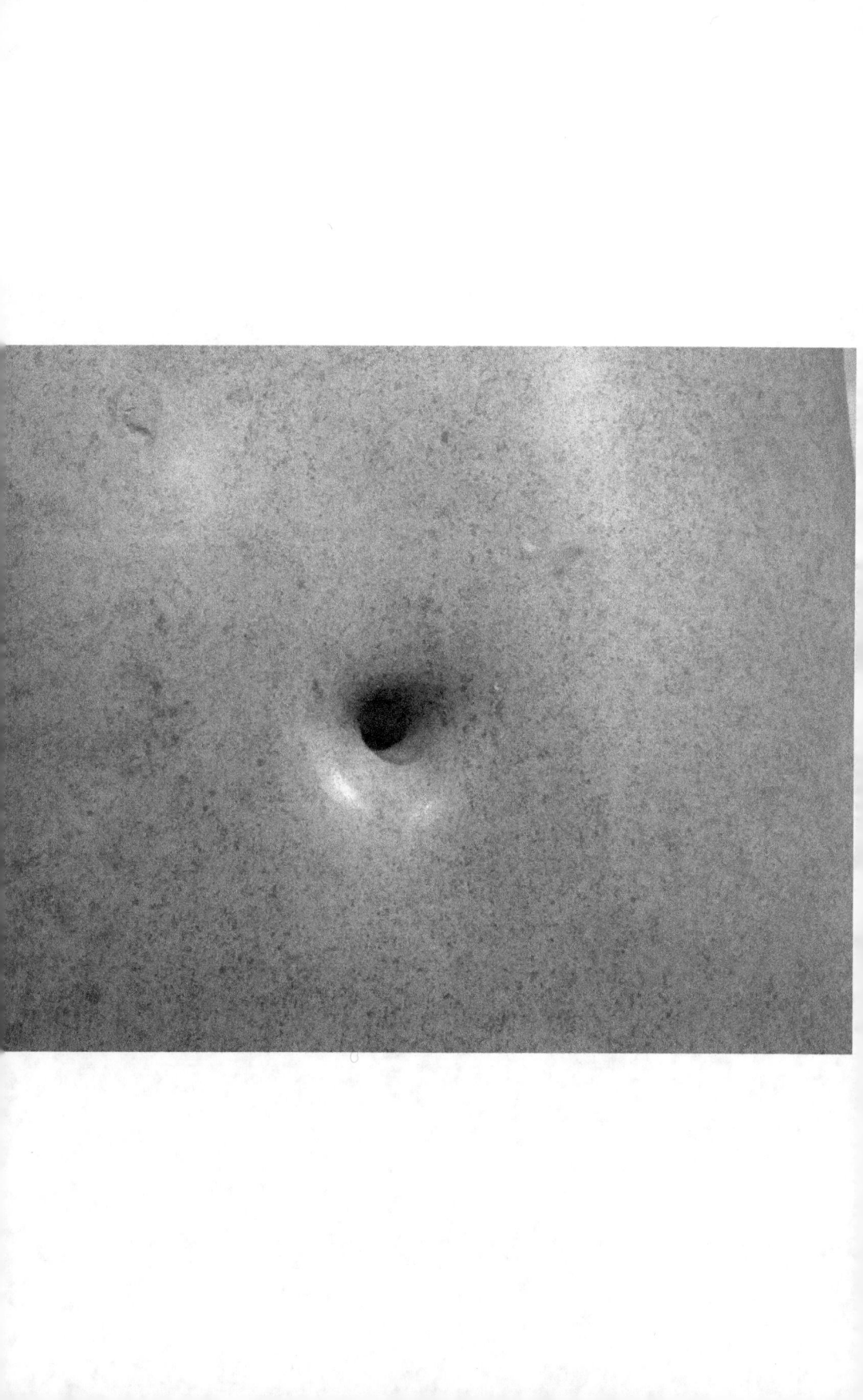

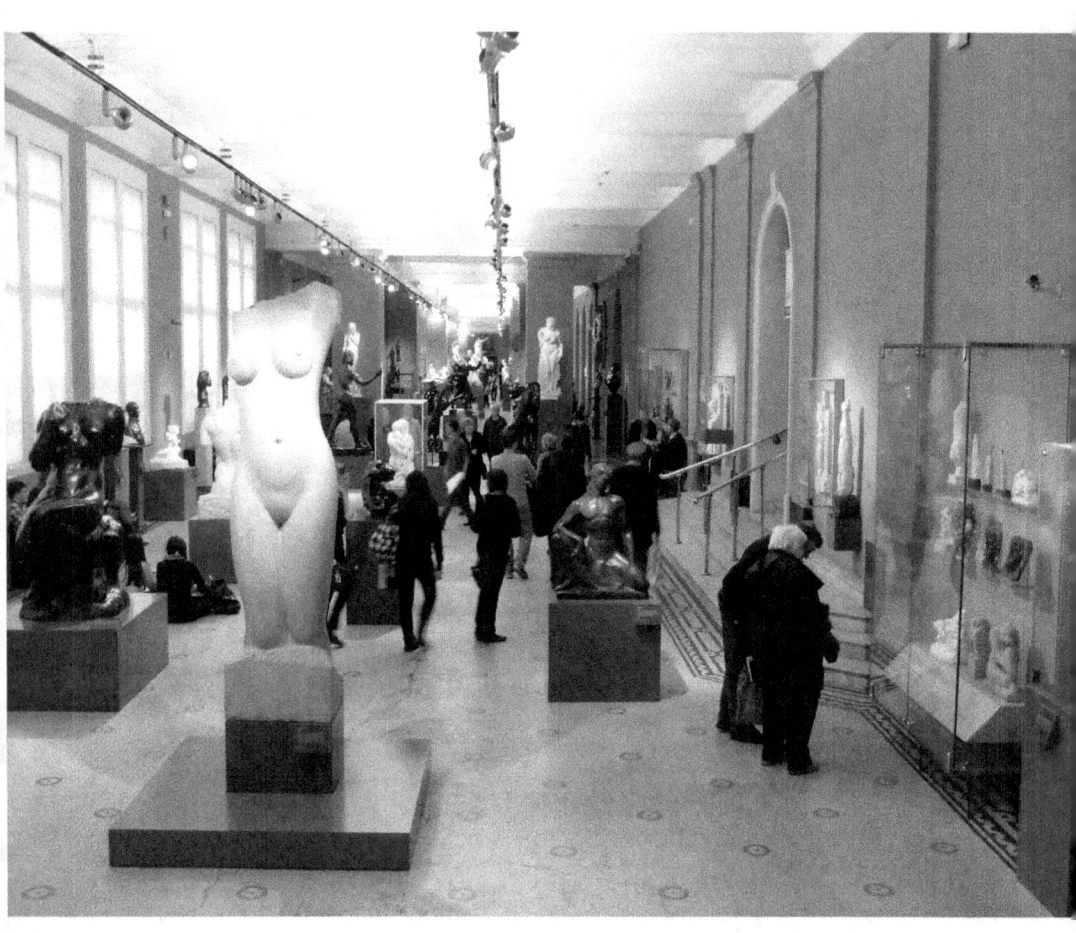

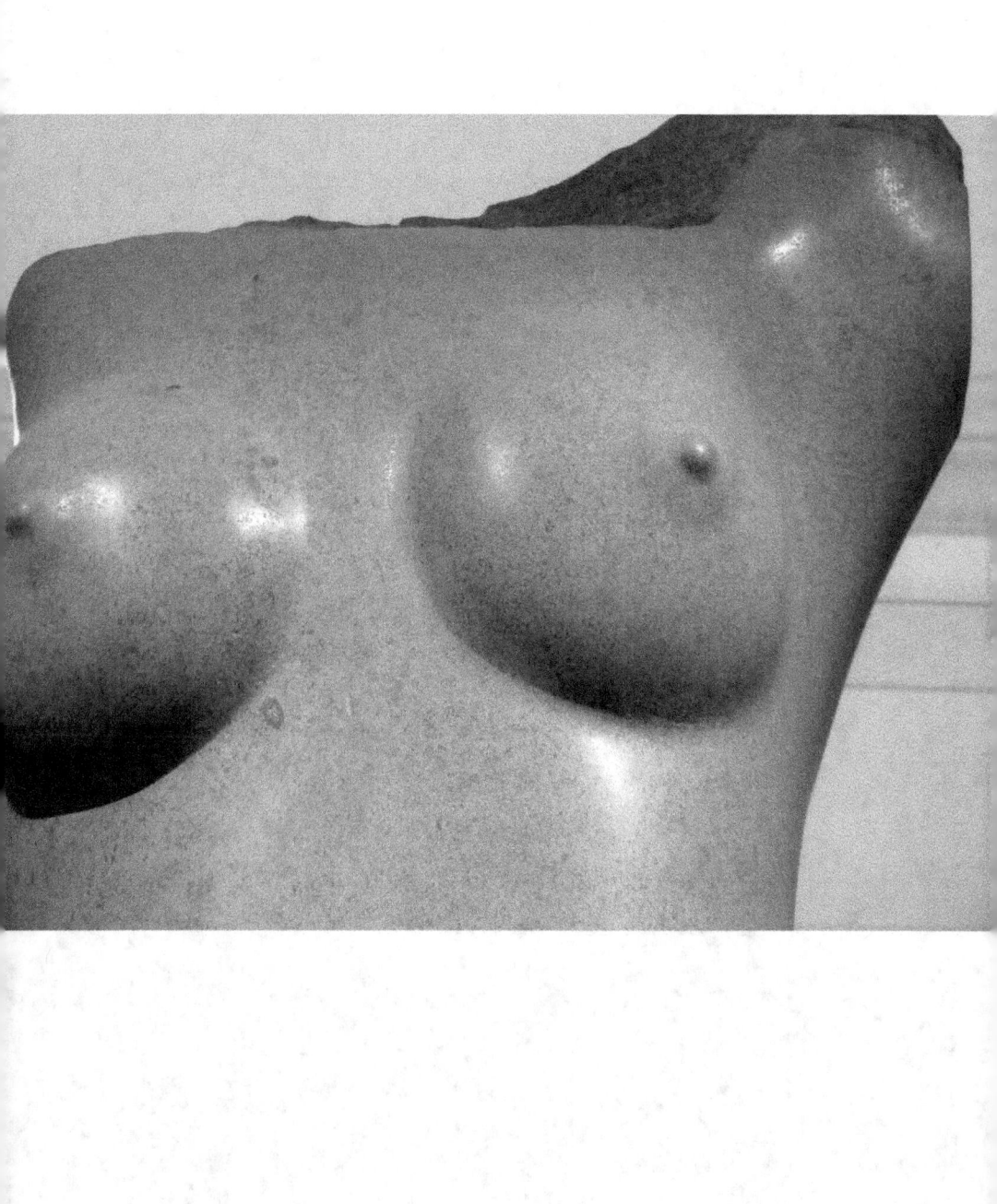

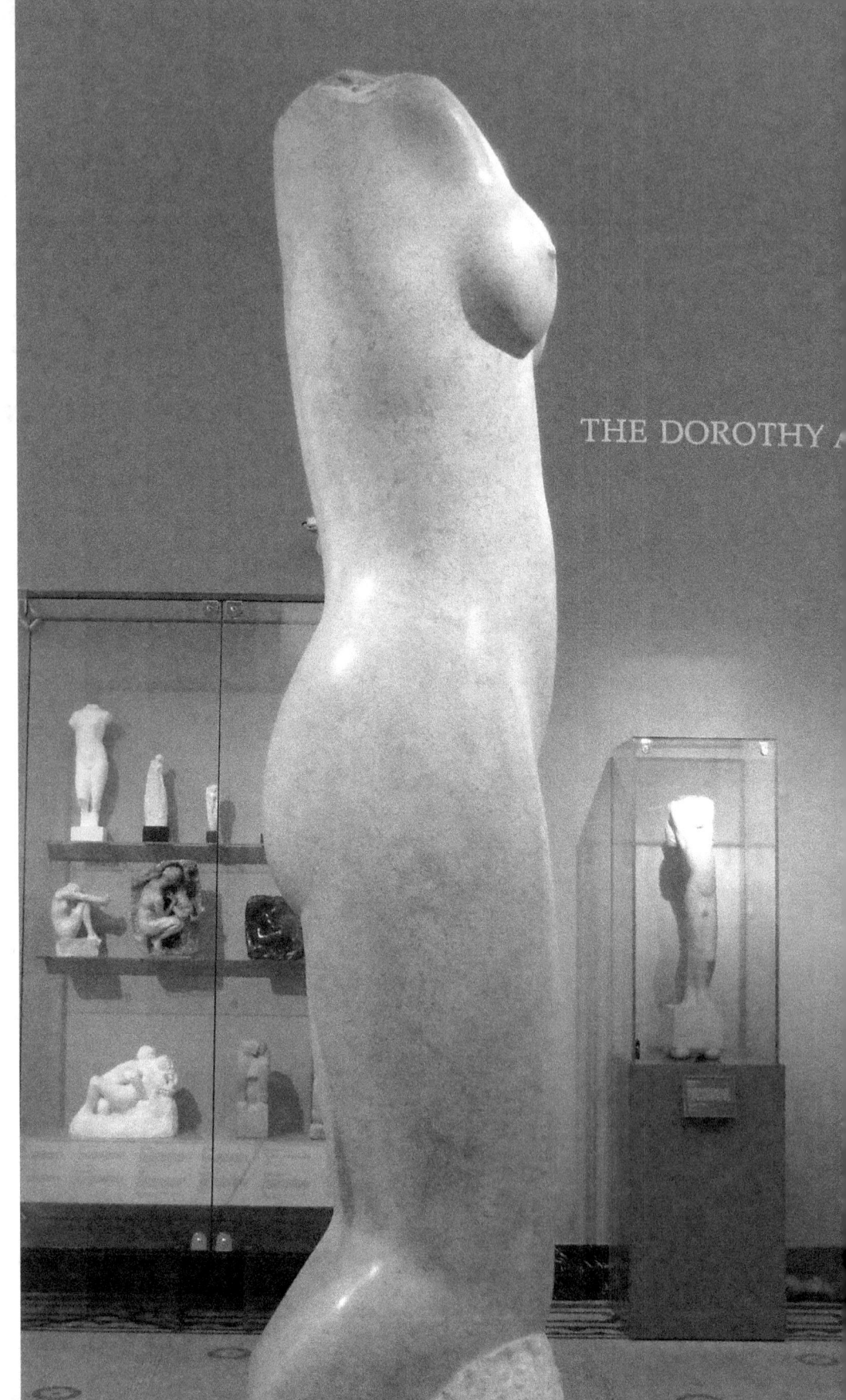

THE DOROTHY A

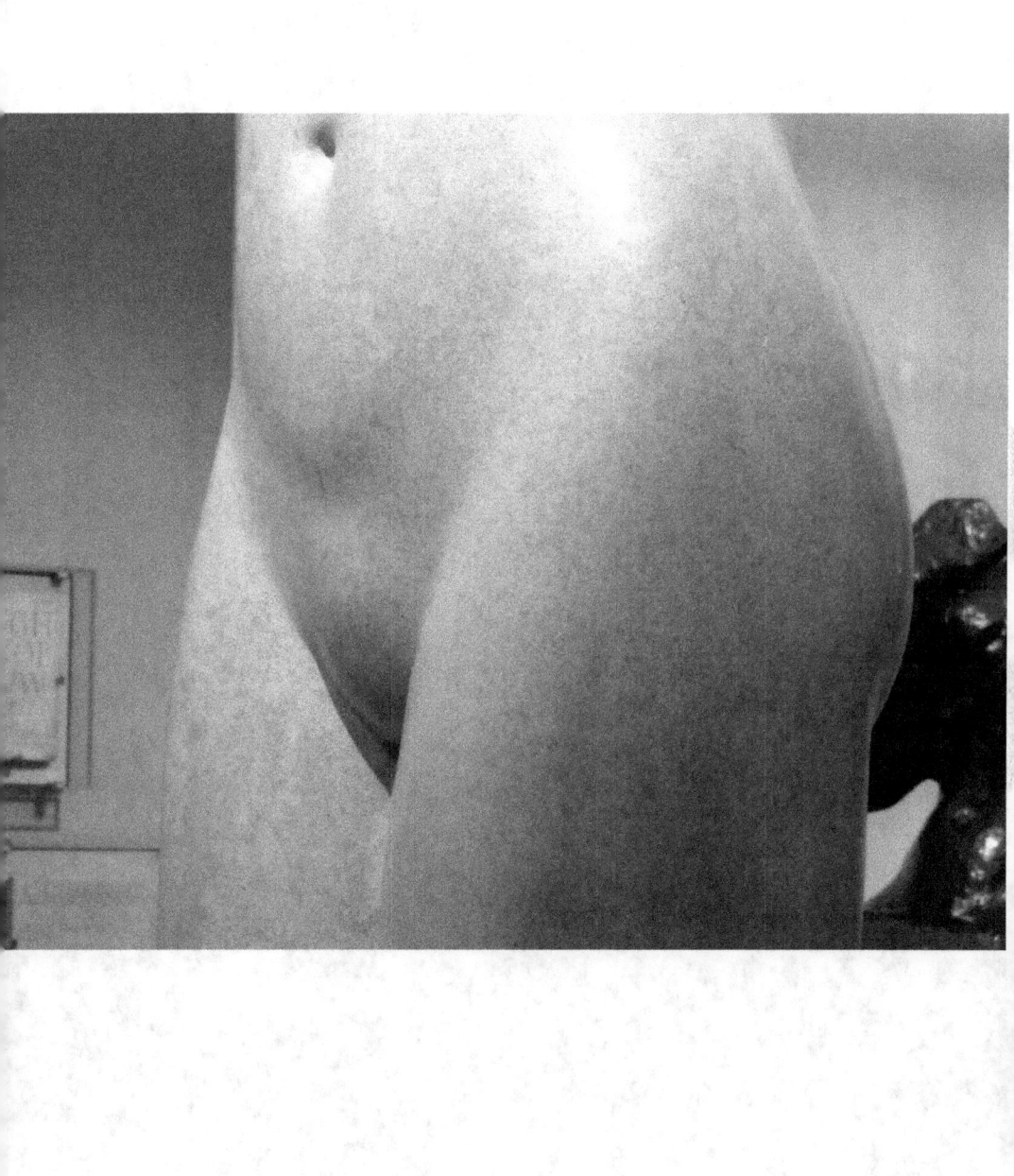

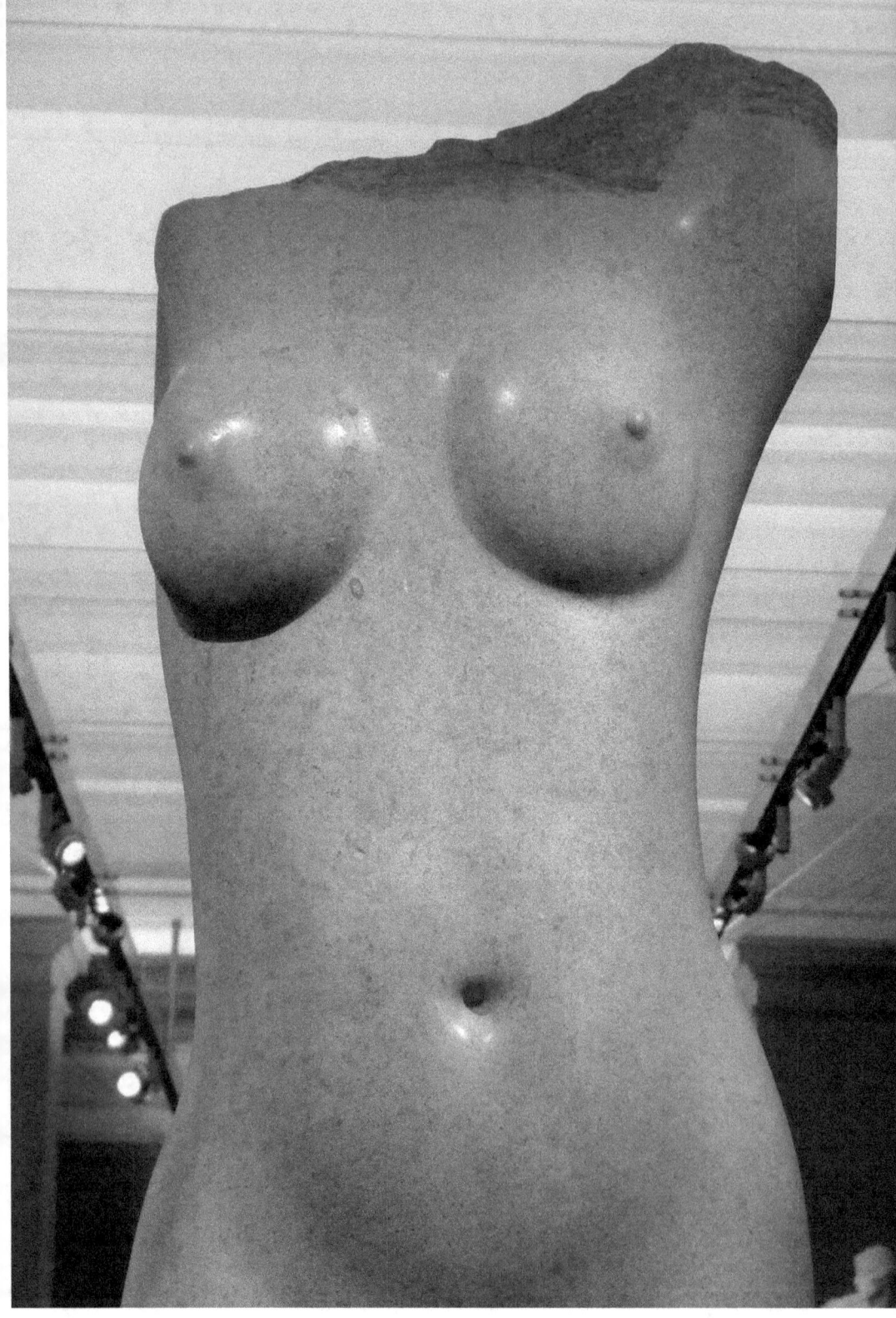

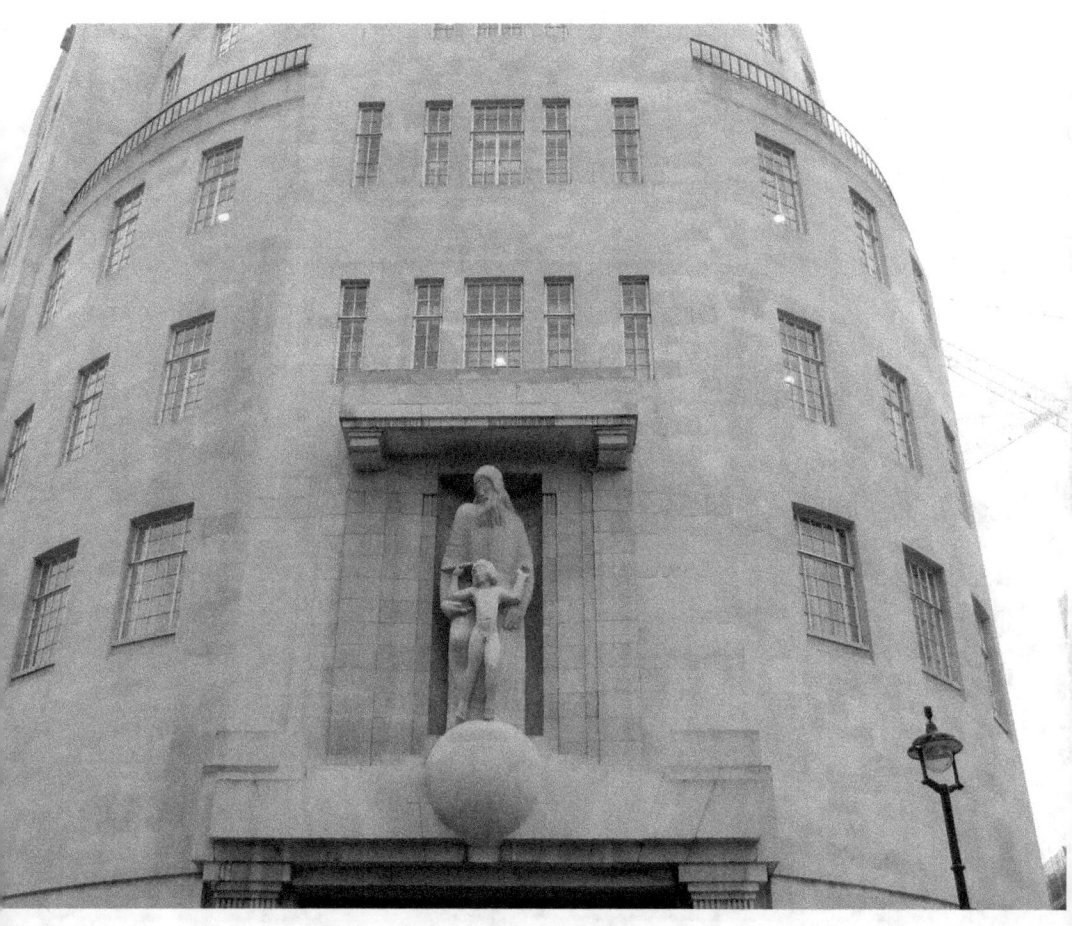

On the following pages, one of Eric Gill's most well-known commissions,
the Prospero piece at the BBC in central London

Photos taken in 2008 by Jeremy Robinson.

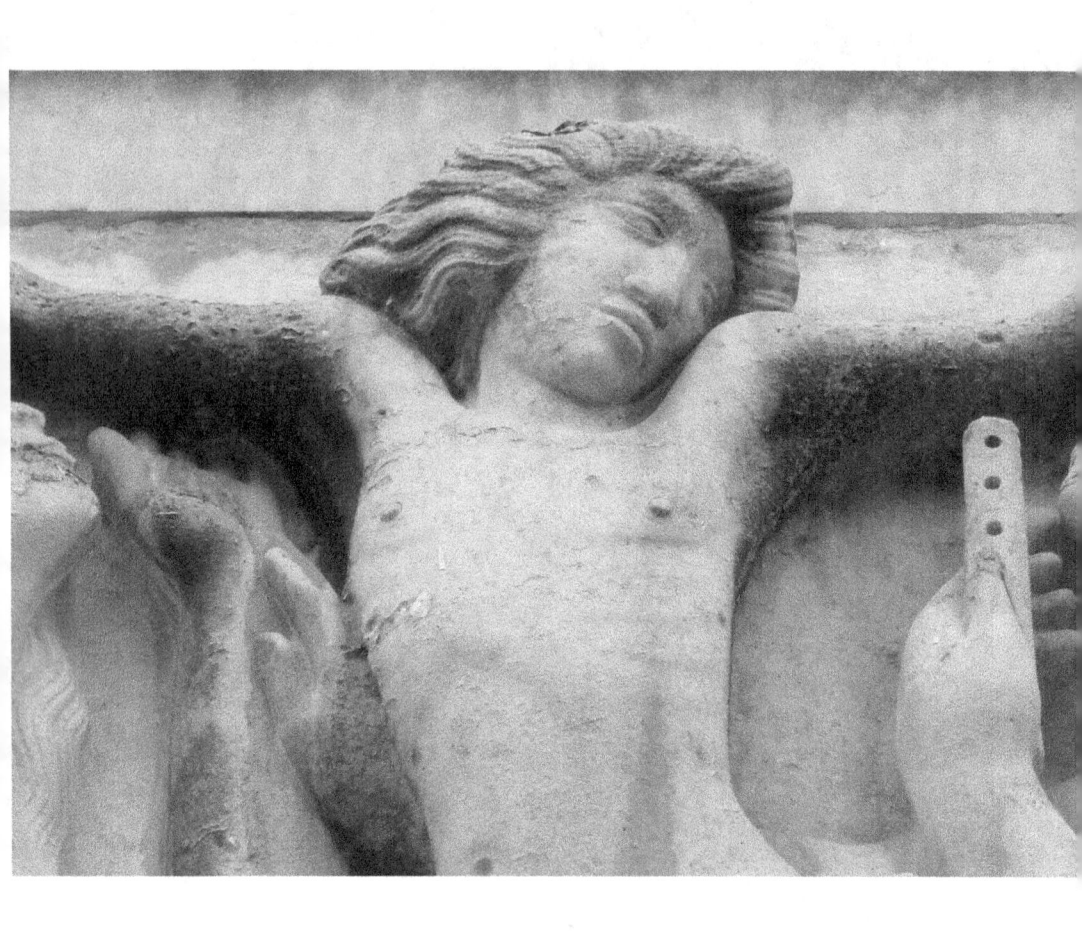

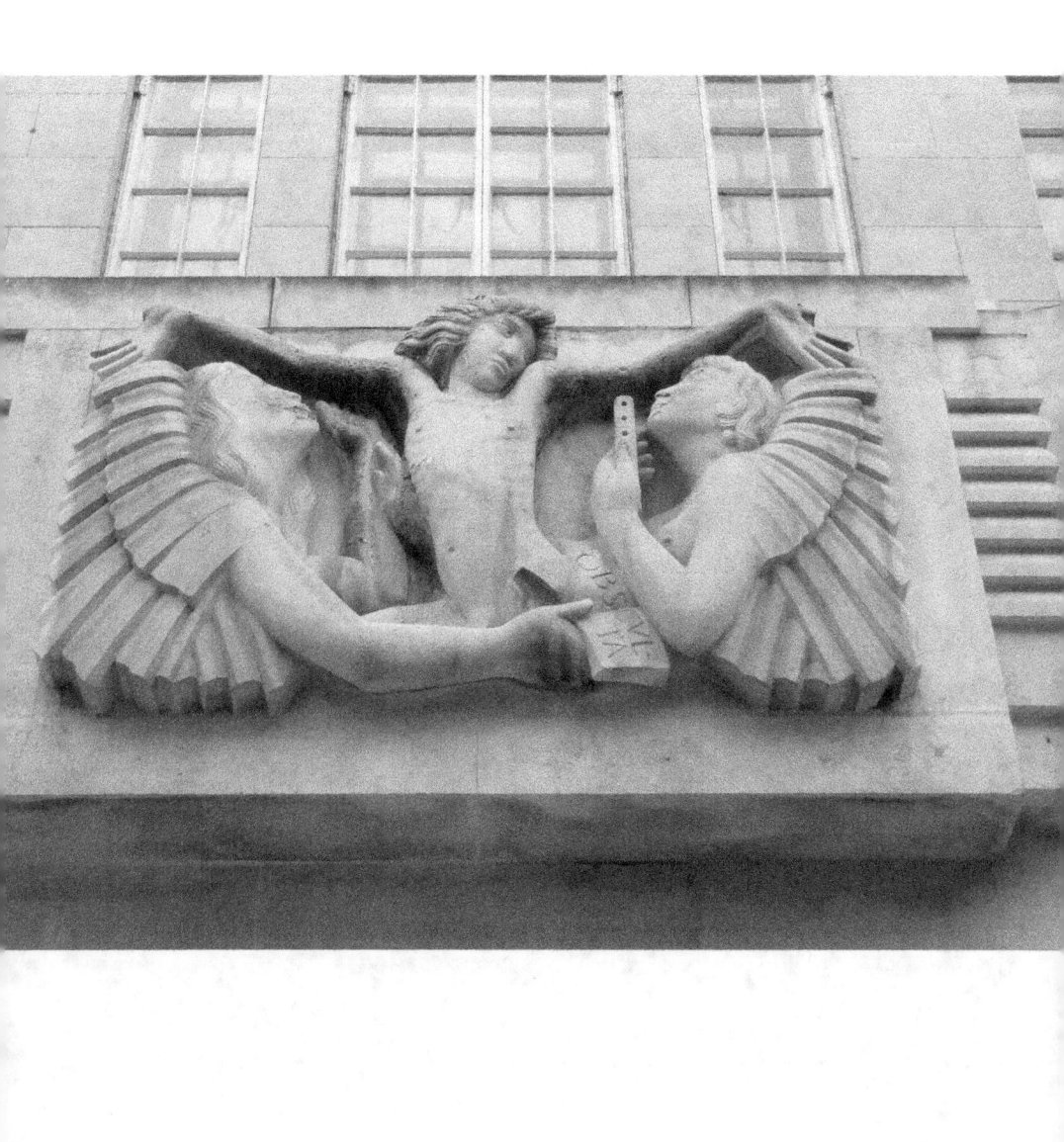

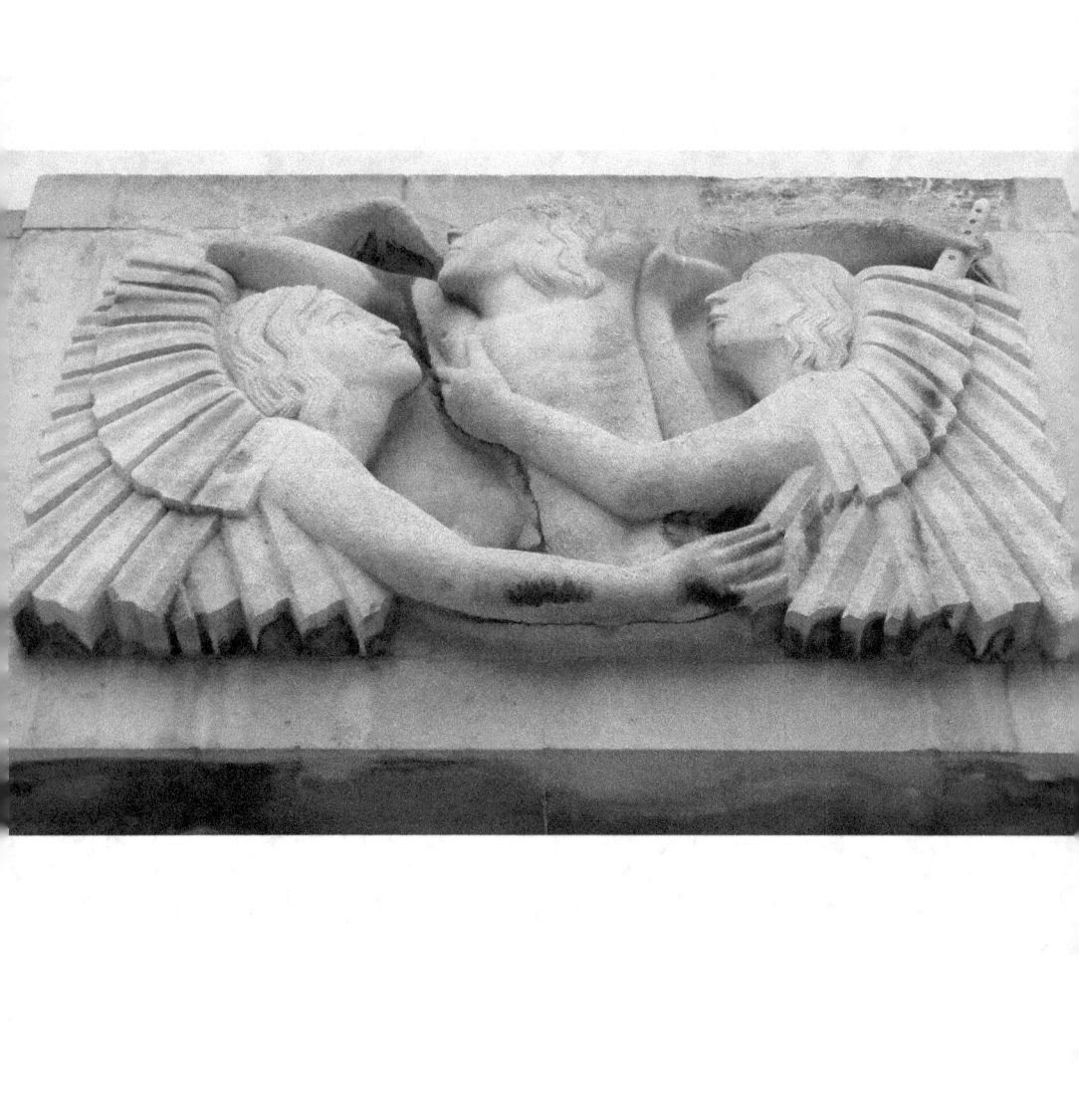

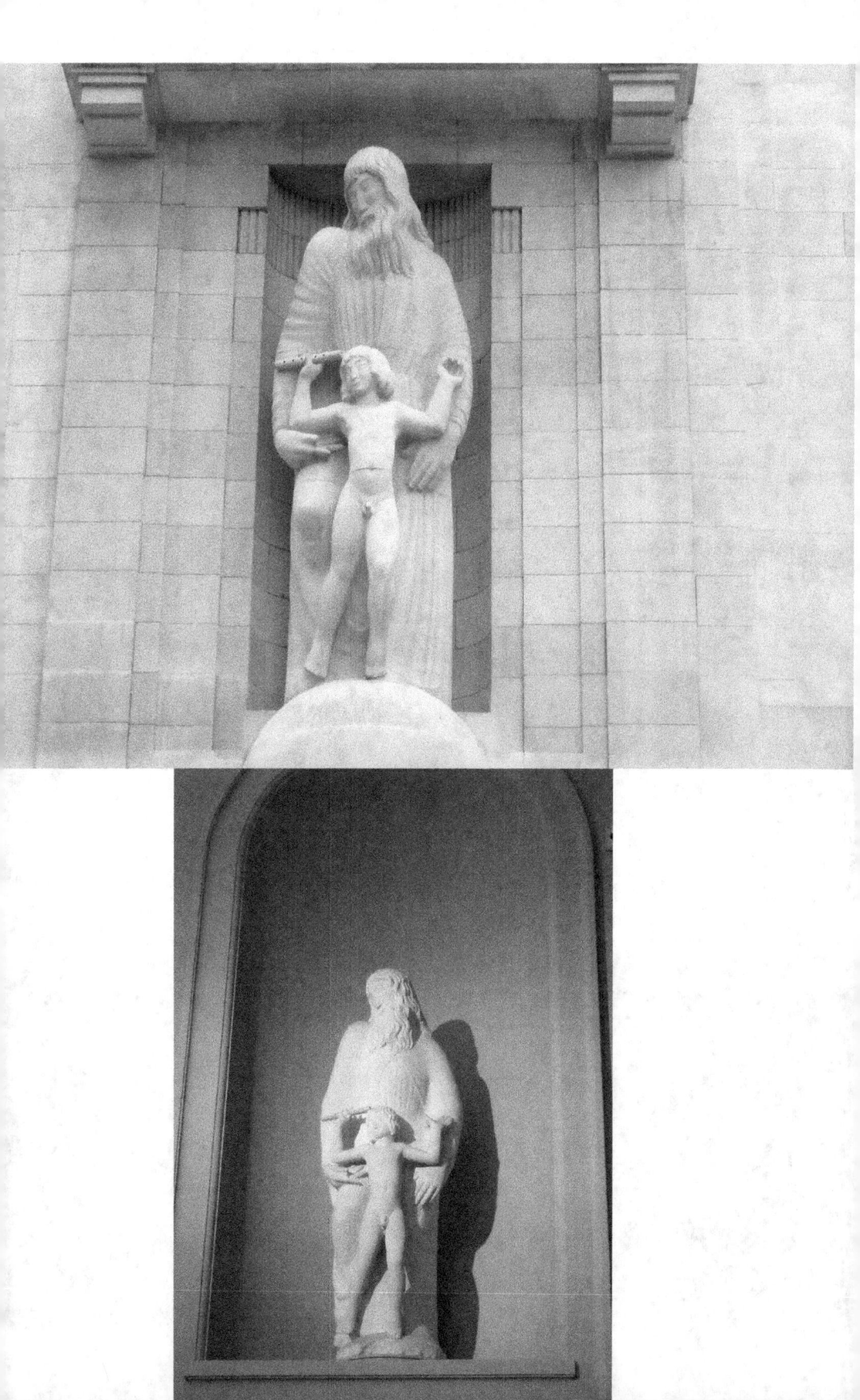

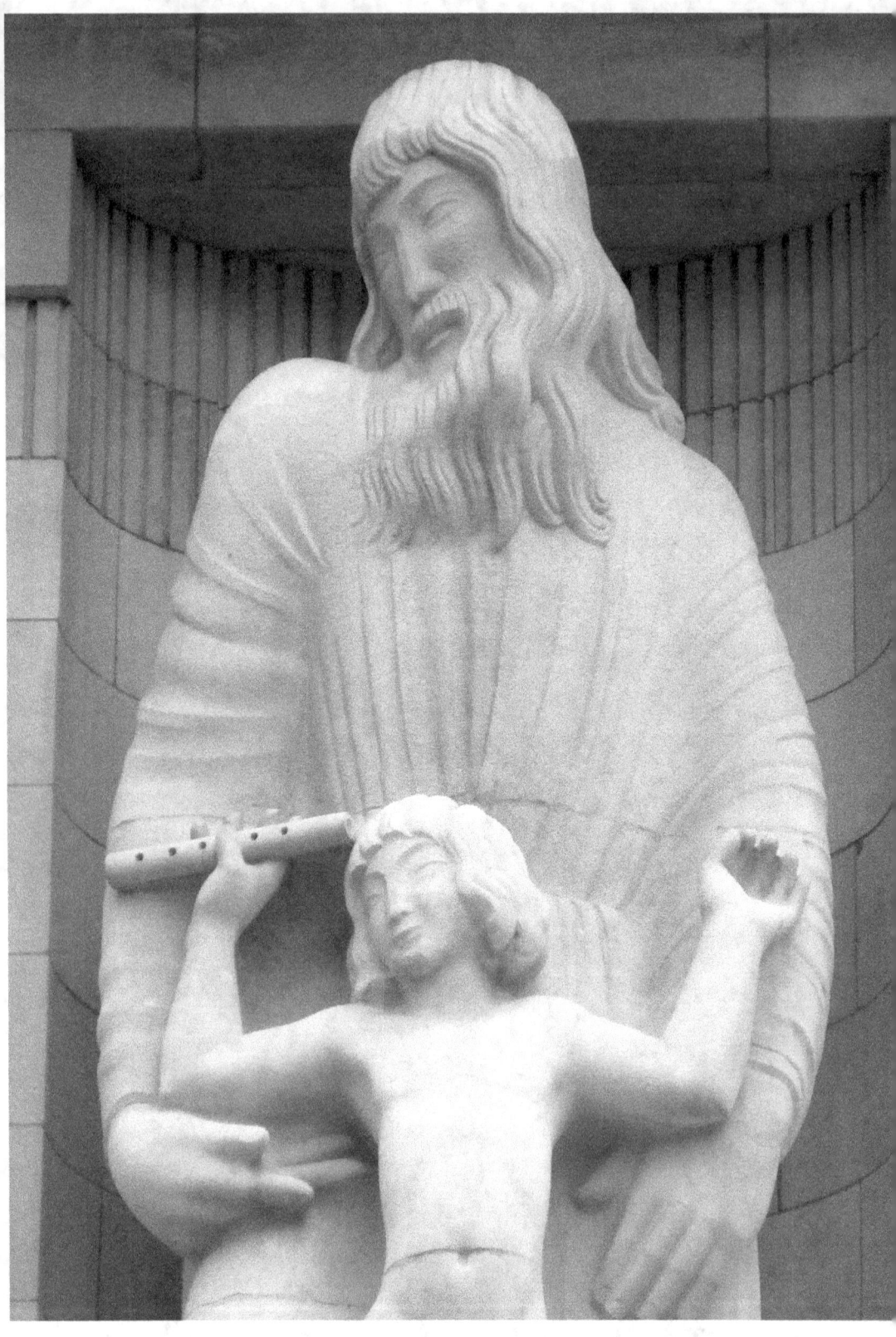

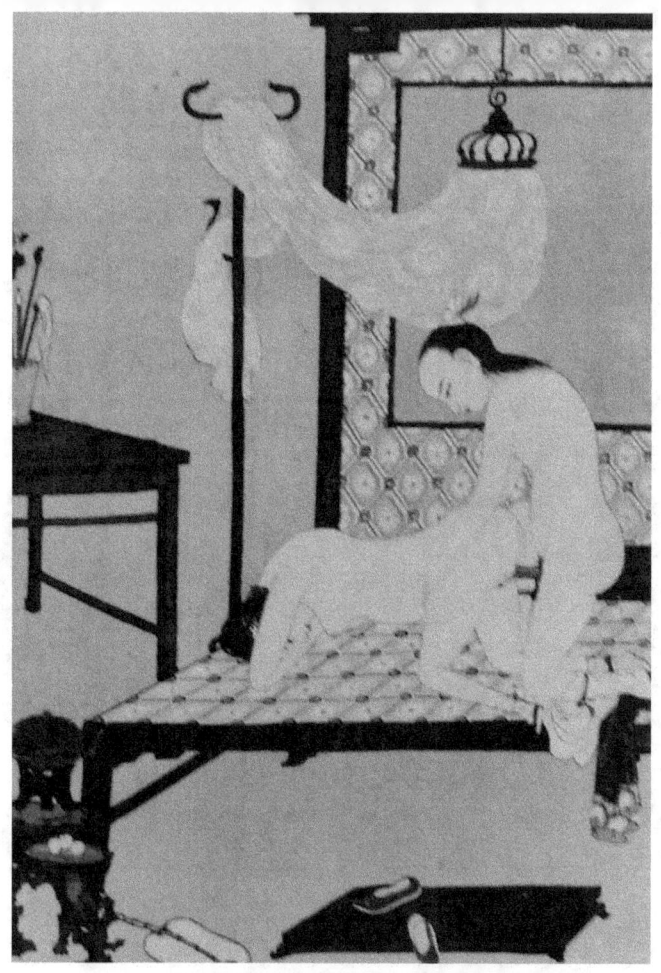

Chinese erotic art: erotic album, above.
Painted scroll, ukiyo-e school, c. 1640, below

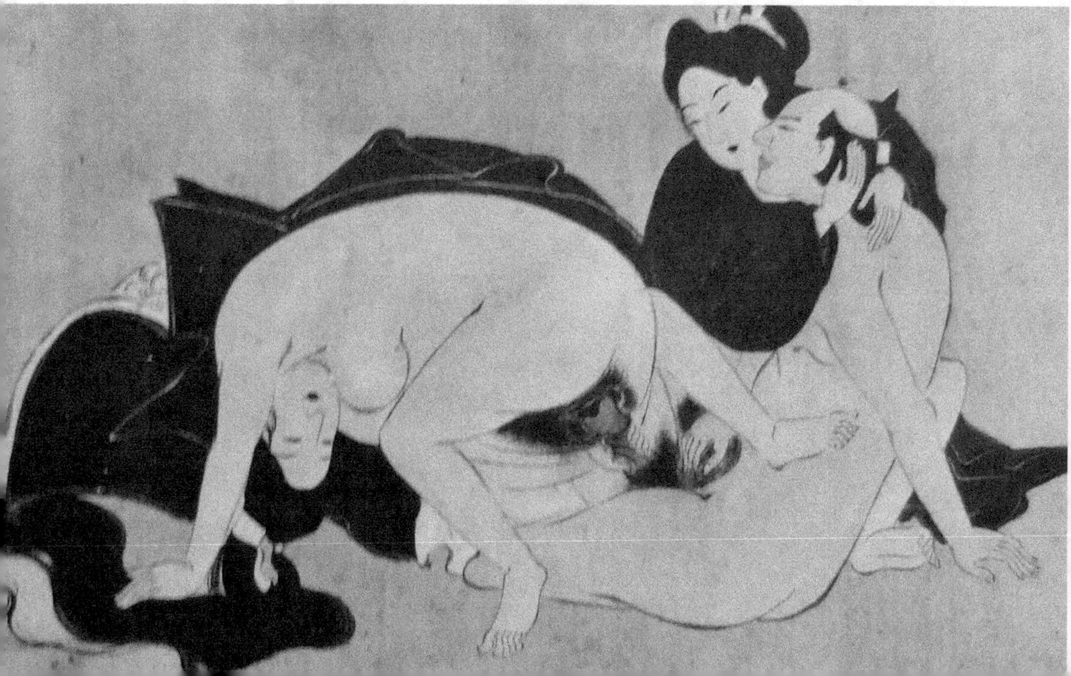

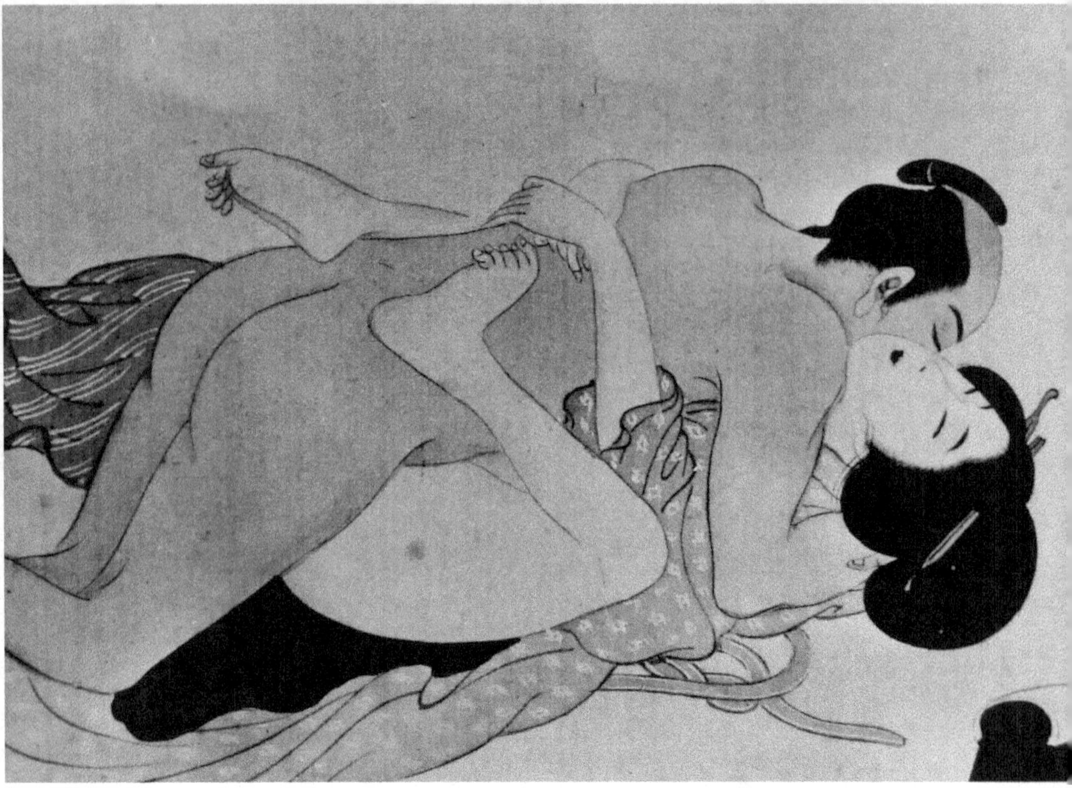

Two Hokusai school pictures: woodblock, 19th century, below.
Hokusai school, c. 1830, above.

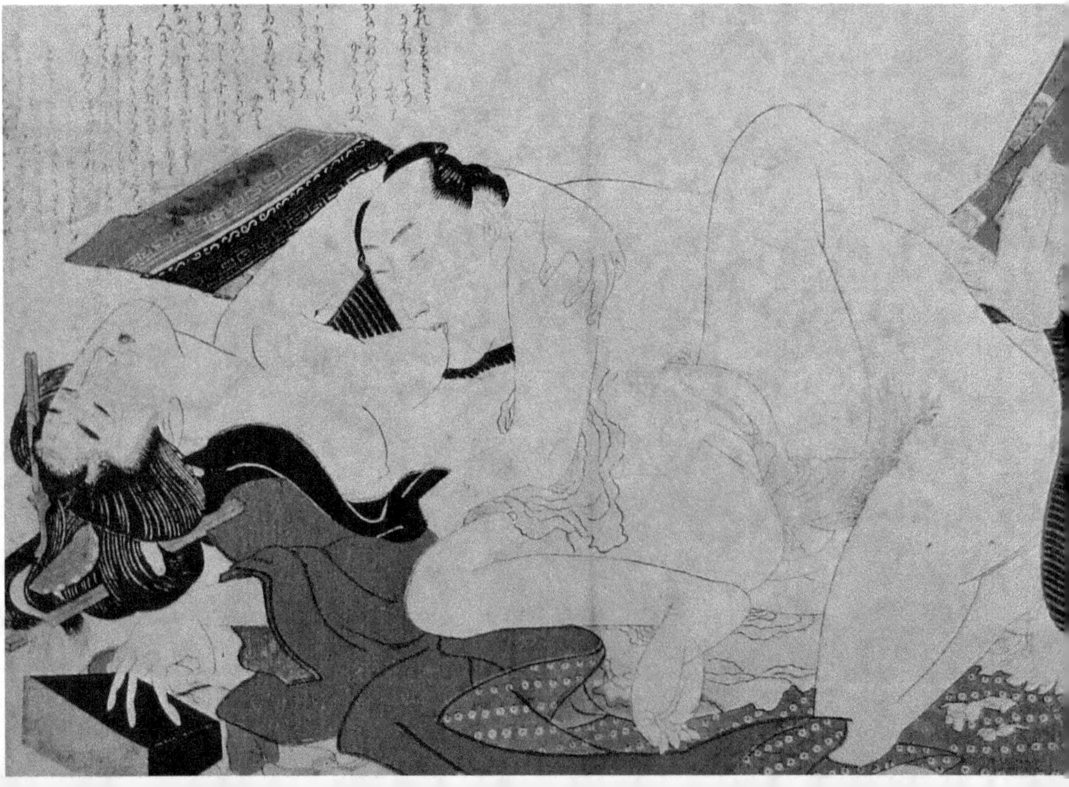

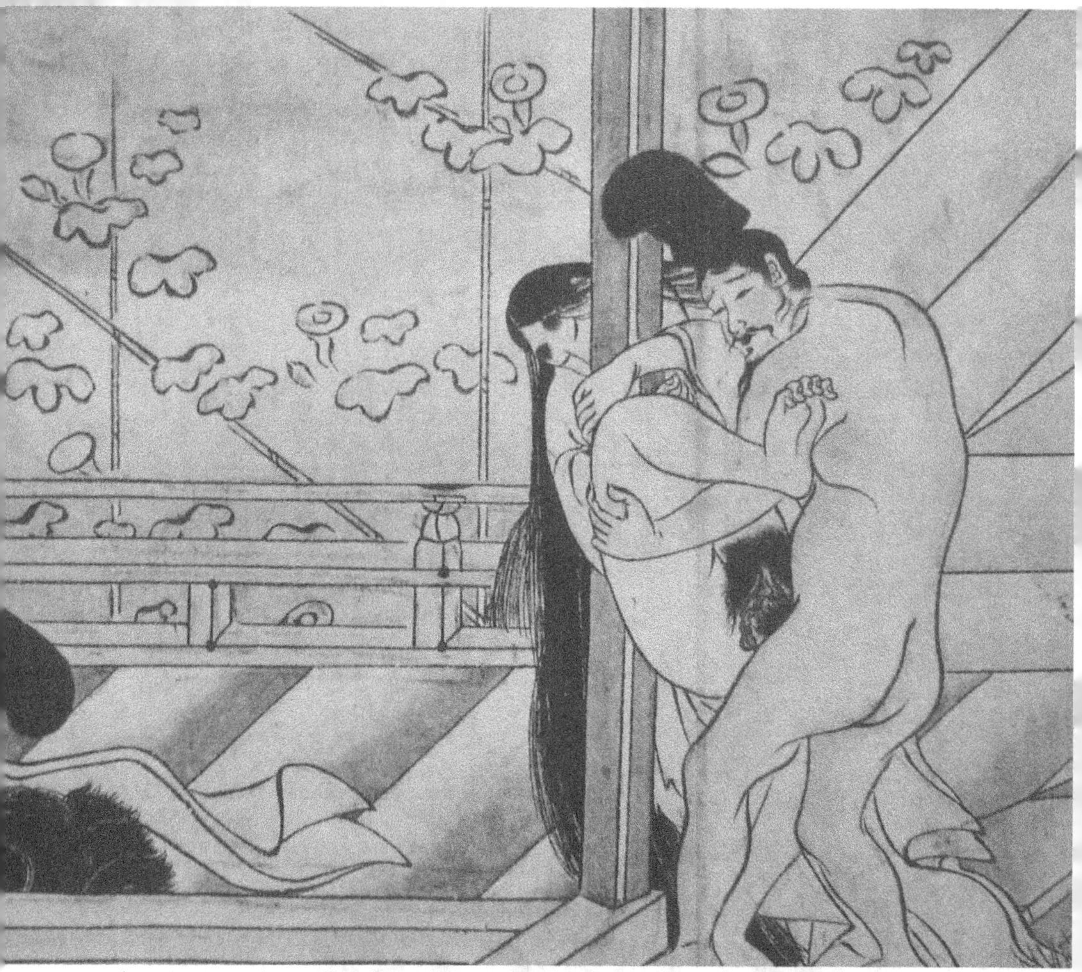

Japanese erotic art. Brushwood fence scroll, 1800s, above. Woodblock, below

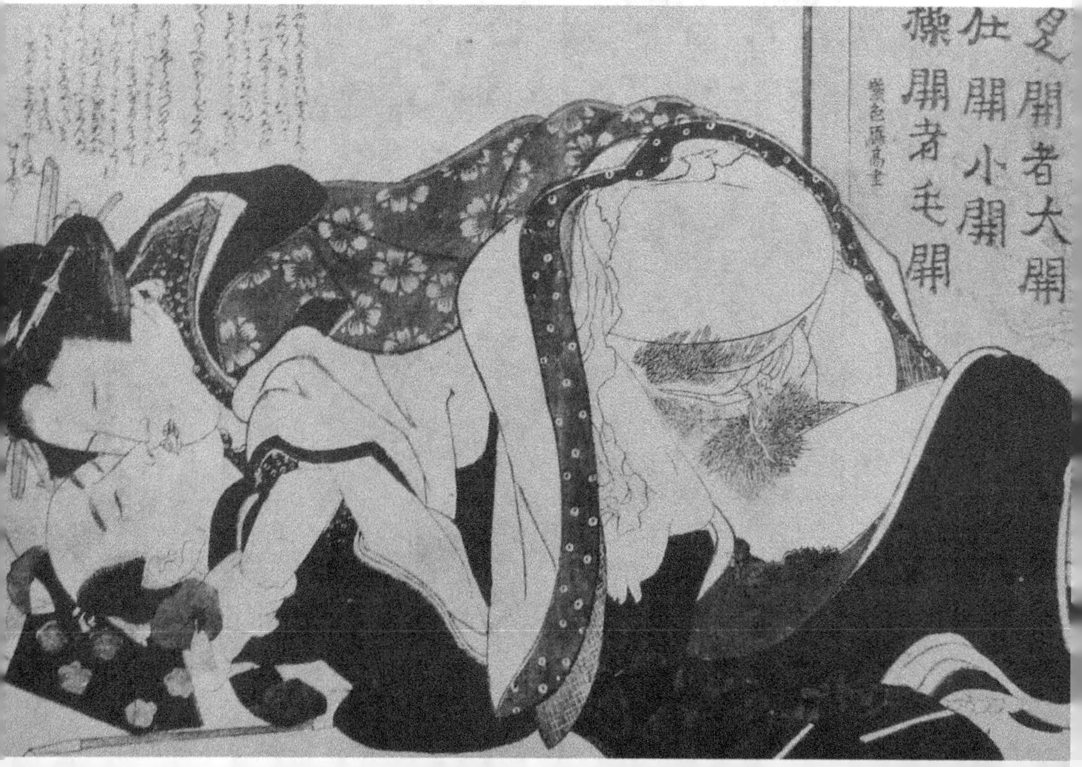

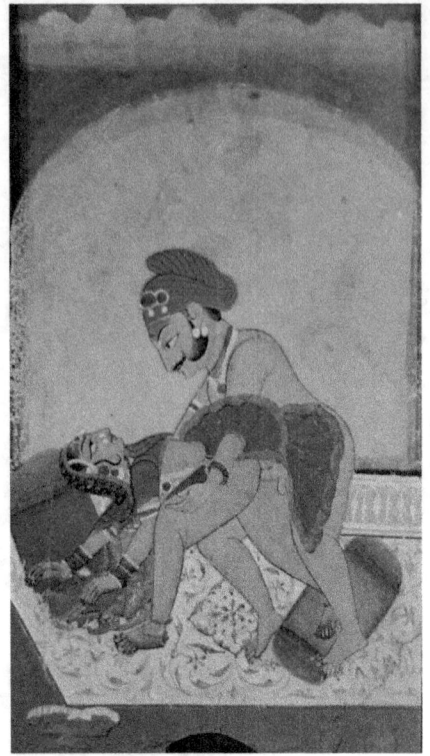

Indian erotic art:
Rajput, late 18th century, above.
Mogul style, 18th century, below.

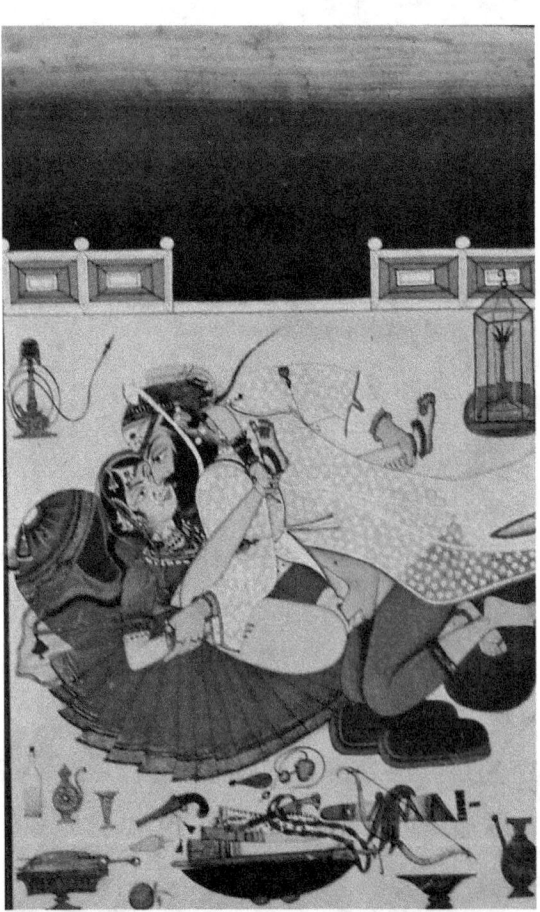

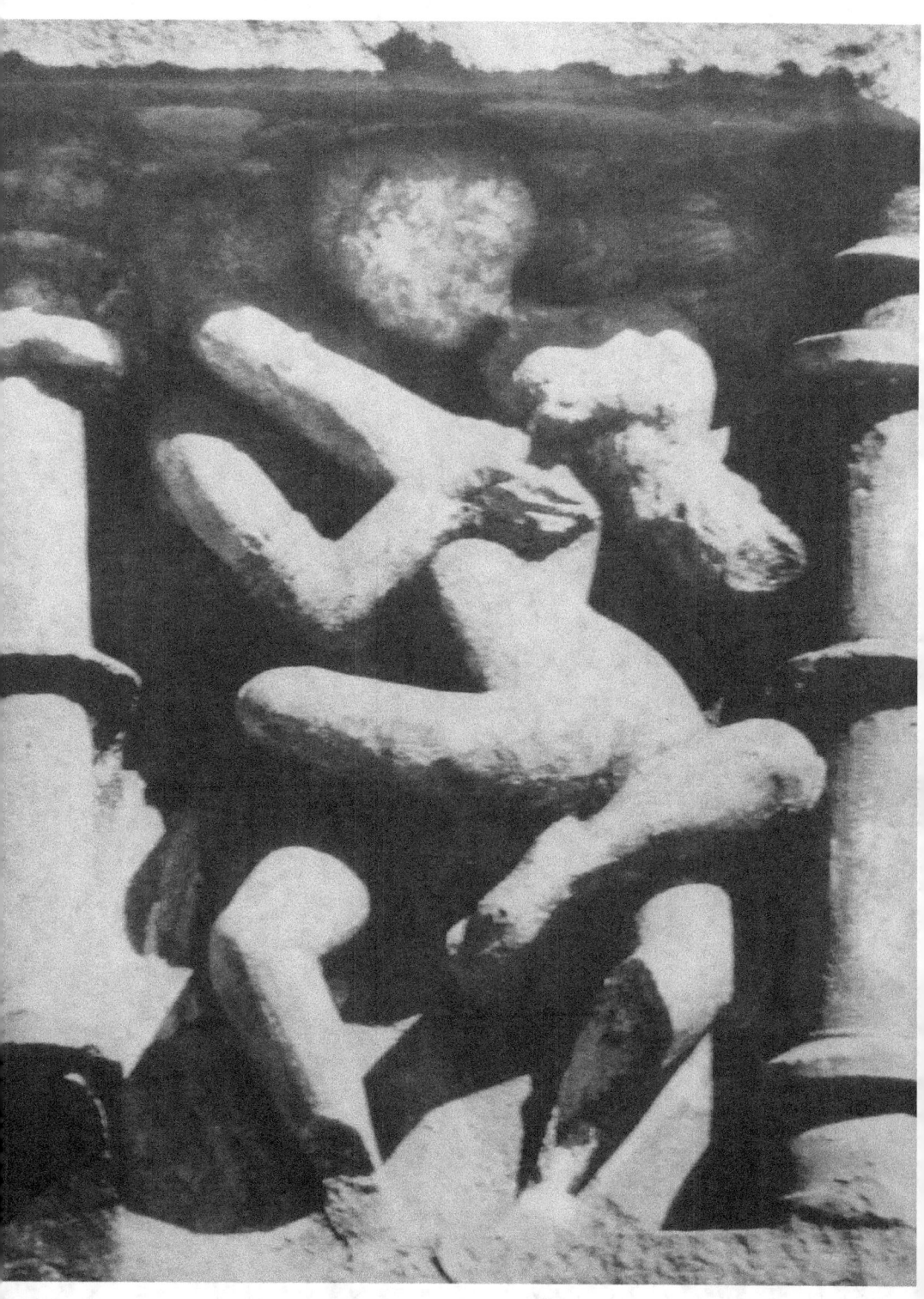

Khajuraho temple, 9th-11th century, North India

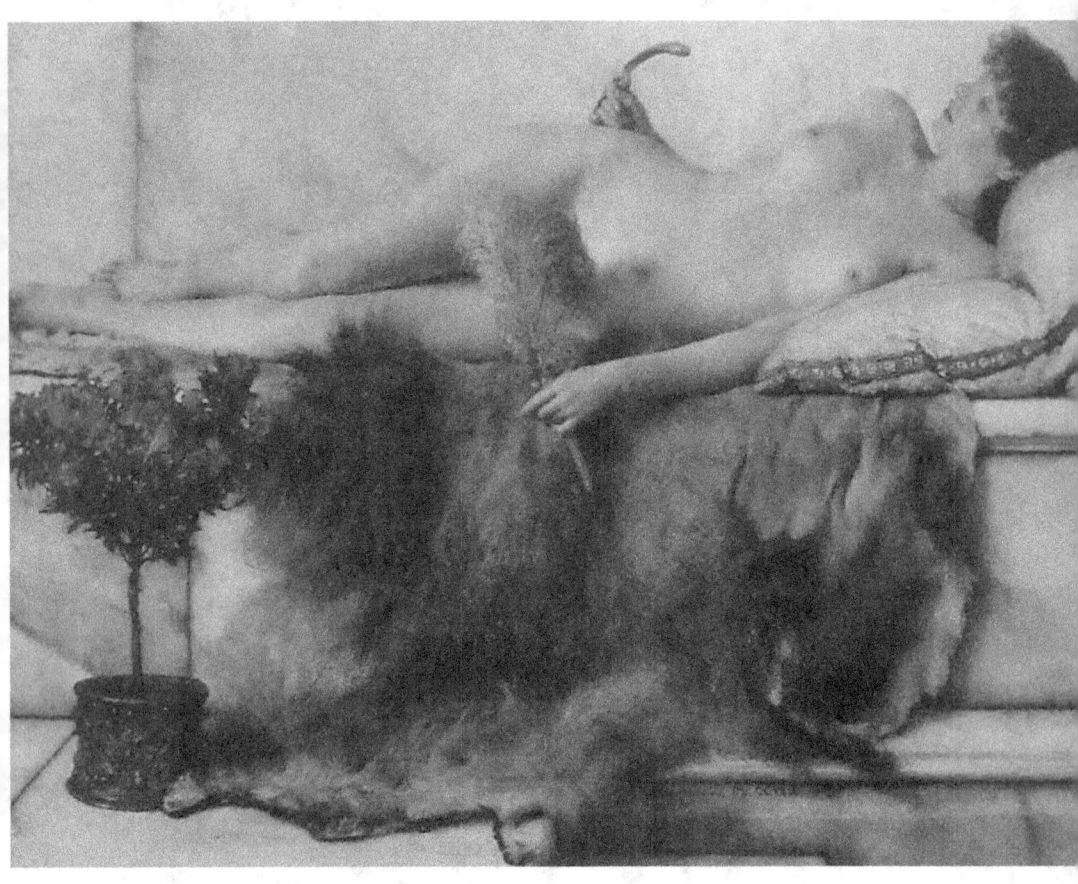

Lawrence Aldma-Tadema, In the Tepidarium, 1881, Lady Lever Art Gallery, Liverpool

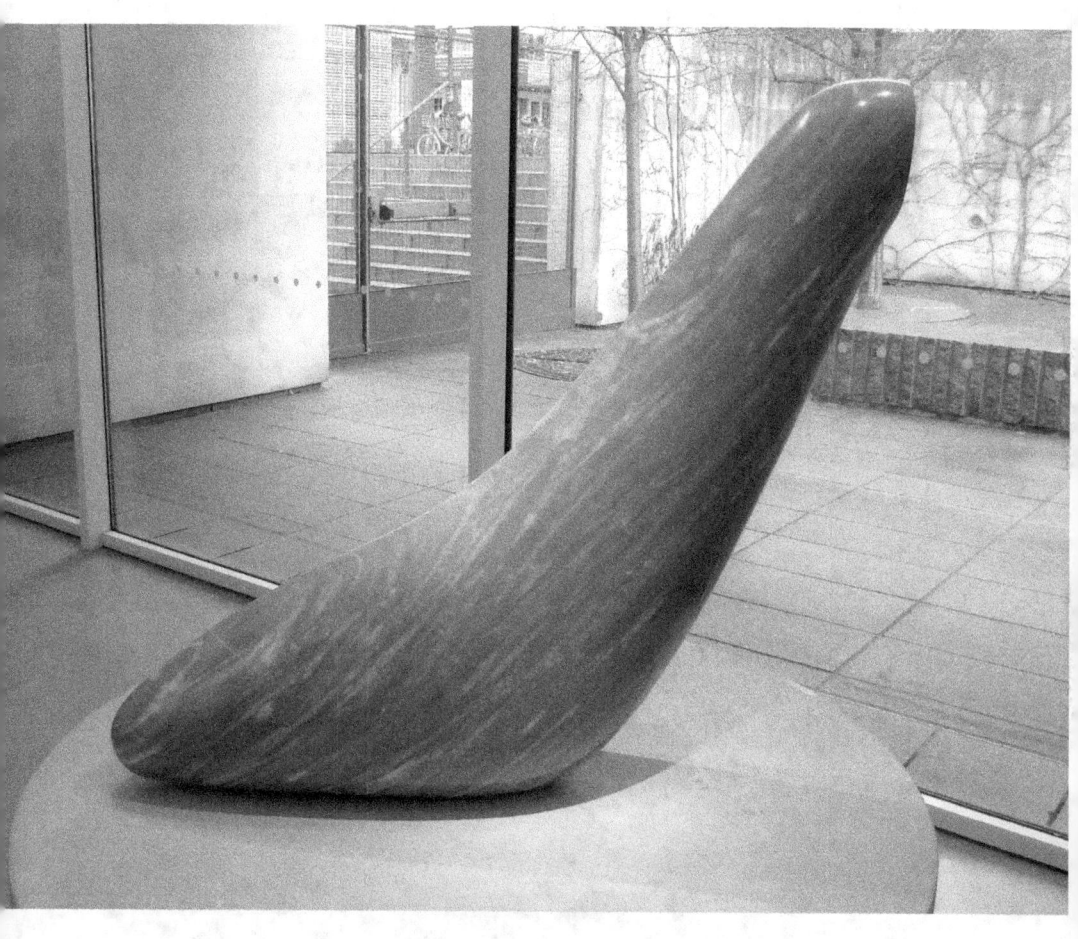

Constantin Brancusi

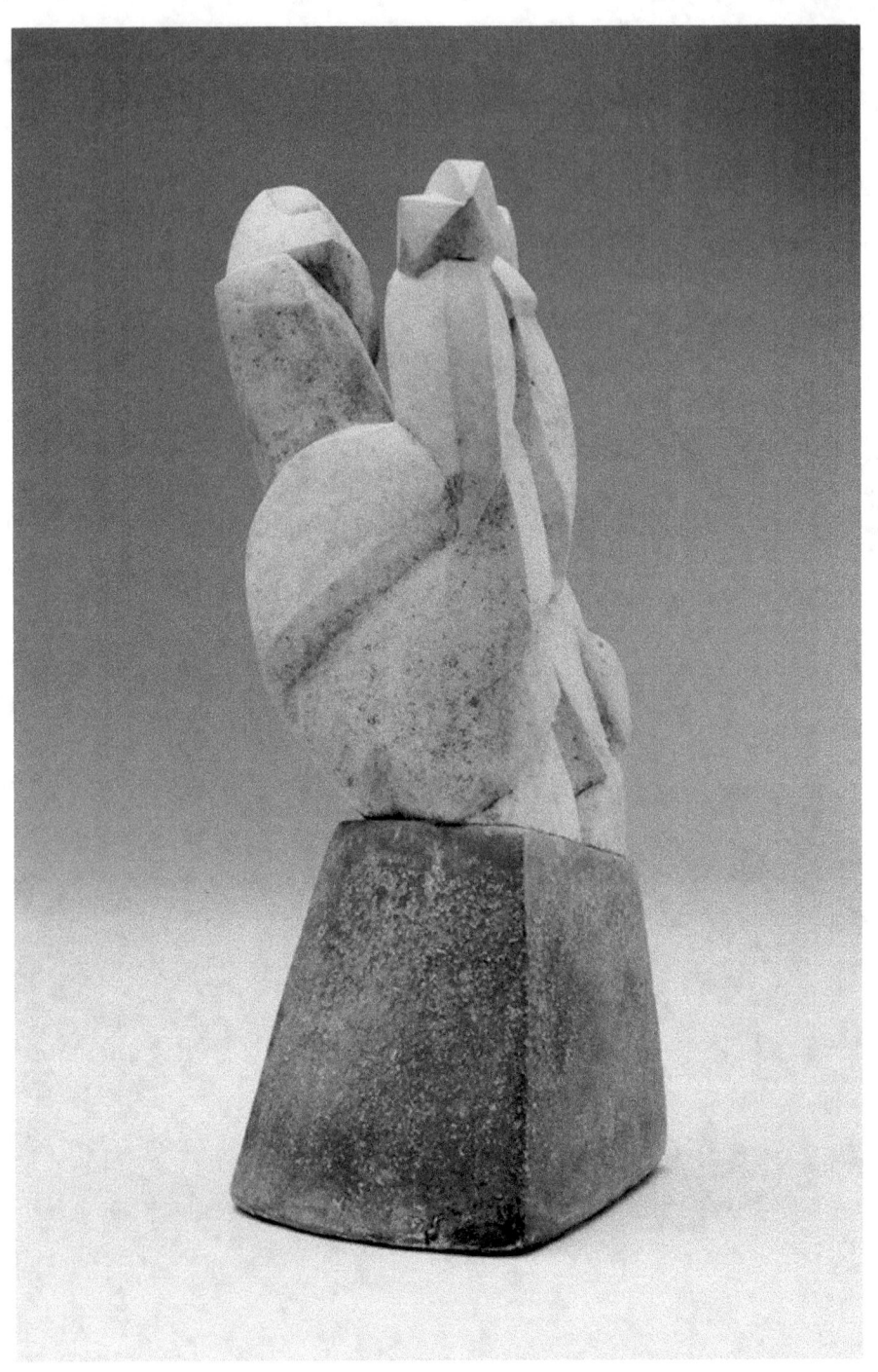

Henri Gaider-Brzeska,

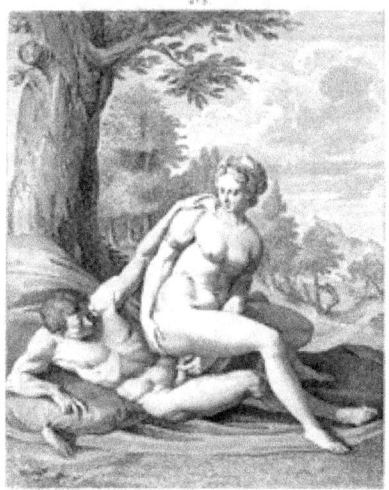

ANGÉLIQUE ET MÉDOR.

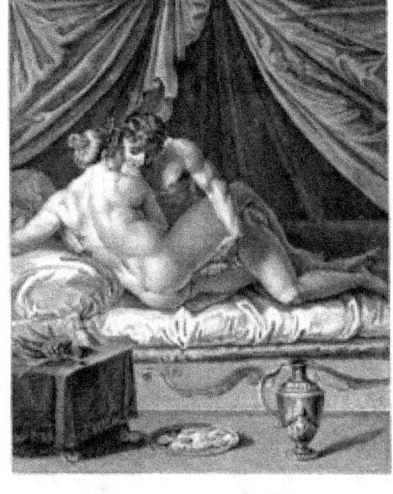

ANTOINE ET CLÉOPATRE.

Agostino Carracci, I Modi, 1524

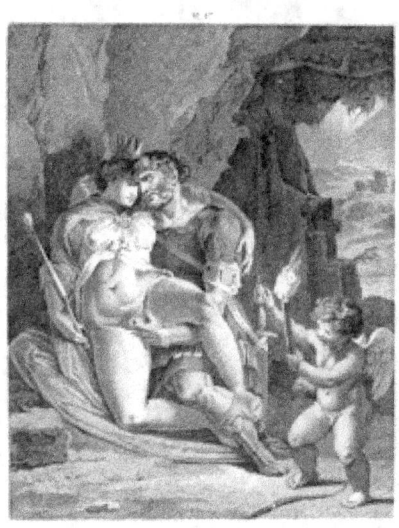

ÉNÉE ET DIDON.

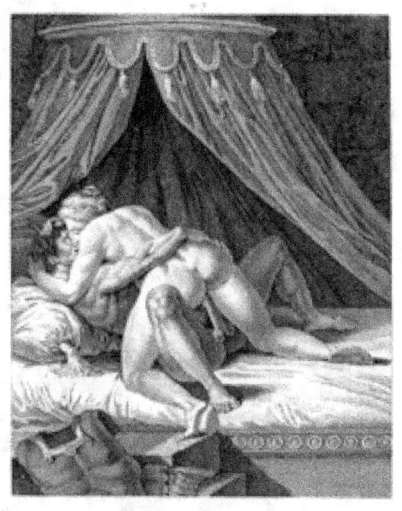

MARS ET VÉNUS.

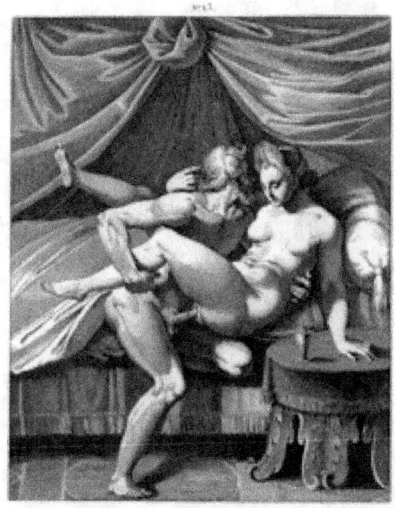

JUPITER ET JUNON.

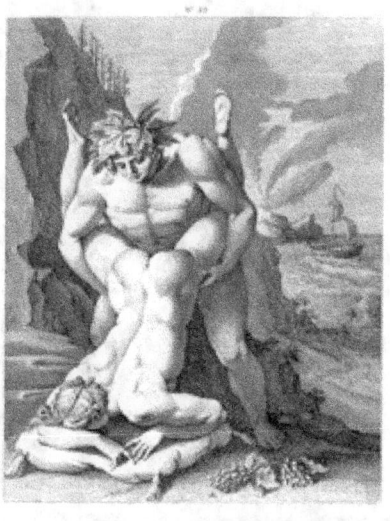

BACHUS ET ARIANE.

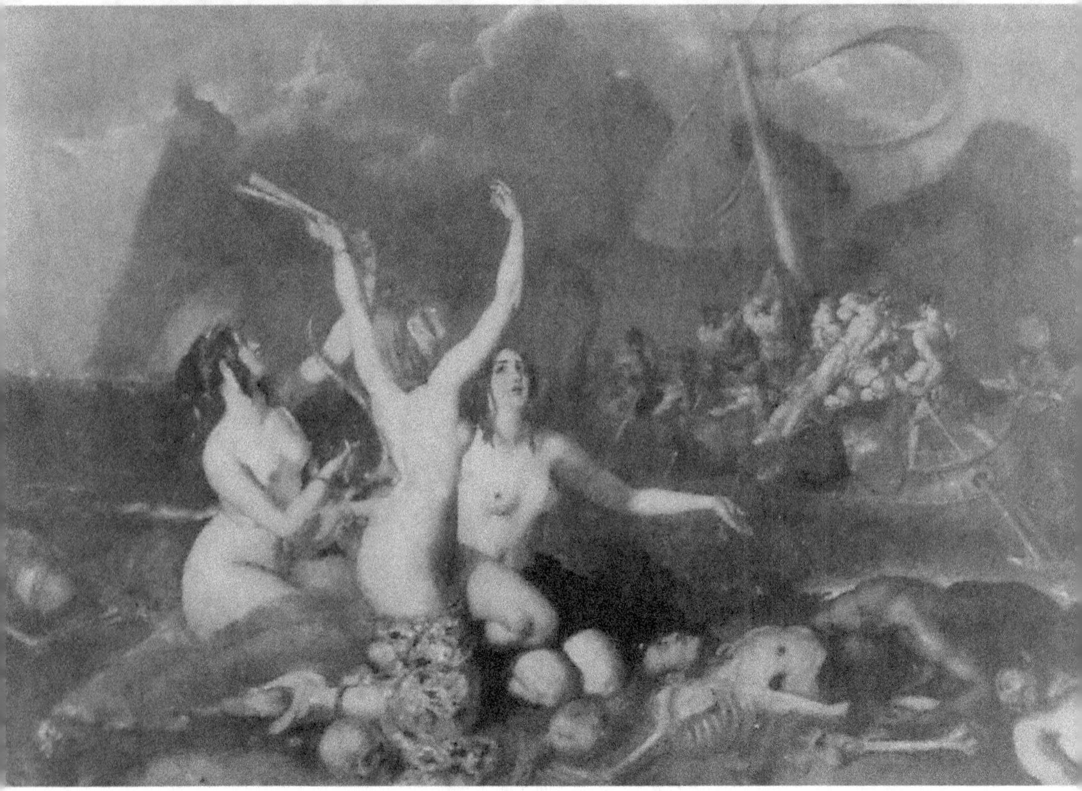

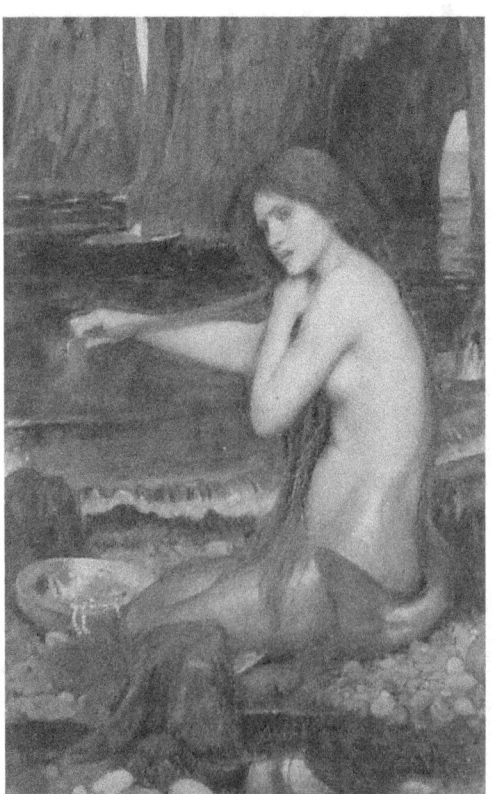

William Etty's The Sirens and Ulysses, 1837, Manchester. above.

J.W. Waterhouse, A Mermaid, 1901, Royal Academy London, below.

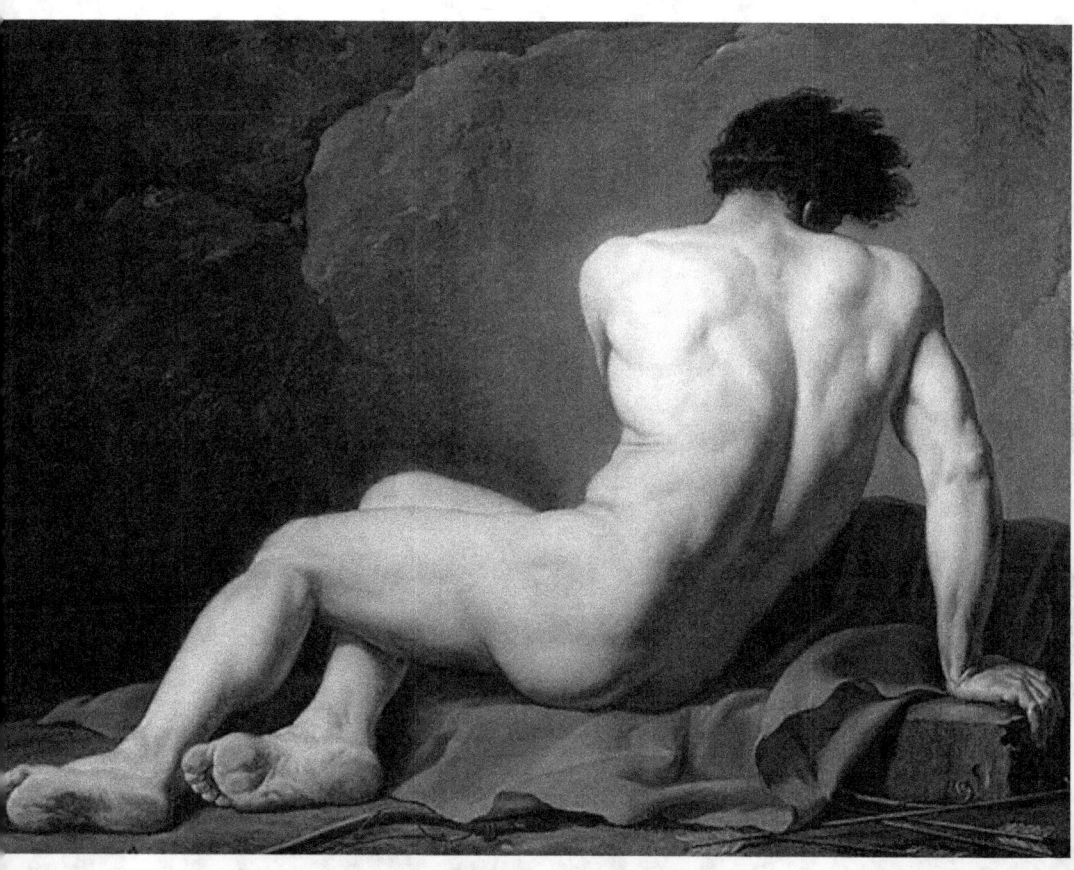

A classical French male nude painting
by Jacques-Louis David (known as Patrocles)

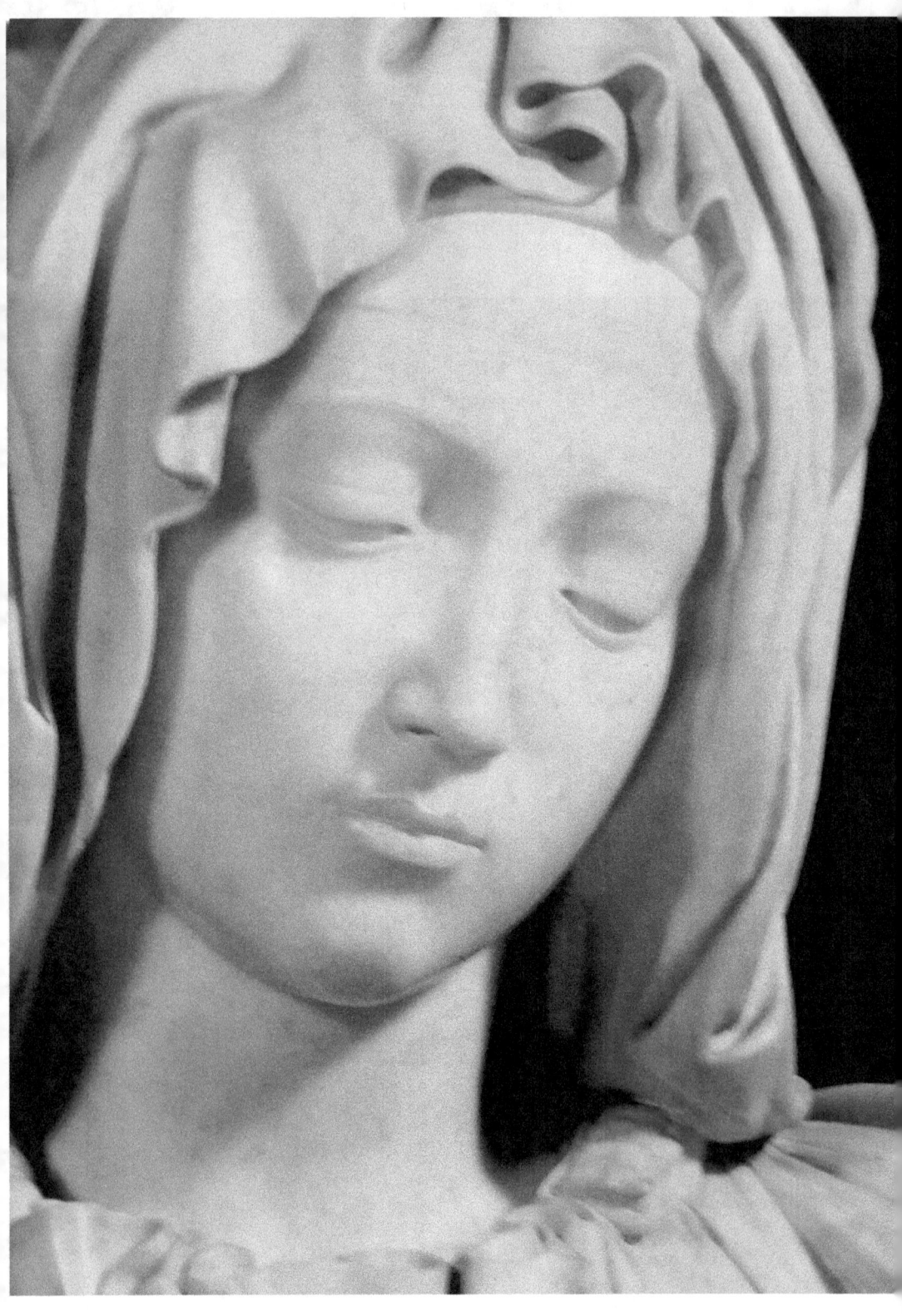

Michelangelo, Pietà, detail, Vatican, Rome

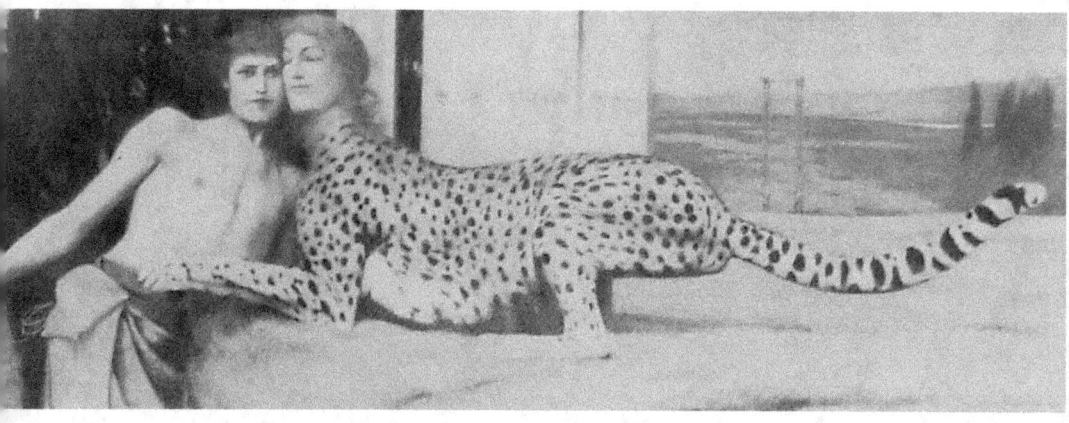

Franz Knopff, Caresses of the Sphinx, 1896, above.
Gustav Klimt, The Bride, 1917-18 (unfinished), below.

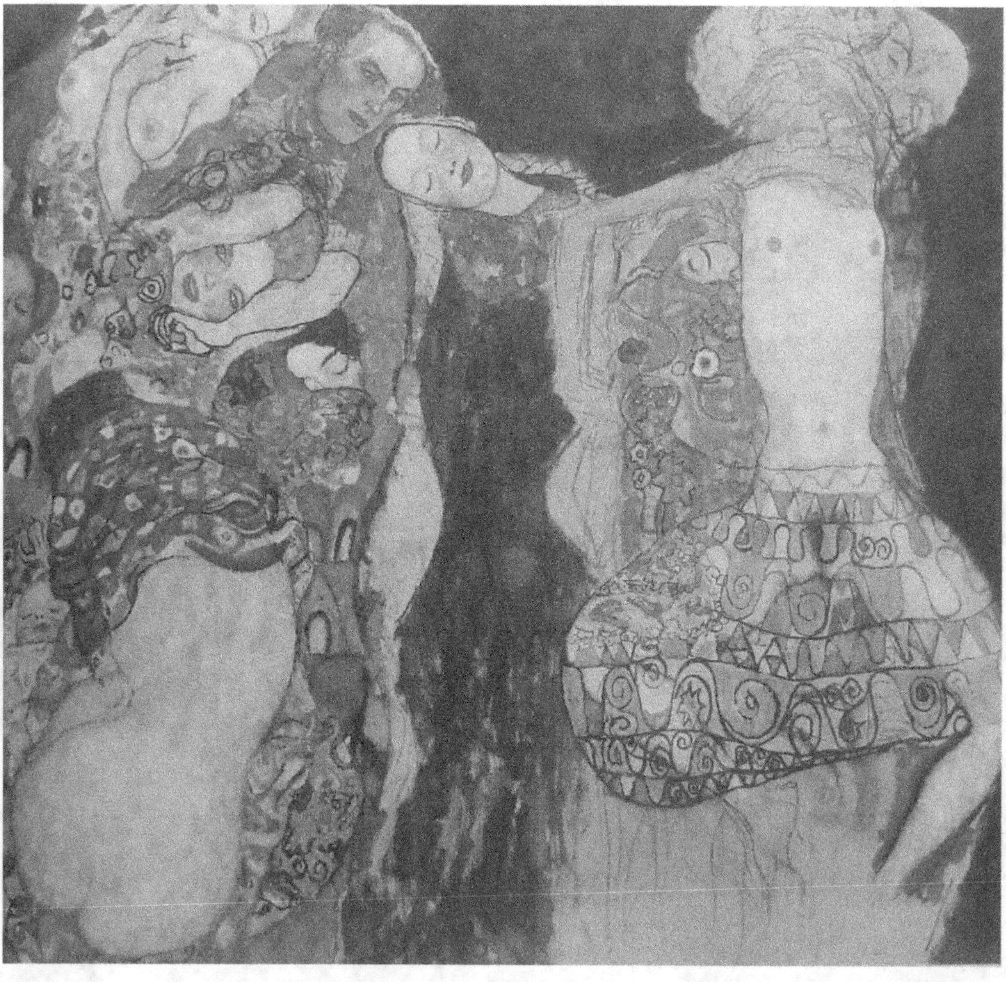

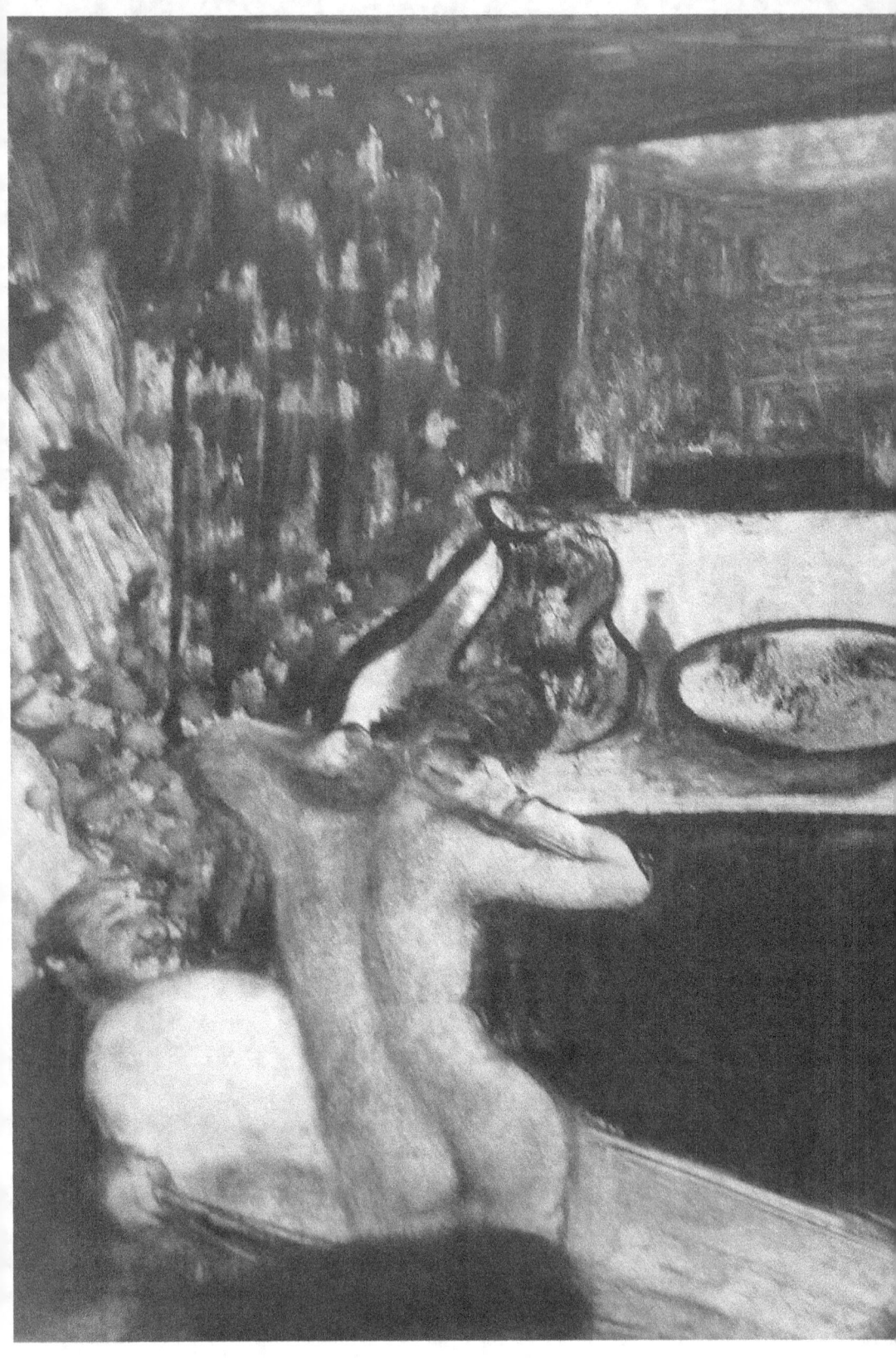

Edgar Degas, The Bath

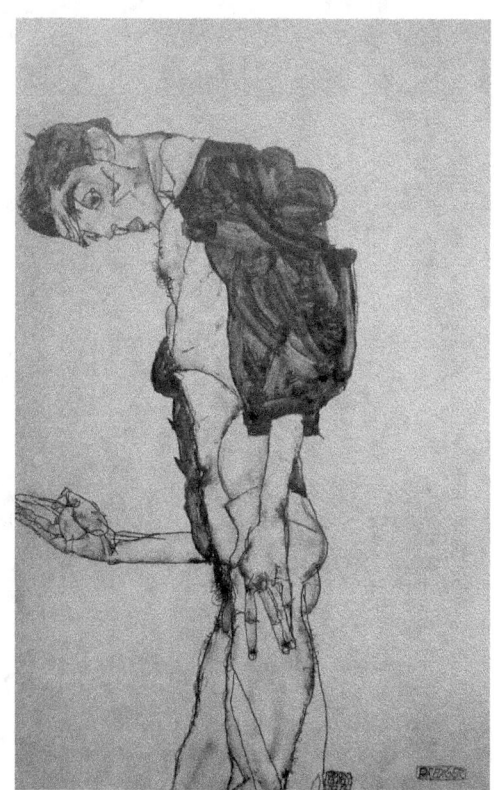

Two Egon Schiele
figures:
Preacher, 1913,
above.
And Standing Nude
Girl With Stockings,
1914, below.

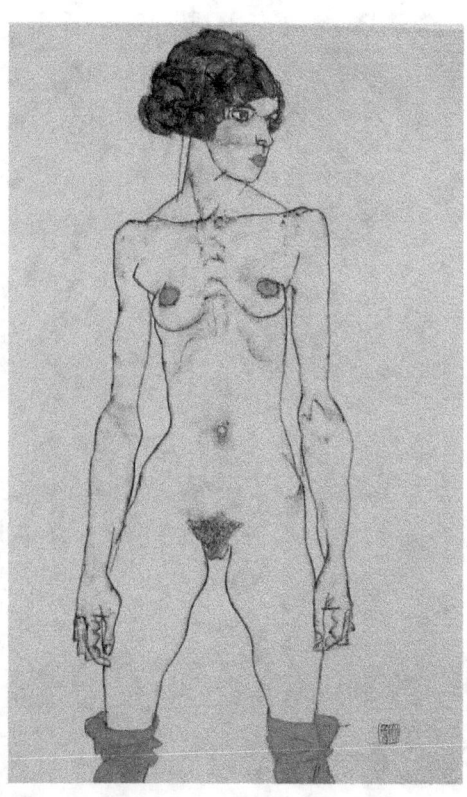

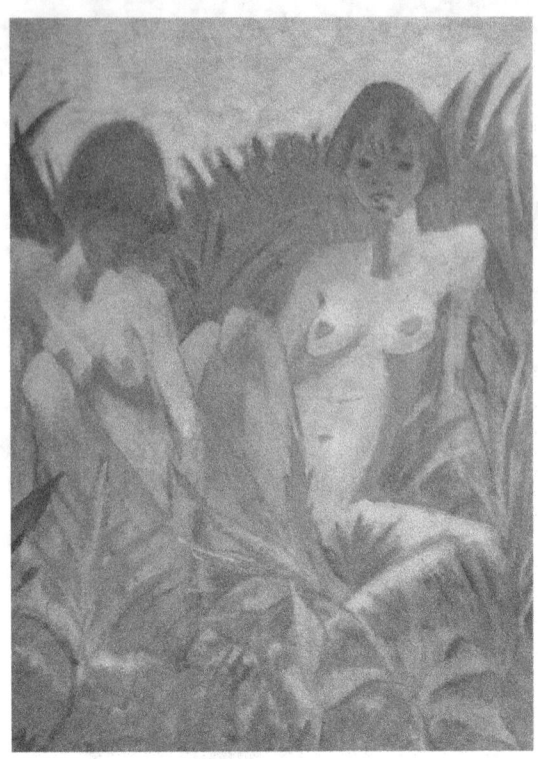

Expressionism: Otto Mueller, Two Girls In the Grass, above.
Ernest Ludwig Kirchner, Semi-Nude Woman With Hat, below.

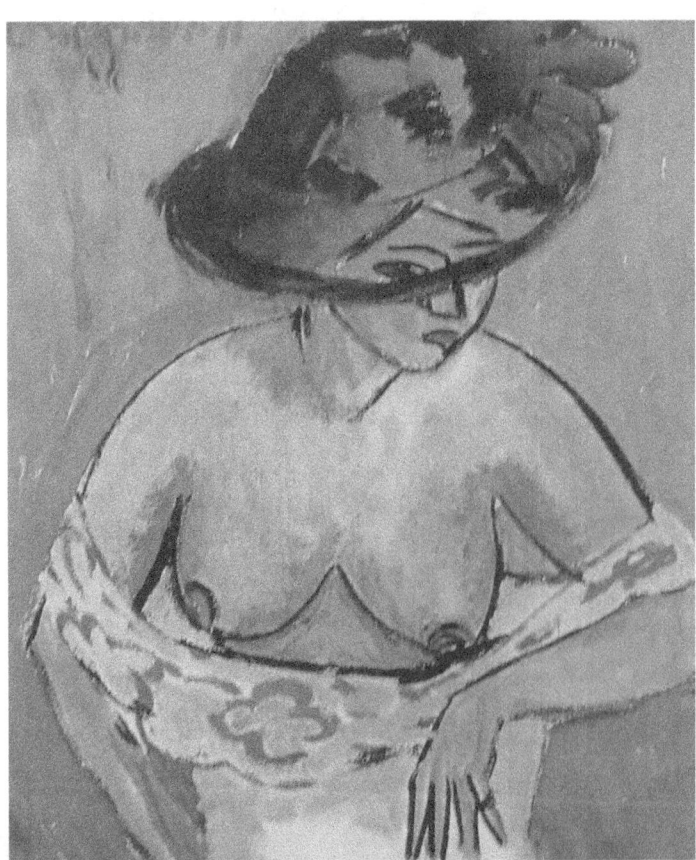

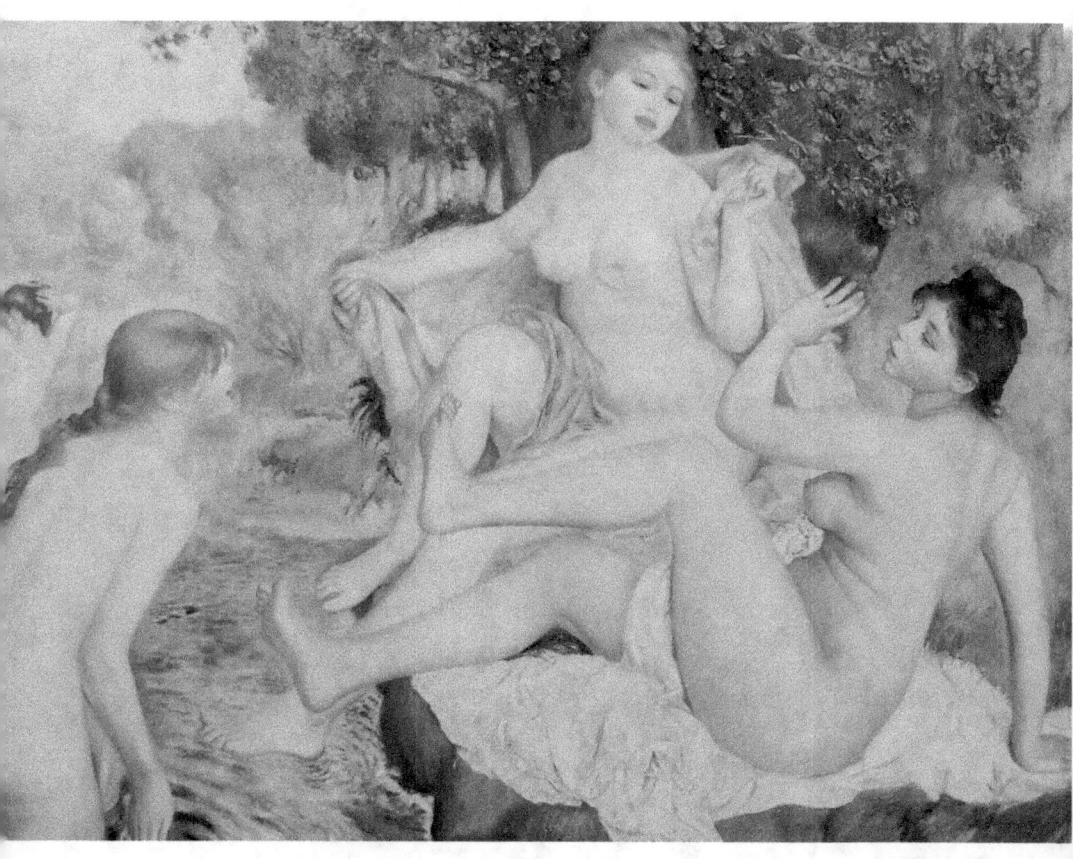

Pierre Renoir, The Bathers, 1887, Philadelphia

NOTES

I INTRODUCTION

1. Wyndham Lewis, letter to T. Sturge Moore, c. February 1911, University of London Library;
Roger Fry in Nation, February 15, 1911.
2. Augustus John, in M. Holroyd: Augustus John: The Years of Innocence, 1974, 363.

3 WOMEN

1. Toril Moi, 99f; Anika Lemaire: Jacques Lacan, Routledge & Kegan Paul, 1977; Elizabeth
Wright: Psychoanalytic Criticism, Methuen, 1984.
2. Pierre Renoir: Bather Arranging Her Hair, 1885, canvas, 92 x 73cm, Sterling and Francis
Clark Institute, Williamstown, Mass.; Lawrence Alma-Tadema: In the Tepidarium, 1881, wood,
24 x 33cm, Lady Lever Art Gallery, Port Sunlight.

5 GILL, RODIN, MAILLOL, KLIMT AND SCHIELE

1. A. Rodin: The Metamorphoses of Ovid, plaster, height 13in.

6 FUCKING

1. E. Gill: The Dancer, 1925, engraving, page 25 of The Song of Songs, 2.4 x 4.2in; Earth
Waiting, 1926, page 8 of Procreant Hymn, engraving, 4.5 x 3.5in; from Twenty-Five Nudes,
J.M. Dent, 1938, engraving, 9.2 x 5.6in, all Victoria & Albert Museum.

7 PHALLUS

1. See Julius Evola, 174; A. De Marchi: Il Culto Privato in roma Antica, Milan 1896
1. E. Gill: The 'Most Precious Ornament', 1937, print, Victoria & Albert Museum.

2. E. Gill's diary, in the William Andrews Clark Memorial Library, UCLA.

8 MIRRORS AND LOOKING

1. Luce Irigaray: *Speculum of the Other Woman*, tr. Gillian C. Gill, and *This Sex which Is Not One*, tr. Catherine Porter, both Cornell University Press, New York, 1985; see also: Dorothy Leland: "Lacanian psychoanalysis and French feminism: toward an adequate political psychology", *Hypatia*, 3 (3), Winter, 1989, 81-103.

2. R. Rilke, letter to Clara Rilke, 8 March, 1907, in *Gesammalte Briefe 1892-1926*, Insel Verlag, Leipzig, 1940, II, 279f.

3. Jack Zipes: *Don't Bet on the Prince: Contemporary Feminist Fairy Tales in North America and England*, Gower, Aldershot, 1986, 258.

4. Maggie Humm: "Is the gaze feminist? Pornography, film and feminism", *Perspectives on Pornography*, eds. G. Day & C. Bloom, Macmillan, 1988; Lorraine Gamran & Margaret Marshment, eds: *The Female Gaze*, Women's Press, 1988; E.D. Pribram, ed: *Female Spectators: looking at film and television*, Verso, 1988.

5. C. Jung: *The Development of Personality*, vol. 17, Routledge, 1954, 198; Marie-Louise von Franz: *The Psychological Meaning of Redemption Motifs in Fairy Tales*, Inner City Books, Toronto, 1980, 39f.

6. Emma Jung & Marie-Louise von Franz: *The Grail Legend*, tr. Andrea Dykes, Sigo Press, Boston, Mass., 1980, 64.

7. E. Gill: *Artist and Mirror*, 1932, wood engraving, 4.8 x 2.6in, Victoria & Albert Museum.

9 DESIRE

1. Larysa Mykyta: "Lacan, Literature and the Look", *SubStance* (39), 1983, 54.

2. See Laura Mulvey: "Visual pleasure and narrative cinema", *Screen*, vol 16, no.3, 1975, 6-19.

3. Annette Kuhn: *Women's Pictures: Feminism and the Cinema*, Routledge & Kegan Paul, 1982, 63.

4. John Berger: *Ways of Seeing*, Penguin, 1972, 47.

5. Catherine King: "The Politics of Representation: A Democracy of the Gaze", in Frances Bonner et al, eds. *Imagining Women Cultural Representations and Gender*, Polity Press, Cambridge, 1992, 136.

6. E. Gill to Helena Wright, 31 Jan, 1933, in B. Evans, *Freedom to Choose*, Bodley Head, 1984.

7. Eric Gill: *Lady C*, 1931, print, 2nd state, Victoria & Albert Museum.

10 LADY C

1. Eric Gill: *Mellors*, 1930, wood engraving, 5.4 x 1.8in, Victoria & Albert Museum.

2. Rembrandt: *The Jewish Bride*, c. 1666, Rijksmuseum, Amsterdam.

3. Antonio Canova; *Cupid and Venus*, marble, Villa Carlota, Lake Como.

12 FLESH

1. Eric Gill: "The Priesthood of Craftsmanship", *Blackfriars*, in R. Goldwater, 456-7.

2. Eric Gill: *Earth Wrestling*, 1926, engraving on copper, Victoria & Albert Museum; *Earth*

Receiving, 1926, engraving on copper, 12.4 x 8.8cm, University of Texas, Austin.

3. Eric Gill: *Ibi Dabo Tibi*, 1925, Victoria & Albert Museum.

4. Eric Gill: *Approaching Dawn*, 1927, in *Troilus and Cresseyde*, Golden Cockerel Press; *Lovers, The Raised Bottom*, 1934, Victoria & Albert Museum.

5. Eric Gill: *The Invisible Man*, 1924, wood engraving, 5 x 3.6in, Victoria & Albert Museum.

6. Eric Gill: *Lot's Daughter*, 1926, pencil and watercolour, 13.5 x 1.6cm, University of Texas, Austin.

7. *The Leaping White Tiger*, album leaf in ink and colours on silk, Chinese K'ang-hsi period (1622-1722), C. T. Loa Collection, Texas.

8. Eric Gill: *Votes for Woman*, 1910, stone, private collection; F. MacCarthy, 104.

9. Eric Gill: *The Juice of My Pomegranates*, illustration for page 40 of *The Song of Songs*, 1925, wood engraving, 2.4 x 4.2in, Victoria & Albert Museum.

10. Eric Gill: *Leda Loved*, 1929, wood engraving, 5.4 x 3.2in, Victoria & Albert Museum.

13 MYTHOLOGY

1. St John of the Cross, *Dark Night of the Soul*, tr. E.A. Peers, Doubleday, New York, 1959, 175.

14 PAIN

1. Eric Gill: *Deposition*, 1924, black hopton wood stone, 76cm high, King's School, Canterbury.

2. E. Gill to J. Raverat, 3 Sept, 1991, in Clark Library, UCLA.

3. Eric Gill: *St Sebastian*, 1919-20, Portland stone, 100.3 x 20.3 x 25.4cm, Victoria & Albert Museum.

15 ORIENT

1. Eric Gill: *Lovers*, bas relief, stone, 38.5 x 19.5 x 7.5cm, University of California, Los Angeles.

2. *I Ching*, tr. James Legge, Dover, New York 1963, 1.

3. Couple from the 'heaven bands' of a temple, Rajasthan, 13th century, sandstone, 11in high; naked ascetic coupling with a Yogini, from Laksmana temple at Khajuraho.

4. Harunobu: *A Fantasy*, late 1760s, anonymous: *Trio in a Garden*, 18th century, China; *The Attack from the Rear*, or '*The Leaping White Tiger*', painting on silk from an album of the K'ang-hsi period, 1662-1722, C.T. Loo Collection, Paris; *In the Garden on a Rocky Seat*, painting on silk, K'ang-his period, C.T. Loo Collection, Paris.

16 VULVA

1. Coco-de-mer, South India, 19th century, 17in high; Icon, 11th century, Hyderabad, stone, from a temple; Holy water container, Bengal, 18th century, copper, 12in long.

2. M. Eliade: *The Myth of the Eternal Return*, Princeton University Press, New Haven, 1971, 36.

3. See D.H. Lawrence in *Book Collector's Quarterly*, Oct-Dec, 1933; Gill's letter to Frieda

Lawrence, 17 April, 1933, Clark Library, UCLA.
  4. E. Gill to Frieda Lawrence, ibid.

17   POWER

  1. Eric Gill: *Eve*, 1926, print, Victoria & Albert Museum.
  2. Eric Gill: *God Sending*, 1926, engraving on copper, Victoria & Albert Museum.
  3. D.H. Lawrence: *The Complete Short Novels*, Penguin, 1982. 596.
  4. *The Collected Letters of D.H. Lawrence*, ed. H.T. Moore, 2 vols, Heinemann, London, 1962, 975.

18   MARRIAGE

  1. Eric Gill, letter, 12 September, 1934, in the Harry Ransom Humanities Research Center, University of Texas, Austin.
  2. Eric Gill: *The Domestic Hose*, 1929, woodcut, Victoria & Albert Museum.
  3. Eric Gill: *Splits II*, 1923, bath stone with added colour, Harry Ransom Humanities Research Center, University of Texas, Austin.
  4. Constantin Brancusi: *The Kiss*, 1907-8, stone, 11in high, Museum of Art, Craiova, Romania; see also Eric Shanes: *Brancusi*, 19f.

BIBLIOGRAPHY

BY ERIC GILL

Art-Nonsense and Other Essays, Cassell, London, 1929
Engravings by Eric Gill: A Selection, ed. D. Cleverdon, Bristol, 1929
Clothes, Cape, London, 1931
An Essay on Typography, Sheed & Ward, London, 1931
Beauty Looks After Herself, Sheed & Ward, London, 1933
Art and a Changing Civilisation, Bodley Head, London, 1934
Money and Morals, Faber, London, 1934
Engravings 1928-33, Faber, London, 1934
Work and Leisure, Faber, London, 1935
The Necessity of Belief, Faber, London, 1936
Trousers and the Most Precious Ornament, Faber, London, 1937
Twenty-Five Nudes, 1938
Autobiography, Cape, London, 1940
Drawings From Life, Hague and Gill, London, 1940
Last Essays, Cape, London, 1942
In a Strange Land, Cape, London, 1944
The Letters of Eric Gill, ed. Walter Shewring, Cape, London, 1947
From the Jerusalem Diary, 1953
Bibliography of Eric Gill, Evan, Gill, Cassell, London, 1953
The Engraved Work of Eric Gill, HMSO, London, 1977
A Holy Tradition of Working, Norwich, 1983
The Inscriptional Work of Eric Gill, Cassell, London, 1984
Eric Gill: The Engravings, ed. C. Skelton, Herbert Press, London, 1990
Eric Gill: Engravings, A & C Black, London, 1997
Eric Gill: Inscriptions, A & C Black, London, 1997
Eric Gill: Sculpture, A & C Black, London, 1997
Eric Gill: Complete Sculpture, A & C Black, London, 1997

OTHERS

P. Anson. *A Roving Recluse*, Mercier Press, Cork, 1946

D. Attawater. *A Cell of Good Living: The Life, Work and Opinions of Eric Gill*, Chapman, London, 1969

—. *Eric Gill: Workman*, Devin-Adar, New York, NY, 1947

C.H. Badaracco. *Trading Words: Poetry, Typography and Illustrated Books in the Modern Literary Economy*, John Hopkins University Press, Baltimore, 1995

O. Benesch. *Egon Schiele As a Draughtsman*, Vienna, 1950

Blackfriars, Eric Gill Memorial Number, 22, 251, Feb, 1941

R. Brewer. *Eric Gill: The Man Who Loved Letters*, Muller, 1973

B. Brezianu. *Brancusi in Romania*, Editura Academiei R.S.R., Bucharest, Romantia, 1976

J. Campbell. *The Power of Myth*, with B. Moyers, ed. B. Sue Flowers, Doubleday, New York, NY, 1988

S. Carter. *20th Century Type Designers*, Trefoil, 1987

Chesterton Review, Eric Gill Centenary Number, 8, 4, Nov, 1982

H.B. Chipp, ed. *Theories of Modern Art*, University Press of California, LA, CA, 1968

D. Chute. "Eric Gill", *Blackfriars*, XXXI, 369, 1950

W.A. Clark Memorial Library, Eric Gill archive, University of California, Los Angeles

D. Cleverdon. "Fifty Years", *The Private Library*, 1978

J. Collins. *Eric Gill, Sculpture*, Lund Humphries, 1992

A. Dworkin. *Intercourse*, Arrow, 1988

—. *Pornography: Men Possessing Women*, Women's Press, 1984

M. Eliade. *Ordeal by Labyrinth*, University of Chicago Press, Chicago, IL, 1984

—. *Symbolism, the Sacred and the Arts*, Crossroad, New York, NY, 1985

P. Faulkner. *William Morris and Eric Gill*, William Morris Society, 1975

Fine Print, Eric Gill issue, 8, 3, San Francisco, July, 1982

J.G. Fletcher. "Eric Gill", *The Arts*, Feb, 1928

P. Fuller. *Images of God*, Chatto, 1985

S. Geist. *Brancusi: The Kiss*, Harper & Row, New York, NY, 1978

R. Gibbings. "Memories of Eric Gill", *Book Collector*, 2, 2, Summer, 1953

C. Gill, B. Warde & D. Kindersley. *The Life and Work of Eric Gill*, Clark Library Symposium, University of California, LA, CA, 1968

E. Gill & D. Peace, eds. *Eric Gill*, Herbert Press, London, 1994

R. Goldwater & M. Treves, eds. *Artists on Art*, John Murray, 1975

N. Gray. "William Morris, Eric Gill and Catholicism", *Architectural Review*, 89, March, 1941

R. Hague. "A Personal Memoir", *Blackfriars*, Feb, 1941

R. Harling. *The Letter Forms and Type Designs of Eric Gill*, Westerham Press, 1976

R. Heppenstall. *Four Absentees*, Sphere, 1988

M. Hoffman: *Sculpture Inside and Out*, Norton, New York, NY, 1939

P. Holliday. *Eric Gill In Ditchling*, Oak Knoll Press, 2002

L. Irigaray. *The Irigaray Reader*, ed. M. Whitford, Blackwell, Oxford, 1991

A. John. *Chiaroscuro*, Cape, 1952

D. Jones. "Eric Gill", *The Tablet*, 30 Nov, 1940

—. "Eric Gill as Sculptor" *Blackfriars*, Feb, 1941

C.G. Jung. *Memories, Dreams, Reflections*, Collins, 1967

H. Kessler. *The Diaries of a Cosmopolitan*, 1971

D. Kindersley et al. Eric Gill, Kettle's Yard, Cambridge, 1979
—. Eric Gill: Further Thoughts by an Apprentice, Wynkyn de Worde Society, 1982
R.E. Krauss. Passages in Modern Sculpture, Thames & Hudson, London, 1977
J. Kristeva. About Chinese Women, tr. A. Barrows, Boyars, 1977
—. Desire in Language: A Semiotic Approach to Literature and Art, ed. L.S. Roudiez, tr. Thomas Gora et al, Blackwell, Oxford, 1982
—. Powers of Horror: An Essay on Abjection, tr. L.S. Roudiez, Columbia University Press, New York, NY, 1982
—. Revolution in Poetic Language, tr. M. Walker, Columbia University Press, New York, NY, 1984
—. The Kristeva Reader, ed. T. Moi, Blackwell, Oxford, 1986
—. Tales of Love, tr. L.S. Roudiez, Columbia University Press, New York, NY, 1987
J. Lacan and the École Freudienne. Feminine Sexuality, ed. Juliet Mitchell and Jacqueline Rose, Macmillan, 1982
J. Laver. "As I Knew Him: Eric Gill", The Listener, 3 May, 1951
D.H. Lawrence. Selected Essays, Penguin, London, 1950
—. Lady Chatterley's Lover, Penguin, London, 1960
—. Phoenix, Heinemann, 1956
—. Phoenix II, Heinemann, 1968
—. A Selection from Phoenix, ed. A.A.H. Inglis, Penguin, London, 1971
—. The Complete Poems, eds. V. de Sola Pinto & W. Roberts, 2 vols, Heinemann, London, 1972
—. The First Lady Chatterley, Penguin, London, 1973
—. John Thomas and Lady Jane, Penguin, London, 1973
—. The Complete Short Novels, Penguin, 1982
I.M. Lippman. The Engravings of Eric Gill: A Study of 20th Century Hieratic Arts, M.A. thesis University of Texas, Austin, 1975
E. Lucie-Smith. Sculpture Since 1945, Phaidon 1987
—. Sexuality in Western Art, Thames & Hudson, London, 1991
F. MacCarthy. Eric Gill, Faber, London, 1989
E. Marks & Isabelle de Courtivron, eds. New French Feminisms: an Anthology, Harvester Wheatsheaf, 1981
E. Powys Mathers. The Garden of Bright Waters One Hundred and Twenty Asiatic Love Poems
J. Miles. Eric Gill and David Jones At Capel-y-Ffin, Seren Books, 1992
K. Millet. Sexual Politics, Doubleday, New York, NY, 1970
T. Moi. Sexual/ Textual Politics: Feminist Literary Theory, Routledge, 1988
S. Morison. On Type Desigs Past and Present, Ernest Benn, 1962
—. Politics and Script, Oxford University Press, Oxford, 1972
John Mumford: Ecstasy Through Tantra, Llewellyn Publications, St Paul, Minnesota 1988
L. Nead. Female Nude: Art, Obscenity and Sexuality, Routledge, 1992
New Blackfriars, Eric Gill issue, LXIII, 745/6, Summer, 1982
Pax Bulletin, Eric Gill issue, 20, Feb, 1941
D. Peace. Addenda and Corrigenda to the Inscriptional Work of Eric Gill, San Francisco, CA, 1972
C. Pepler. "A Study in Integrity: The Life and Teaching of Eric Gill", Blackfriars, XXVIII, 326, May, 1947
D. Potter. My Time with Eric Gill, Walter Ritchie, Kenilworth, 1980
P. Rawson. The Art of Tantra, Thames & Hudson, London, 1973a
—. The Erotic Art of the East, Weidenfeld & Nicolson, 1973b
H. Read. A Coat of Many Colours, Routledge, 1945
H.P. Roche: "L'Enterrement de Brancusi", Homage de la Sculpture à Brancusi, Paris, 1957

J. Rothenstein. Eric Gill, Ernest Benn, 1927

B. Sewell. "Aspects of Eric Gill", Chesterton Review, 8, 4, Nov, 1982

E. Shanes. Constantin Brancusi, Abbeville, New York, NY, 1989

C. Skelton. The Engraved Bookplates of Eric Gill, San Francisco, CA, 1986

—. A Book of Alphabets For Douglas Cleverdon Drawn By Eric Gill, September Press,
   Wellingborough, 1987

W. Shewring. Making and Thinking, Hollis & Carter, 1957

R. Smith. "Eric Gill and Today's Problem", Good Work, 29, 1, New York, Winter, 1966

R. Speaight. The Life of Eric Gill, Methuen, 1966

J. Thorp. Eric Gill, Cape, 1929

A. Tilly. Erotic Drawings, Phaidon, Oxford, 1986

B. Warde. "Eric Gill", Fleuron VIII, Doubleday, 1930

—. Crystal Goblet, Sylvan Press, 1955

— ed. Monotype Recorder, Eric Gill issue, Oct, 1958

—. "The Diuturnity of Eric Gill", Penrose Annual, LIII, 1959

M. Warner. Alone Of All Her Sex: The Myth and Cult of the Virgin Mary, Picador, 1985

—. From the Beast to the Blonde, Vintage, 1995

P. Webb. The Erotic Arts, Secker & Warburg, 1983

F. Whitford. Egon Schiele, Thames & Hudson, London, 1981

M. Yorke. Eric Gill: Man of Flesh and Spirit, Constable, 1981

CRESCENT MOON PUBLISHING

ARTS, PAINTING, SCULPTURE

The Art of Andy Goldsworthy: Complete Works
Andy Goldsworthy: Touching Nature
Andy Goldsworthy in Close-Up
Andy Goldsworthy: Pocket Guide
Andy Goldsworthy In America
Land Art: A Complete Guide
The Art of Richard Long: Complete Works
Richard Long: Pocket Guide
Land Art In the UK
Land Art in Close-Up
Land Art In the U.S.A.
Land Art: Pocket Guide
Installation Art in Close-Up
Minimal Art and Artists In the 1960s and After
Colourfield Painting
Land Art DVD, TV documentary
Andy Goldsworthy DVD, TV documentary
The Erotic Object: Sexuality in Sculpture From Prehistory to the Present Day
Sex in Art: Pornography and Pleasure in Painting and Sculpture
Postwar Art
Sacred Gardens: The Garden in Myth, Religion and Art
Glorification: Religious Abstraction in Renaissance and 20th Century Art
Early Netherlandish Painting
Leonardo da Vinci
Piero della Francesca
Giovanni Bellini
Fra Angelico: Art and Religion in the Renaissance
Mark Rothko: The Art of Transcendence
Frank Stella: American Abstract Artist
Jasper Johns
Brice Marden
Alison Wilding: The Embrace of Sculpture
Vincent van Gogh: Visionary Landscapes
Eric Gill: Nuptials of God
Constantin Brancusi: Sculpting the Essence of Things
Max Beckmann
Caravaggio
Gustave Moreau
Egon Schiele: Sex and Death In Purple Stockings
Delizioso Fotografico Fervore: Works In Process 1
Sacro Cuore: Works In Process 2
The Light Eternal: J.M.W. Turner
The Madonna Glorified: Karen Arthurs

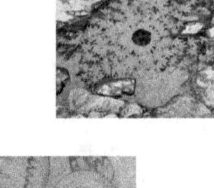
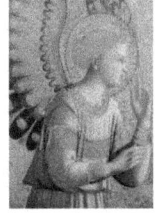
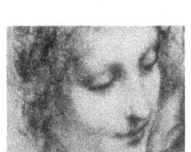
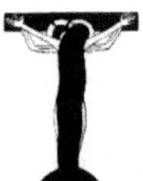
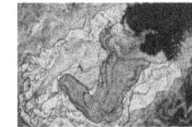

LITERATURE

J.R.R. Tolkien: The Books, The Films, The Whole Cultural Phenomenon
J.R.R. Tolkien: Pocket Guide
Tolkien's Heroic Quest
The *Earthsea* Books of Ursula Le Guin
Beauties, Beasts and Enchantment: Classic French Fairy Tales
German Popular Tales by the Brothers Grimm
Philip Ullman and *His Dark Materials*
Sexing Hardy: Thomas Hardy and Feminism
Thomas Hardy's *Tess of the d'Urbervilles*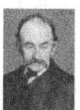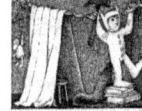
Thomas Hardy's *Jude the Obscure*
Thomas Hardy: The Tragic Novels
Love and Tragedy: Thomas Hardy
The Poetry of Landscape in Hardy
Wessex Revisited: Thomas Hardy and John Cowper Powys
Wolfgang Iser: Essays and Interviews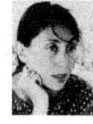
Petrarch, Dante and the Troubadours
Maurice Sendak and the Art of Children's Book Illustration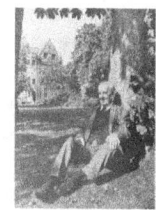
Andrea Dworkin
Cixous, Irigaray, Kristeva: The *Jouissance* of French Feminism
Julia Kristeva: Art, Love, Melancholy, Philosophy, Semiotics and Psychoanalysis
Hélene Cixous I Love You: The *Jouissance* of Writing
Luce Irigaray: Lips, Kissing, and the Politics of Sexual Difference
Peter Redgrove: Here Comes the Flood
Peter Redgrove: Sex-Magic-Poetry-Cornwall
Lawrence Durrell: Between Love and Death, East and West
Love, Culture & Poetry: Lawrence Durrell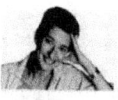
Cavafy: Anatomy of a Soul
German Romantic Poetry: Goethe, Novalis, Heine, Hölderlin
Feminism and Shakespeare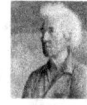
Shakespeare: Love, Poetry & Magic
The Passion of D.H. Lawrence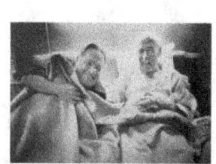
D.H. Lawrence: Symbolic Landscapes
D.H. Lawrence: Infinite Sensual Violence
Rimbaud: Arthur Rimbaud and the Magic of Poetry
The Ecstasies of John Cowper Powys
Sensualism and Mythology: The Wessex Novels of John Cowper Powys
Amorous Life: John Cowper Powys and the Manifestation of Affectivity (H.W. Fawkner)
Postmodern Powys: New Essays on John Cowper Powys (Joe Boulter)
Rethinking Powys: Critical Essays on John Cowper Powys
Paul Bowles & Bernardo Bertolucci
Rainer Maria Rilke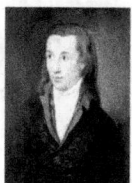
Joseph Conrad: *Heart of Darkness*
In the Dim Void: Samuel Beckett
Samuel Beckett Goes into the Silence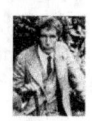
André Gide: Fiction and Fervour
Jackie Collins and the Blockbuster Novel
Blinded By Her Light: The Love-Poetry of Robert Graves
The Passion of Colours: Travels In Mediterranean Lands
Poetic Forms

POETRY

Ursula Le Guin: Walking In Cornwall
Peter Redgrove: Here Comes The Flood
Peter Redgrove: Sex-Magic-Poetry-Cornwall
Dante: Selections From the *Vita Nuova*
Petrarch, Dante and the Troubadours
William Shakespeare: *The Sonnets*
William Shakespeare: Complete Poems
Blinded By Her Light: The Love-Poetry of Robert Graves
Emily Dickinson: Selected Poems
Emily Brontë: Poems
Thomas Hardy: Selected Poems
Percy Bysshe Shelley: Poems
John Keats: Selected Poems
D.H. Lawrence: Selected Poems
Edmund Spenser: Poems
Edmund Spenser: *Amoretti*
John Donne: Poems
Henry Vaughan: Poems
Sir Thomas Wyatt: Poems
Robert Herrick: Selected Poems
Rilke: Space, Essence and Angels in the Poetry of Rainer Maria Rilke
Rainer Maria Rilke: Selected Poems
Friedrich Hölderlin: Selected Poems
Arseny Tarkovsky: Selected Poems
Novalis: *Hymns To the Night*
Paul Verlaine: Selected Poems
Arthur Rimbaud: Selected Poems
Arthur Rimbaud: *A Season in Hell*
Arthur Rimbaud and the Magic of Poetry
D.J. Enright: By-Blows
Jeremy Reed: Brigitte's Blue Heart
Jeremy Reed: Claudia Schiffer's Red Shoes
Gorgeous Little Orpheus
Radiance: New Poems
Crescent Moon Book of Nature Poetry
Crescent Moon Book of Love Poetry
Crescent Moon Book of Mystical Poetry
Crescent Moon Book of Elizabethan Love Poetry
Crescent Moon Book of Metaphysical Poetry
Crescent Moon Book of Romantic Poetry
Pagan America: New American Poetry

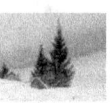
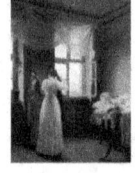
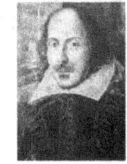
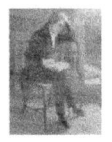
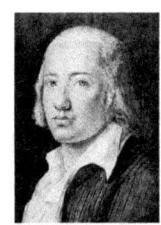
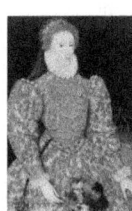

MEDIA, CINEMA, FEMINISM and CULTURAL STUDIES

J.R.R. Tolkien: The Books, The Films, The Whole Cultural Phenomenon
J.R.R. Tolkien: Pocket Guide
The *Lord of the Rings* Movies: Pocket Guide
The Cinema of Hayao Miyazaki
Hayao Miyazaki: *Princess Mononoke*: Pocket Movie Guide
Hayao Miyazaki: *Spirited Away*: Pocket Movie Guide
Tim Burton
Ken Russell
Ken Russell: *Tommy*: Pocket Movie Guide
The Ghost Dance: The Origins of Religion
The Peyote Cult

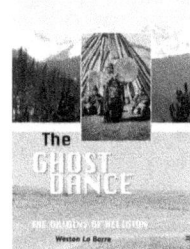

Cixous, Irigaray, Kristeva: The *Jouissance* of French Feminism
Julia Kristeva: Art, Love, Melancholy, Philosophy, Semiotics and Psychoanalysis
Luce Irigaray: Lips, Kissing, and the Politics of Sexual Difference
Hélene Cixous I Love You: The *Jouissance* of Writing
Andrea Dworkin
'Cosmo Woman': The World of Women's Magazines
Women in Pop Music
Discovering the Goddess (Geoffrey Ashe)
The Poetry of Cinema
The Sacred Cinema of Andrei Tarkovsky
Andrei Tarkovsky: Pocket Guide
Andrei Tarkovsky: *Mirror*: Pocket Movie Guide
Andrei Tarkovsky: *The Sacrifice*: Pocket Movie Guide
Walerian Borowczyk: Cinema of Erotic Dreams
Jean-Luc Godard: The Passion of Cinema
Jean-Luc Godard: *Hail Mary*: Pocket Movie Guide
Jean-Luc Godard: *Contempt*: Pocket Movie Guide
Jean-Luc Godard: *Pierrot le Fou*: Pocket Movie Guide
John Hughes and Eighties Cinema
Ferris Bueller's Day Off: Pocket Movie Guide
Jean-Luc Godard: Pocket Guide
The Cinema of Richard Linklater
Liv Tyler: Star In Ascendance
Blade Runner and the Films of Philip K. Dick
Paul Bowles and Bernardo Bertolucci
Media Hell: Radio, TV and the Press
An Open Letter to the BBC
Detonation Britain: Nuclear War in the UK
Feminism and Shakespeare
Wild Zones: Pornography, Art and Feminism
Sex in Art: Pornography and Pleasure in Painting and Sculpture
Sexing Hardy: Thomas Hardy and Feminism

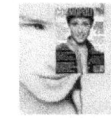
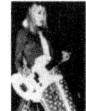
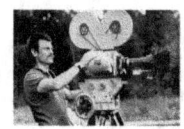
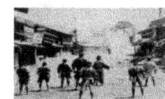
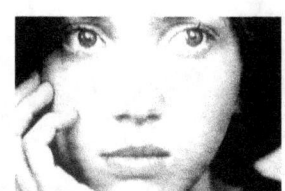

In my view *The Light Eternal* is among the very best of all the material I read on Turner. (Douglas Graham, director of the Turner Museum, Denver, Colorado)

The Light Eternal is a model monograph, an exemplary job. The subject matter of the book is beautifully organised and dead on beam. (Lawrence Durrell)

It is amazing for me to see my work treated with such passion and respect. (Andrea Dworkin)

CRESCENT MOON PUBLISHING
P.O. Box 1312, Maidstone, Kent, ME14 5XU, Great Britain. www.crmoon.com

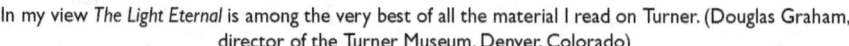